CRIME SCENE
INVESTIGATION, CRIMINALISTICS, AND THE LAW

CRIME SCENE INVESTIGATION, CRIMINALISTICS, AND THE LAW

Thomas Buckles

THOMSON

DELMAR LEARNING™

Australia Canada Mexico Singapore Spain United Kingdom United States

THOMSON
™
DELMAR LEARNING

WEST LEGAL STUDIES

CRIME SCENE INVESTIGATION, CRIMINALISTICS, AND THE LAW

Thomas Buckles

Career Education Strategic Business Unit:

Vice President:
Dawn Gerrain

Managing Editor:
Robert L. Serenka , Jr.

Acquisitions Editor:
Shelley Esposito

Director of Production:
Wendy A. Troeger

Senior Content Project Manager:
Betty L. Dickson

Director of Marketing:
Wendy Mapstone

Marketing Manager:
Gerard McAvey

Cover Design:
Dutton and Sherman Design

Cover Image:
©Getty Images

COPYRIGHT © 2007
Thomson Delmar Learning, a part of the Thomson Corporation. Thomson, the Star Logo, and Delmar Learning are trademarks used herein under license.

Printed in the United States
1 2 3 4 5 ML 10 09 08 07 06

For more information contact
Delmar Learning, 5 Maxwell Drive, P.O. Box 8007, Clifton Park, New York 12065.

Or find us on the World Wide Web at
http://www.westlegalstudies.com

All rights reserved. No part of this work covered by the copyright hereon may be reproduced or used in any form or by any means—graphic, electronic, or mechanical, including photocopying, recording, taping, Web distribution or information storage and retrieval systems— without written permission of the publisher.

For permission to use material from this text or product, contact us by
Tel(800) 730-2214
Fax(800) 730-2215
www.thomsonrights.com

Library of Congress Cataloging-in-Publication Data

Buckles, Thomas.
  Crime scene investigation, criminalistics, and the law / Thomas Buckles. p. cm.
  Includes index.
  ISBN 1-4018-5929-1
1. Crime scenes. 2. Criminal investigation. 3. Evidence, Criminal. I.Title. HV8073.B75 2007
363.25--dc22
                    2006019023

NOTICE TO THE READER

This book is dedicated to my son, Cris (who worked a few crime scenes of his own during his time in CID) and to all professionals involved in crime scene investigation. I've had the honor of working with many of them over the years, in the investigation of more than 4,000 crime scenes. If asked why they do this work, their responses often remind me of some of the words written on the FBI's dedication stone to its newest crime lab, built in 2003:

"Behind every case is a victim –
man, woman, or child –
and the people who care for them.
We dedicate our efforts ...
to those victims."

—Written on dedication stone for FBI's crime lab

BRIEF CONTENTS

TABLE OF CONTENTS

TABLE OF CASES

This book is about crime scene investigation and criminalistics, and the laws that govern them. Aimed at all personnel involved in the many aspects of crime scene investigation, this book focuses on how a crime scene should be investigated, searched, and processed for evidence, with an emphasis on the legal admissibility of these procedures, the forensic value of physical evidence, and the role of forensic science and criminalistics in analyzing this evidence and presenting it in court in the form of scientific testing and expert testimony.

How a crime scene is investigated can make or break a case. A good defense team can and *will* challenge the investigative procedure used at the crime scene and any subsequent analysis, testing, or evaluation of evidence. Therefore, it is essential for those involved in the investigation, prosecution, or defense of a crime involving a crime scene to understand the *proper* procedures and techniques involved in the investigation of a crime scene. It is equally essential to know the laws governing crime scene investigation and the potential *evidentiary challenges* that may be faced by either side.

GOALS OF THIS BOOK

My goals in writing this book are to show:

- How a crime scene *should* be investigated
- The role of the *crime lab* and *criminalistics* in crime scene investigation
- What *evidentiary value* can be gained from the physical evidence collected and analyzed from the crime scene
- *Laws that govern* crime scene investigation, analysis of crime scene evidence, and the admission of this evidence in court
- How crime scene *evidence* is presented *in court*
- *Legal and evidentiary challenges* that can be raised if a crime scene investigation is not conducted properly.

FEATURES OF THIS BOOK

Setting a new standard in crime scene education and training texts, this is the first book that not only covers the exciting field of *crime scene investigation* but the *laws* that govern it! Designed to provide a student-friendly, readable format with a rich variety of learning features, this text includes photos, illustrations, checklists, exhibits, and actual cases to enhance reading and learning. In addition, the book has a wealth of pedagogical features, allowing readers to apply and practice what they learn.

Learning Features

Presented in a reader-friendly, understandable format, each chapter begins with a *Chapter Outline* for the exciting topics to be covered, and an *Introduction* to the learning in that chapter. *Definitions* are provided in the margins throughout each chapter. Relevant Internet sites are included that allow students to continue their study and research into chapter concepts, as well as to provide valuable online resources. At the end of every chapter, there is a *Summary* and *Key Terms* review, as well as the *Web Sites* referred to or recommended within the chapter. Throughout the book, there are examples, exhibits, and checklists to help students better understand the concepts and techniques used. To help facilitate understanding of what is learned, there are thought-provoking questions, case problems, exercises, and practical, hands-on applications in each chapter. These features not only reinforce learning, but also serve to strengthen and assess competencies and essential skills. Included in each chapter are:

- **Critical Thinking Questions**
- **Crime Scene Analysis Exercises**
- **Forensic Research Using The Internet Applications**
- **Exhibits**
- **Practice Tips**
- **CSI Checklists**

Critical Thinking Questions challenge students to examine, discuss, and reflect crime scenes investigation techniques, and the procedures and concepts covered in the readings. *Crime Scene Analysis Exercises* applications require students to apply what they have learned to a crime scene case problem using proper CSI investigative methods and legal challenges. Some may use crime lab comparison problems for students to get hands-on practice of how criminalists and crime labs analyze and compare physical evidence found at the crime scene. *Forensic Research* skills are emphasized by integrating them with the use of the Internet. Students are given a series of research assignments on the Internet, not only developing their research, but also their technology skills. As a bonus, many of these assignments ask the student to research and compare his or her own state resources, procedures, and laws governing crime scene investigation with those studied in the text, ensuring both a more rounded understanding and a knowledge of the considerable. *Exhibits* supplement the readings with a rich assortment of examples and illustrations. *Practice Tips* offers practical "how-to" help and tips on conducting crime scene investigations. *CSI Checklists* tie important concepts together through visual checklists outlining what is needed to prove or investigate a specific crime scene topic. Some chapters include *Special Investigative Challenges*, which focus on some of the special crime scene issues or challenges that might come up during an investigation. Many chapters also include timely *Crime Scene Cases* to help students better understand legal issues and rules by examining leading cases that govern CSI investigative procedures, seeing how they are applied and analyzing the court's reasoning behind their decision.

Timely and Important Court Cases

The book includes leading cases that have shaped and governed crime scene investigative procedures and admissibility of crime scene evidence. These include Unites States Supreme Court cases that deal with fire scene and death scene investigations, and a wealth of other recent state and federal cases that deal with crime scene search and seizure, forensic experts, and testing, whether there is "implied" consent to search a crime scene, what constitutes an "exigency" at a crime scene, chain of custody, scientific testing, admissibility of crime scene evidence, the admissibility of bloodstain analysis, fingerprints, and DNA.

Who Is This Book Designed For?

Crime Scene Investigation, Criminalistics, and the Law is designed for both students and in-service personnel in criminal justice, law enforcement, criminalistics, paralegal, pre-law, legal studies, criminology, forensic science, police sciences, and law enforcement training academies, as well as those readers who just want to know more about the fascinating topics of crime scene investigation, criminalistics, and the law.

ACKNOWLEDGMENTS

Simply put, I could not have written this book without the support and encouragement of my family. I thank them all for it. (A very special thanks to forensic artist and photographer Lou Buckles.)

I want to acknowledge and thank my original acquisition editor, Pamela Fuller, for her belief in this project. Thank you, Ellen Kitchel, for conducting much of the initial caselaw research. Thanks also to Adriana Colonno, for her assistance as Rights and Permissions Specialist. Thanks to Sandra Mitchell and her team at GEX Publishing Services, and Betty Dickson, Senior Content Project Manager at Thomson, for their expertise with the production process. A special thank you to development editor Diane Colwyn for guiding me through the many months of writing and revisions. Her support, suggestions, and professionalism are always greatly appreciated.

Thank you to the following reviewers who braved the drafts of this book, providing many valuable comments and suggestions that were incorporated in this revision:

Rodney Brewer	University of Louisville
Anne Cucinelli	Community College of Vermont (Vermont State Colleges)
Jeff Engel	Pikes Peak Community College
Paul Friedman	Palm Beach Community College
William Kelly	Auburn University
Richard Li	Sam Houston State University
Steve Lickiss	San Diego Miramar College
Peter Massey	Henry C. Lee Institute of Forensic Science
Marilyn Miller	Virginia Commonwealth University
Thomas Petee	Auburn University
John Wyant	Illinois Central College

A special acknowledgment to above reveiwer Anne Cucinelli. Her career as an investigator and attorney (former FBI agent and prosecutor), and her expertise in forensics and crime scene investigation exemplify the dedication and professionalism for these important fields.

INTRODUCTION TO CRIME SCENE INVESTIGATION, CRIMINALISTICS, AND THE LAW

"Every Contact Leaves A Trace..."

—Edmond Locard, (1877–1966), established first workable crime laboratory and founded Institute of Criminalistics in Lyons, France 1910

"One should always look for a possible alternative and provide against it. It is the first rule of Criminal Investigation."

—Sherlock Holmes, in Sir Arthur Conan Doyle's *Adventure of Black Peter*

Chapter Outline

- Every Contact Leaves a Trace
- What is Criminalistics?
- Why is Law Important to Crime Scene Investigation?
- What is an Investigation?
- What is a Crime Scene Investigation?
- What is a Crime Scene?
- Who Are Crime Scene Investigators?
- What Do Crime Scene Investigators Look For?
- What is Crime Scene Evidence Used For?

criminalist
One who applies science and scientific method to crime scene investigation.

crime scene
Location where crime was committed or continued.

trace evidence
Minute amounts of evidence, such as fibers, hairs, or specks of dirt.

exchange theory
Whenever two surfaces come into contact with each other, there is a partial transfer or exchange of material from one to the other.

criminalistics
forensic science
Application of science and scientific method to crime scene investigation.

INTRODUCTION: "EVERY CONTACT LEAVES A TRACE."

In 1910, Edmond Locard, a French **criminalist** who founded the first police crime laboratory in France, wrote that every time a criminal entered a **crime scene**, he left something behind in the way of **trace evidence** and took something with him. According to this "**Exchange Theory**," whenever two surfaces come into contact with each other, there is a partial *transfer* or *exchange* of material from one to the other. Therefore, Locard believed, investigators should, whenever possible, focus on the crime scene for evidence that might prove or disprove their case.

Throughout the years, Locard's *exchange theory* has remained the guiding principle for crime scene investigators. The emerging role of the criminalist and the development of the modern crime lab have become an integral part of the crime scene investigation. Today, however, there is also a renewed interest in the crime scene by other professionals in criminal law. Dramatic advances in the fields of **criminalistics** and **forensic science** in the past decade have contributed new and revolutionary improvements to investigative efforts and legal proof in both the prosecution and defense of criminal cases.

In this chapter, we will begin to look at how crime scene investigation has blended with criminalistics and the law. Like an investigation itself, this book will examine, step-by-step, each of these fields, how they are used to work together in the investigation of a crime, and the legal challenges that face each step of the process.

WHAT IS A CRIME?

crime
Act or omission to act that violates a law for which there is a prescribed sanction or punishment.

Before we focus on crime scene investigation and criminalistics, we need to define crime. A **crime** is an act or omission to act that violates a law for which there is a prescribed sanction or punishment. A crime is a violation against the state or society. Even though it involves individual victims, the "state" is the prosecutor in a criminal action.

Felony and Misdemeanor

felony
Serious crime, generally punishable by more than one year of imprisonment.

misdemeanor
Less serious crime, punishable by less than one year of incarceration.

Crimes are classified as a **felony** or **misdemeanor**, depending on their seriousness and the punishment prescribed. In most states, a felony is a crime that, upon conviction, may be punishable by more than one year imprisonment, or, in some states (like Vermont), more than two years. Misdemeanors are those crimes punishable by less than one year.

Corpus Delicti

The definitions for crimes are generally found in state or federal criminal codes. These definitions include the **elements** of that crime, each of which must be proven in order to establish that a crime has been committed and that a particular suspect committed the crime. This process is also referred to as establishing the **corpus delicti**, or "body" of the crime; to show that a crime has been committed and to help prove or disprove every element of that crime. For example, a burglary may require an unlawful entry into a building with the intent to commit a crime or steal something inside. Physical evidence found at the crime scene showing evidence of forced entry on a door or damage to an interior cash drawer would help to establish these elements of burglary.

elements of a crime
Every part of a definition for a particular crime must be established and proven in order to convict a defendant of that crime.

corpus delicti
Latin for "body of the crime," or the elements necessary to prove that a crime has been committed.

WHAT IS CRIMINALISTICS?

Criminalistics is the application of science and scientific method to crime scene investigation. It identifies and analyzes physical evidence discovered at the crime scene by applying scientific principles and testing procedures. It is different, however, from **criminology**, which is the behavioral study of crime and criminals. Criminalistics is a term that is often interchanged with forensic science and **crime lab**.

criminology
Behavioral study of crime and criminals.

crime lab
Laboratory where evidence from crime scenes is tested and analyzed.

Criminalistics Merges Science with Investigation

Criminalistics merges the principles of physical science with those of criminal investigation and law in order to fulfill the mission of law enforcement in solving crimes. Through the identification, collection, preservation, and evaluation of physical evidence found at the crime scene and the extended crime environment, criminalistics attempts to determine whether a crime has been committed, how and when it was committed, where it was committed, why it was committed, and who did or did not commit the crime.

Through the proper collection, identification, and evaluation of physical evidence found at the crime scene, investigators can now utilize the concepts of forensic evidence and the science of criminalistics to discover valuable information that will aid in solving crimes.

A successful crime scene investigator must understand the role of **physical evidence** found at the crime scene and how criminalistics can be utilized to evaluate this evidence. Investigators must understand the importance of following proper procedure to ensure that the crime scene is processed in a thorough and systematic manner, and that all potential evidence is properly identified, collected, preserved, and evaluated.

physical evidence
Objects or materials that can be seen, touched, or felt, such as the murder weapon, blood stains, or fingerprints.

Evaluating Physical Evidence by Matchable Characteristics

Some physical evidence must be compared to other samples. For example, a bullet from a body is compared to a bullet fired from a suspect's gun; fingerprints found at scene are compared to those of the suspect. This evidence and the samples obtained are compared to find the number of **Matchable Characteristics**, or identifying features that might prove the evidence is the same or from the same source as the sample.

Class versus Individual Characteristics

Matchable characteristics are classified as either **Class Characteristics** or *individual characteristics*. When the characteristics of physical evidence are common to a group of objects or persons, they may be termed as belonging to a *Class*. Regardless of how thoroughly examined, such evidence can only offer generalizations. An individual identification cannot be made as there is a possibility of more than one source for the material found. An example of this is carpet fiber. An opinion could be offered as to whether a particular fiber generally matched a type of carpet or was similar to a particular carpet, but it could not be said positively that a fiber came from a specific carpet.

Unlike *class*, evidence with **individual characteristics** can be identified as having originated from a particular person or source. Every person and many objects have individual characteristics that are unique to it and different from all others. Examples of this include fingerprints, ballistics, and DNA.

Matchable Characteristics
Identifying features that might prove the evidence is the same or from the same source as the sample.

Class Characteristics
Characteristics of physical evidence that are common to a group of objects or persons.

individual characteristics
When the characteristics of physical evidence can be identified as having originated from a particular person or source.

PRACTICE TIP 1.1

Job Opportunities in Forensic Science

Want to find out more about how to work in a crime lab or in the field of forensic science? Research the following Web sites:

American Academy of Forensic Sciences
http://www.aafs.org/
American Society of Crime Laboratory Directors
http://www.ascld.org/forensicstudents.html

These sites provide resources that answer important questions for those seeking employment in the forensic sciences, such as what type of education is needed, what else might help get a job in a crime lab, and other information.

WHY IS LAW IMPORTANT TO CRIME SCENE INVESTIGATION?

How the crime scene is investigated can make or break a case. Anyone who has been involved in the investigation, prosecution, or defense of a criminal case involving a crime scene understands the importance of a proper and legal crime scene investigation. Since the O.J. Simpson trial (with its televised focus on the crime scene, crime lab analysis, and DNA), the Jon Benet Ramsey investigation, the growing use of DNA evidence, and the recent spate of popular television shows focusing on crime scenes, there has been growing attention to and interest in the evidentiary value and legal challenges to crime scene investigation and criminalistics.

Every person who works in any capacity in the investigation, analysis, reporting, prosecution, or defense of a criminal case *should* know how and why a crime scene is investigated, and understand the evidentiary and courtroom value, admissibility, and legal challenges involved in crime scene evidence. This includes law enforcement personnel who are involved in the primary investigation, processing, or analysis of a crime scene. It includes other professionals, reporters, forensic experts, and analysts involved in the testing and analysis of crime scene evidence.

It also includes the attorneys, legal investigators, and paralegals involved in and charged with the direct responsibility of prosecuting or defending a criminal case. By understanding the proper procedures and laws governing crime scene investigation, they can competently conduct the follow-up evaluation of reports, testing, witnesses, and evidence.

But, what is an investigation? What is a crime scene? Who are crime scene investigators? And, what type of evidence are we looking for?

investigation
From the Latin *investĭgāre*, meaning to track, inquire into, search for, or examine systematically.

WHAT IS AN INVESTIGATION?

Investigation comes from the Latin *investĭgāre*, meaning to track, inquire into, search for, or examine systematically. Crime scene investigation focuses on the scene of the crime, in an effort to locate any evidence that may tend to prove or disprove guilt.

WHAT IS A CRIME SCENE INVESTIGATION?

crime scene investigation
A methodical investigation initially carried out at the crime scene to determine what happened, how it happened, why it happened, and who or what was responsible.

A **crime scene investigation** is a methodical process that involves identifying, documenting, collecting, preserving, and evaluating information and **evidence** at a crime scene to determine what happened, how it happened, why it happened, and who or what was responsible. A crime scene investigation is a specialized part of a criminal investigation.

Crime Scene Investigation and Deductive Reasoning

evidence
Anything that tends to prove or disprove a fact at issue in a criminal action.

When a crime has been committed and the crime scene is investigated, the investigator is starting with the *general* and trying to obtain evidence to narrow it down to a *specific*. This is called **deductive reasoning** or **deduction**.

deductive reasoning or deduction
To narrow reasoning from the general to the specific.

Investigation may be Inculpatory and Exculpatory

A proper crime scene investigation is both **inculpatory** and **exculpatory**. It not only seeks to identify the suspect or possible suspects and uncover evidence of their guilt, called *inculpatory*, but also to collect information that may *exculpate* or prove that someone did not commit the crime, called *exculpatory* evidence.

inculpatory evidence
Evidence used to incriminate or prove guilt.

exculpatory evidence
Evidence used to clear a party of blame or guilt.

Evidence is Information

Everything considered evidence relating to a crime is information subject to use. As you will learn in this book, the good investigator knows when and how to make the best use of the information obtained.

Effect of Time on Information

Some information may be *time-critical*, meaning that failure to identify and retrieve it at the right time will cause it to be lost forever. Examples of this include the description of a getaway car leaving the scene of a crime, or deterioration of physical evidence at the scene by weather, traffic, cleaning, or people walking through the crime scene.

WHAT IS A CRIME SCENE?

Not every crime has a crime scene and some crimes may have scenes but require no formal crime scene investigation. This is usually the case when there is no physical evidence present or recoverable at the scene. Examples of this might include petty thefts, such as someone taking a purse from a shopping cart in a store. Investigators may want to interview witnesses and check for security cameras, but unless there is additional information that warrants a crime scene investigation, there typically would not be any processing for physical evidence.

This may be the case in other crimes, such as forgery (although the forged document or instrument constitutes a "crime scene"), fraud, some robberies, and most minor crimes. On the other hand, if the crime involves the possibility of physical evidence being left or impacted somewhere (Locard's Exchange Theory), then there likely will be a crime scene that requires processing and investigating. Most major crimes involve a crime scene, such as crimes of violence, burglary, arson, sexual assault, kidnapping, and many robberies.

WHO ARE CRIME SCENE INVESTIGATORS?

Law enforcement officers and crime lab specialists have the primary responsibility for responding, securing, and examining crime scenes. However, there are many other types of investigative positions that require knowledge of crime scene techniques and procedures.

Law Enforcement Officers and Investigators

When a crime is reported, law enforcement patrol officers are among the first to respond to the scene. Depending on a law enforcement department's size, these patrol officers may have a variety of responsibilities at the scene. In large departments, the first officer on the scene is responsible for determining whether a crime has been committed, checking for suspects and victims, and securing the crime scene until investigators and crime lab specialists can arrive to take over the investigation.

Most law enforcement departments around the country are small and may lack the specialist resources of the larger departments. In these smaller departments, the patrol officer has the additional responsibility of investigating the crime scene and collecting evidence. In major crimes, smaller departments usually can call on county or state crime scene and lab resources to assist. In either case, the officers must secure the crime scene until this assistance can arrive. (See Exhibit 1.1.)

EXHIBIT 1.1 Patrol Officer - First Responder

Law enforcement patrol officers are routinely dispatched to reports of crimes in progress or having just occurred, and are typically the first responders to crime scenes. The first law enforcement officer to arrive at the scene of the crime is in charge until he or she is properly relieved by a ranking officer or investigator. As one patrol officer described the duties, "If I arrive first at a crime scene, my primary responsibilities are to assist any injured, detain suspects, and to protect that scene and freeze it; don't let anyone in or out. Based on the seriousness of the crime, there may be investigators and crime scene personnel called out, or I may also be responsible for the follow-up investigation."

Crime Lab Specialists

Assisting law enforcement in the initial investigation of the crime scene are a variety of civilian investigative personnel, including criminalists, crime lab technicians, forensic specialists, and other specialists who have received training or education in forensic science, fingerprinting, investigative photography, or ballistics. (See Exhibit 1.2.)

Medico-Legal and Arson Investigators

Depending on the crime, there may be other types of investigators at the initial crime scene in addition to law enforcement officers. If a death has occurred, many states have coroner's investigators or medico-legal investigators to oversee the death investigation for the coroner or medical examiner's office. A crime scene with a fire of suspicious origins will bring arson investigators from the police and/or fire departments.

Investigators from Other Agencies

Crime scenes involving offenders under the supervision of a Department of Corrections may require a probation or parole officer, or a corrections investigator to conduct a separate investigation.

Serious violent crimes and major felonies may result in criminal investigators from the prosecutor's or attorney general's offices being present. Other investigators who may be called out or become involved include military investigators, security investigators, or investigators from other agencies who may have had a particular connection with the crime or the victim.

Paralegals and Legal Investigators

Paralegals, when trained and educated properly, are legal investigators. Their duties and responsibilities, although varied by specialization, focus primarily on assisting their attorney team in the

EXHIBIT 1.2 Crime Lab Job Descriptions

Crime Lab Technicians

Crime Lab Technicians are primarily responsible for maintaining and operating crime lab equipment. Although they may assist crime scene personnel in collecting evidence at the crime scene, they typically spend much of their time in the crime lab, performing lab work in support of the analyses and testing being conducted by criminalists. An associate or bachelor's degree, with coursework in science and knowledge of general chemistry, is generally required for this position.[1]

Crime Scene Analysts

Crime Scene Analysts are primarily responsible for documenting and processing crime scenes to collect and preserve evidence. As the job description for a Crime Scene Analyst with the Las Vegas Crime Lab states, major duties may include the conducting of "detailed inspections of crime scenes for the presence of evidence... Respond to the morgue to evaluate, photograph, fingerprint, and recover any trace or physical evidence from deceased persons ... Document crime scenes to include general and comparison photography, notetaking and sketching and diagramming crime scenes. Evaluate ... and conduct latent fingerprint processing ... Photograph crime scenes, victims, autopsies ...Collect and process evidence from various body areas of living and deceased persons. Process collected evidence and maintain appropriate chain of custody to preserve crime scene evidence for presentation in court. Complete detailed written reports ... Maintain accurate records and logs ... Testify as an expert witness." The education required for this position is an associate degree "with major course work in biology, chemistry, forensic technology, forensic science, physical science or a related field, including specialized training in crime scene investigation."[2]

Criminalist

Criminalists are primarily responsible for the forensic testing and analyses of crime scene evidence. This can include the identification and collection of evidence at the crime scene, and, as stated in the job description for Criminalist at the Las Vegas Crime Lab, the performing of "a variety of scientific laboratory analyses on physical evidence to provide scientific consultation; to interpret test results and form conclusions; to prepare reports; and to testify as an expert witness." The education required for this position is a bachelor or master's degree "with major course work in criminalistics, forensic science, chemistry, biology, or a related field..."[3]

EXHIBIT 1.3   District Attorney's Investigator

District Attorney investigators typically do not go to the initial crime scene. Their responsibilities revolve more around case investigation and preparation. As one investigator described her job, "Usually, my main job is to review the crime scene reports and re-interview the victims, witnesses, and officers to ensure that everything was done properly, all of the elements can be proven, and that the evidence is present for a strong case."

management and preparation of cases by interviewing witnesses, reviewing reports and documents, inspecting and evaluating evidence, preparing releases, forms, papers, and court documents, legal research and writing, and the conducting of all other investigative functions to assist the team in preparing for trial. A paralegal's job is to review the case with a fine-tooth comb, finding the holes in the opposition's arguments and plugging the holes in their own. Most prominent criminal attorneys admit that the real success or failure of a criminal case rests with the findings and preparation efforts of their paralegal and investigative team. (See Exhibit 1.3.)

Some paralegals and legal investigators who work with the prosecution team may be called to the initial crime scene to help oversee case management, usually in a major or particularly sensitive crime. As a representative of the prosecution team, these paralegal investigators are there to assist the prosecutor in ensuring that all legal procedures are followed, that the evidence is properly collected and documented, and that all witnesses are interviewed.

Most paralegals and legal investigators, however, are not afforded the opportunity to be at the initial crime scene. They must conduct their investigations after the fact, sometimes months or even years after the initial crime allegedly occurred. Relying on the crime reports, photographs, and demonstrative evidence filed by the initial investigators at the scene, these paralegals and legal investigators must sift through reports and paperwork to insure that the case is properly and thoroughly prepared for trial.

Whether they represent the prosecution or defense team, these investigators must review every report filed, talk to every witness, and often revisit and attempt to reconstruct the crime scene in order to search for strengths and weaknesses in their case. The very success of their team's case may depend on their findings and what they find depends largely on how familiar they are with proper criminal investigation and crime scene investigative techniques and procedures. (See Exhibit 1.4.)

EXHIBIT 1.4   Public Defender Paralegal/Investigator

The duties of public defender investigators and paralegals revolve around case preparation and management. They don't get called to the initial crime scene, but spend time in going back over the crime scene before trial, and verifying investigative reports and witness accounts. As one investigator noted, "Usually, I go out later, examine all of the different reports, interview witnesses, and reconstruct the crime scene to see whether the police missed anything or did something wrong. Many of our cases are won on errors by police at the crime scene."

PRACTICE TIP 1.2

Job Opportunities as Crime Scene Investigator

For more information on job opportunities as a crime scene investigator, visit the following Web site:
        Crime-Scene-Investigator.Net
        http://www.crime-scene-investigator.net/

WHAT DO CRIME SCENE INVESTIGATORS LOOK FOR?

At the crime scene, investigators look for *evidence* that will help them establish whether a crime has been committed, who committed the crime, and evidence to prove their case. Evidence is the legal means by which one attempts to prove or disprove something. Evidence can include almost anything submitted to the jury or trier of fact for consideration. It can be offered in many forms, from someone's own testimony to material objects, such as weapons or blood stains, to crime scene sketches, diagrams, photographs, documents, and other types of physical evidence.

What Type of Evidence are Investigators Looking for at Crime Scene?

At the crime scene, investigators are looking for any evidence that will provide information or assistance that may be relevant to their case. Physical evidence is one of the most important forms of evidence sought at the crime scene, and is something which can be seen, touched, or felt, and identified by its own nature. Physical evidence is said to "speak for itself" and therefore is considered more reliable than other forms of evidence. Generally, physical evidence may be obtained from five main sources: crime scene, victim, victim's environment, suspect, and the suspect's environment.

Examples of physical evidence include the weapon found at the crime scene, fingerprints, blood stains, semen, hair, fibers, and many other items. In order for physical evidence to be admitted into court, a proper foundation must be presented through a witness who can testify to the authenticity of the evidence.

CSI CHECKLIST 1.1

Sources of Physical Evidence

Physical Evidence is obtained from five main sources:

❑ Crime scene
❑ Victim
❑ Victim's environment
❑ Suspect
❑ Suspect's environment

WHAT IS CRIME SCENE EVIDENCE USED FOR?

Crime scene evidence is used to help determine whether a crime has been committed, how and when it was committed, where it was committed, why it was committed, and who did or who did not commit the crime. It is used to identify and locate a suspect and to connect that suspect to the crime and the crime scene. It is also used to establish legal proof in a criminal trial that a crime has been committed and that the defendant committed the crime. For the defense, crime scene evidence may be used for the opposite purpose—to disprove that a crime was committed or that the defendant committed the crime.

PRACTICE TIP 1.3

Think Ahead!

When gathering crime scene evidence, be sure to think ahead to the ultimate goal. What will be admissible at trial? How will the opposing side challenge this evidence and what additional evidence must be found in order to overcome that challenge?

How Do We Know What Evidence to Look for at the Crime Scene?

To know what *is* evidence, consider what type of crime was committed. The relative importance of crime scene evidence depends on its ability to establish that a crime was committed, and to show *how, when*, and *by whom* it was committed.

SUMMARY

A crime scene investigation is a methodical process that involves identifying, documenting, collecting, preserving, and evaluating information and evidence at a crime scene to determine what happened, how it happened, why it happened, and who or what was responsible. The emerging role of the criminalist and development of the modern crime lab have become an integral part of the crime scene investigation. Based on Locard's Exchange Theory, that whenever two surfaces come into contact with each other, there is a partial *transfer* or *exchange* of material from one to the other, criminalistics merges the principles of physical science with those of criminal investigation and law in the detection of crimes. Through the identification, collection, preservation, and evaluation of physical evidence found at the crime scene and the extended crime environment, criminalistics attempt to determine whether a crime has been committed, how and when it was committed, where it was committed, why it was committed, and who did or who did not commit the crime. A crime scene investigator must understand the role of physical evidence found at the crime scene and how criminalistics can be utilized in evaluating this evidence.

How the crime scene is investigated can make or break a case. It is imperative for anyone involved in the investigation, prosecution, or defense of a crime to understand the *proper* procedures and techniques involved in the investigation of a crime scene. It is equally essential to know the laws governing crime scene investigation and the potential *evidentiary challenges* that faced by either side.

KEY TERMS

Class Characteristics	Criminalist
Corpus Delicti	Criminalistics
Crime	Criminology
Crime Lab	Deduction
Crime Scene	Deductive Reasoning
Crime Scene Investigation	Elements of a Crime

Evidence	Individual Characteristics
Exchange Theory	Investigation
Exculpatory Evidence	Matchable Characteristics
Felony	Misdemeanor
Forensic Science	Physical Evidence
Inculpatory Evidence	Trace Evidence

REVIEW QUESTIONS

1. Define *Locard's Exchange Theory* and explain how it is used.

2. Distinguish *criminalistics* from *criminology*.

3. Describe the difference between *class* and *individual characteristics*, and provide an example of each.

4. Assess why law is important to crime scene investigation, and how laws influence the investigation of a crime scene and the gathering of evidence. Provide examples.

5. Discuss what a crime scene is and what type of crime may not involve a crime scene.

6. Distinguish between the different types of crime scene investigators and what they look for at a crime scene.

7. Describe what crime scene evidence is used for.

8. Explain what a crime is and what is meant by establishing the *corpus delicti*.

CRITICAL THINKING QUESTIONS 1.1

1. Why do you think we have laws that govern the investigation of a crime scene and what public policy reasons do you think are behind these?

2. What criminal cases in the news can you name that were lost or affected by improper following of legal procedures by crime scene personnel?

FORENSIC RESEARCH USING THE INTERNET

1. Search the Internet for crime scene investigation sites. Assess some of these sites and discuss them in class.

2. Search the Internet for specific laws dealing with crime scene investigations. Discuss whether there are a sufficient number of sites that provide this information. If not, think about how you would find these important laws.

PRACTICE SKILLS:

Practice what you have learned in the following crime scene problem:

Crime Scene Analysis 1.1

Burglary is the unlawful entering of a building or structure with the intent to commit a felony or theft therein.

List at least six different examples of evidence that might be found at the crime scene of a potential burglary to help prove the elements in the definition above. For each, explain which element the evidence would help prove and why.

Crime Scene Analysis 1.2

For each of the above examples of evidence discuss:

1. Whether you think the evidence might have class or individual characteristics

2. Whether the evidence is an example of Locard's Exchange Theory

WEB SITES

American Academy of Forensic Sciences
http://www.aafs.org/

American Society of Crime Laboratory Directors
http://www.ascld.org/forensicstudents.html

City of Beverly Hills, California (Job Opportunities)
http://www.beverlyhills.org

City of Mesa, Arizona, Crime Lab
http://www.ci.mesa.az.us/police/crimelab

ENDNOTES

[1] From the City of Mesa, Arizona web site, *http://www.ci.mesa.az.us/police/crimelab/*

[2] From Crime Scene Analyst I job description, Las Vegas Crime Lab.

[3] From Criminalist I job description, Las Vegas Crime Lab.

INVESTIGATING THE CRIME SCENE: INITIAL RESPONSE AND PLANNING

"It is a capital mistake to theorize before one has data. Insensibly one begins to twist facts to suit theories instead of theories to suit facts."

—Sherlock Holmes, *A Scandal in Bohemia*

"All truths are easy to understand once they are discovered; the point is to discover them."

—Galileo Galilei

Chapter Outline

- Preliminary Investigation Techniques
- Initial Response
- Securing the Crime Scene
- Establishing a Perimeter
- Ensuring Scene Safety
- Emergency Care
- Initial Documentation
- Crime Scene Assessment
- Scene Briefing
- Walk-Through of Crime Scene
- Planning the Crime Scene Investigation
- Planning Steps for a Methodical Process
- Crime Scene Debriefing
- Final Documentation of the Crime Scene
- Final Survey Before Release of Crime Scene
- Legal Challenges

INTRODUCTION

In Chapter 1, we looked at the importance of and relationship between crime scene investigation, criminalistics, and the law. In this chapter, we will begin our focus on how to investigate a crime scene, from the preliminary considerations and initial response to planning the final assessment and release of a crime scene.

PRELIMINARY INVESTIGATION TECHNIQUES

In the United States, unless a federal crime has been committed, local law enforcement agencies (including city police, county sheriffs, and state police) have the primary responsibility for the investigation of most crimes. Typically, it is a patrol officer from one of these local agencies who is the first responder to a crime scene. These patrol officers, and the crime scene investigators called to the scene, assess preliminary investigative considerations and procedures that are followed throughout the investigation. (See Exhibit 2.1.) These considerations include providing a safe and effective initial response, establishing scene security, ensuring safety measures, providing emergency care, and creating initial documentation.

EXHIBIT 2.1   Preliminary Investigation

In many basic law enforcement training academies, officers receive the following guidelines regarding preliminary investigation:
- ❑   Proceed to scene quickly and safely
- ❑   Render aid to injured
- ❑   Effect arrest of offender/suspect
- ❑   Locate and identify witnesses
- ❑   Initiate "be on the lookout" broadcast, if needed
- ❑   Maintain crime scene and protect evidence
- ❑   Interview victims and witnesses—interrogate suspect if needed
- ❑   Note all conditions and remarks
- ❑   Arrange for collection and preservation of evidence
- ❑   Report incident fully and accurately
- ❑   Yield responsibility to specialty investigators or superiors, if required

INITIAL RESPONSE

Law enforcement officers are taught preliminary investigative techniques that stress a quick but safe response to a crime scene. Typically, the first officer on the scene is in charge until properly relieved by the appropriate investigator. In many small departments, the patrol officer will also serve as the lead investigator unless the crime or crime scene is serious or complex enough to require specialized crime lab or investigative support.

Officers should record the date and time of their call, their time of arrival, visibility, weather, and lighting. Upon arriving at the scene, they should note people or vehicles, potential evidence, safety factors, and any objects or conditions that might have a bearing on the crime or the crime scene.

The initial call to a patrol officer regarding a potential crime scene generally comes in one of three different reporting forms: a crime in progress, a crime that just occurred, or a crime that has already occurred and has just been discovered (or reported). Tactics for responding to potential crime scenes will depend on how the call is received by the officer. For example, an officer will proceed quickly and directly to a reported crime in progress. Upon arrival, the officer will employ tactical measures to approach the scene safely, and will search for suspects and victims. Depending on the type of crime reported, the presumption here is that a suspect is still at the scene and there may be victims in need of emergency care. The focus, then, is on safety of the officers, finding the suspect, and tending to the victims.

For a report of a crime that just occurred, a patrol officer will still employ the same safety measures upon arrival, but may adjust her approach in driving to the scene to focus on potential suspects, victims, or witnesses leaving the area.

The patrol officer must balance all of these considerations in the initial response to a crime scene. How to approach, what to observe and note, whether a suspect is still at the scene, whether there is a victim being held hostage or in need of medical care, what environmental conditions or other safety issues need to be dealt with—all of these may be important as the responding officer enters and scans the crime scene. At the center of all of this assessment and tactical decision making is the need to secure the potential crime scene, to avoid destroying or contaminating potential evidence, and to determine whether a crime has been committed.

CSI CHECKLIST 2.1

Initial Response

The initial responding officer(s) should:

❑ Quickly but safely respond to the crime scene
❑ Be observant of and note all conditions, persons, and vehicles at scene
❑ Ensure officer safety when approaching scene
❑ Check for victims or suspects
❑ Take steps to secure and protect the scene
❑ Treat the location as a crime scene until determined to be otherwise

PRACTICE TIP 2.1

Crime Scene Response Guidelines

Want to read more about crime scene response?
Crime Scene Response Guidelines from
http://www.crime-scene-investigator.net/csi-response.html

Securing the Crime Scene

One of the most important steps at a potential crime scene is the protection, security, and control of the scene. This must be done as soon as possible to prevent evidence from being removed, destroyed, or contaminated. It is also done to identify, document, and control people at the scene. The general rule for the first patrol officer to arrive at the scene is to *freeze and protect the scene*; do not let anyone in or out, and freeze or control the movements of those at the scene until an initial assessment can be done of whether a crime has been committed and the type of crime and potential evidence involved. In its crime scene guide for law enforcement, the National Institute of Justice states that "[c]ontrolling the movement of persons at the crime scene and limiting the number of persons who enter the crime scene is essential to maintaining scene integrity, safeguarding evidence, and minimizing contamination."[1]

Controlling the movement of those at the crime scene also involves ensuring that no one touches, moves, or affects any potential evidence before the scene is thoroughly documented and processed. For example, no one should be allowed to eat, drink, smoke, use a bathroom or telephone, open any window or door, adjust a thermostat, pick up, put down, or move anything, or turn on any electronic device (e.g., radio, television, computer) or appliance.

CSI CHECKLIST 2.2

Securing the Crime Scene

The initial responding officer(s) should:

- ❑ Freeze and protect the scene
- ❑ Identify and control movements of all individuals at the scene
- ❑ Secure and separate suspects, witnesses, and victims
- ❑ Keep unauthorized and nonessential personnel from the scene
- ❑ Ensure that no one touches, moves, or affects any potential evidence before the scene is thoroughly documented and processed

---

Establishing a Perimeter

Proper security of a crime scene also involves establishing a perimeter boundary to protect the scene from anyone attempting to enter or leave. The size and extent of a perimeter boundary is guided by the type of crime and location of the scene. Usually, this boundary is set up farther out from the actual crime scene in order to protect potential points of entry or exit that the suspect or victim may have taken, or where evidence may have been moved or left. For example, a crime scene in a wooded or outdoor location may require a large area perimeter extending several hundred yards or more. (See Exhibit 2.2.) The general rule is that a larger perimeter boundary can be more easily reduced in size than it can be expanded. The perimeter boundary should be a physical barrier using crime scene tape or rope. Officers should be assigned to access control points along the boundary, with one central point of entry and exit established. A crime scene sign-in log should be maintained by the access control officer at the main point of entry to document everyone that enters or exits the scene.

EXHIBIT 2.2   Human Skull Found in Woods

In this crime scene, a large perimeter must be established to allow a search for more bones.

The proper protection and security of the crime scene will be a critical element in maintaining the legal integrity of the subsequent investigation and evidence collected.

CSI CHECKLIST 2.3

Establishing Perimeter Boundary at Crime Scene

The initial responding officer(s) should:

- ❑ Establish a perimeter boundary to protect the scene from anyone attempting to enter or leave, and to protect the evidence at the scene
- ❑ Include in the boundaries the potential points and paths of entry and exit for suspects, victims, witnesses, and evidence
- ❑ Assign officers to access control points along the boundary, with one central point of entry and exit established
- ❑ Control and document all individuals entering or leaving the scene
- ❑ Ensure proper protection and security of the crime scene

> ## PRACTICE TIP 2.2
>
> **Electronic Crime Scene Investigation**
>
> *What do you do if the crime scene is a computer? Find out more about the initial response procedure for first responders to electronic crime scenes.*
>
> *Electronic Crime Scene Investigation: A Guide for First Responders*
>
> *http://www.ojp.usdoj.gov/nij/pubs-sum/187736.htm*

Ensuring Scene Safety

After establishing the perimeter boundary to secure a crime scene, the patrol officer or initial responding investigator needs to evaluate the scene to identify potential health or safety hazards that might endanger the crime scene or individuals at the scene. Potential risks can include anything from chemical, biohazards, or bloodborne pathogens, to traffic, weather, structural dangers, animals, or hostile crowds. Protective safety devices or clothing may need to be used and other emergency control agencies (e.g., fire department, hazardous material response team, disaster control, emergency management) may be contacted for assistance.

> ## CSI CHECKLIST 2.4
>
> **Ensuring Safety at Crime Scene**
>
> *To help ensure safety at the crime scene, the following steps should be followed:*
>
> ❑ Evaluate the scene to identify and control any potential health or safety hazards that might endanger the crime scene or those individuals at the scene
> ❑ Contact agencies and specialists to assist when needed (e.g., fire department, public health, hazardous materials team)
> ❑ Identify and control any suspects or persons at the scene who present a danger to themselves or others
> ❑ Ensure safety of all persons at the scene

CSI CHECKLIST 2.5

Contamination Control

It is essential at crime scenes to establish effective contamination control procedures and prevent cross-contamination. The following checklist from the Department of Justice provides an important checklist to help with this:

❑ Limit scene access to people directly involved in scene processing.

❑ Follow established entry/exit routes at the scene.

❑ Identify first responders and consider collection of elimination samples.

❑ Designate secure area for trash and equipment.

❑ Use personal protective equipment (PPE) to prevent contamination of personnel and to minimize scene contamination.

❑ Clean/sanitize or dispose of tools/equipment and personal protective equipment between evidence collections and/or scenes.

❑ Utilize single-use equipment when performing direct collection of biological samples.

Summary: Minimize contamination by being safe, clean, and careful to ensure the welfare of personnel and the integrity of the evidence.

Source: U.S. Department of Justice, National Institute of Justice[2]

Emergency Care

As noted under the "R" in the acronym for *preliminary*, "render aid to the injured" is a primary responsibility for the first responder to a crime scene. The officer or investigator who responds first to a violent crime scene may encounter a victim in need of immediate medical attention. The officer may need to check the victim and render aid, while trying not to contaminate or disturb the crime scene. To compound the potential for contamination, medical first-responder personnel will be arriving at the crime scene, charged with the responsibility of providing emergency medical care to the victim at the scene. This will involve various paramedics or fire personnel going in and out of the scene, setting up medical instruments, moving the victim, and often moving furniture and objects near the victim.

The officers or investigators in charge of the crime scene need to ensure that medical aid is provided to the victim, while trying not to have medical personnel contaminate the scene. To help with this, the officers should document (photograph if there is time) the victim's position, clothing, appearance, and everything around the immediate area of the victim prior to the emergency medical personnel arriving at the scene. This may be difficult or impossible if the victim requires immediate attention before the medical personnel arrive, or if the medical responders arrive at the same time as the patrol officer.

Officers also need to document the medical personnel at the scene, including who they are, where they come from, where they take the victim, their movements at the scene, and what they touch or move. Officers should warn medical personnel about potential evidence, telling them not to move or touch anything unless necessary, and not to cut through or tear any clothing or items that might have evidentiary value, like a shirt with a knife or bullet hole. Many law enforcement agencies conduct specialized training for medical first responders to help them understand the importance of protecting crime scenes and evidence found on the victim or at the scene.

CSI CHECKLIST 2.6

Emergency Care

The initial responding officer(s) should:

❑ Render aid to the injured while trying not to contaminate scene
❑ Request emergency medical assistance, if needed
❑ Document and guide movement of medical personnel and equipment to victim to help reduce contamination of scene
❑ Warn medical personnel about potential physical evidence and instruct them not to move or touch evidence unless necessary
❑ Document any statements/comments made by victims, suspects, or witnesses at the scene
❑ Send officer with victim or suspect if transported to a medical facility to collect and preserve evidence and to document any statements made

Initial Documentation

Throughout the initial response and preliminary investigation of the crime scene, the responding officers or investigators must continue to document in a clear and concise manner all actions taken and observations made. From the time that the call was received to the time of arrival, weather conditions, traffic, vehicles or people at or near the scene, conditions and observations upon arrival, assessments made, actions taken, and personnel involved—any or all of this could be important to the subsequent crime scene investigation.

CSI CHECKLIST 2.7

Initial Documentation

Documentation must be accomplished in a clear and concise manner. The initial responding officer(s) should document:

❑ All activities, conditions, and observations made upon arrival at the scene
❑ Any action or observation made while at the scene
❑ Statements from or observations about witnesses, victims, or suspects at the scene

---

Crime Scene Assessment

After the initial response and preliminary investigative considerations have been dealt with by the first responders, the lead investigators taking charge of the crime scene investigation, whether patrol officers or specialized investigators, must conduct an assessment of the crime scene to determine how to proceed. An assessment of the crime scene may involve a briefing by the initial responder, another walk-through of the scene, an assessment of the type of crime to be investigated, and planning for the level of investigation, personnel, and equipment needed to properly process the crime scene.

A crime scene assessment helps investigators develop a plan for the "coordinated identification, collection, and preservation of physical evidence and identification of witnesses. It also allows for the exchange of information among law enforcement personnel and the development of investigative strategies."[3]

Scene Briefing

The briefing of the lead investigator by the initial responder is an important time for several reasons. It allows the control of the crime scene to be smoothly turned over from the initial responder to the investigator who will be leading the crime scene search. It allows the lead investigator to be made aware of the initial aspects, observations, and relevant information of the crime scene response officers. This might include what the responding officer observed upon arrival, suspects or victims present, personnel in or out of the scene, actions taken, whether or not a crime has been established, and, if so, the type of crime is involved. The briefing alerts the lead investigator to security or safety issues that need to be considered in planning the crime scene investigation. It also allows for the maintenance and continuation of all crime scene documentation and logs.

Walk-Through of Crime Scene

theory of the case
The initial hypothesis of what crime was committed, how it was committed, and where.

Conducting a walk-through of the crime scene gives the lead investigator an overview of the entire scene and helps in planning how the crime scene should be processed. The investigator can see the crime committed, where it was committed, and identify points of entry, exit, and potential evidence at any of these points. The walk-through helps the investigator form an initial hypothesis of the crime, also referred to as the **theory of the case**, to help form an opinion of what crime was committed, how it was committed, and where. This will, in turn, help with planning the focus of the investigation and how to search and process the crime scene. Taking notes and photographing or videotaping the walk-through provides valuable documentation of the condition of the scene as first observed by the investigator.

CSI CHECKLIST 2.8

Crime Scene Assessment

The lead investigators taking charge of a crime scene should conduct a crime scene assessment that includes:

- ❏ Briefing by the initial responder
- ❏ Walk-through of the crime scene
- ❏ Assessment of the type of crime to be investigated
- ❏ Planning for the level of investigation, personnel, and equipment needed to properly process the crime scene.

PRACTICE TIP 2.3

Use Caution in Walk-Through

Caution must be used in conducting the walk-through to ensure that the crime scene is not contaminated or potential evidence destroyed by the movement through the scene.

PLANNING THE CRIME SCENE INVESTIGATION

After a crime scene has been properly responded to and assessed, the plan developed to investigate the scene will be initiated. The crime scene walk-through and assessment helps the investigator properly plan how the crime scene will be investigated and processed for evidence. This planning will include the number of personnel and equipment needed; specific responsibilities of those personnel, time factors, security, and safety considerations; legal issues, including whether a search warrant is needed; size of the scene and whether the initial scene protective boundaries need to be changed; how search personnel will approach the scene; how evidence will be processed and collected; where evidence will be temporarily stored at the scene and how this evidence will be protected and preserved; and how the crime scene investigation and processing will be accurately and thoroughly documented.

Planning Steps for a Methodical Process

A crime scene investigation needs to be a methodical process that proceeds in a logical and thorough manner. Without such a painstaking process, important evidence may not be found or may be collected improperly. As noted in Chapter 1, a crime scene investigation involves identifying, documenting, collecting, preserving, and analyzing information and evidence at a crime scene to determine what happened, how it happened, why it happened, and who or what was responsible. The basic steps of the crime scene investigative process are:

1. Identification

Relevant evidence at the crime scene must first be found and identified by the investigator, from the possible drops of blood that look like black paint to the reluctant witness who may have heard the crime being committed but does not want to get involved.

2. Documentation

Once found and identified, evidence must be properly documented so that a permanent record is available for further reference in the investigation, as well as at trial. Proper documentation includes photographs and videotaping of the evidence, notes describing the evidence and who found it, and a sketch detailing where evidence was found in relation to the crime scene and other evidence at the scene.

3. Collection

After it is identified as possible physical evidence, evidence must then be collected. Dried blood must be properly gathered and stored in the proper container. The reluctant witness must be located and convinced to cooperate.

4. Preservation

chain of custody
The proper preservation and protection of crime scene evidence in order to ensure its physical and legal integrity.

Evidence must be properly maintained and protected in order to preserve its legal integrity. This is called maintaining the **chain of custody**. Blood samples must be sealed and accounted for until trial. A written statement from the witness must be obtained.

5. Analysis

After it has been collected and preserved, the evidence must be analyzed to determine its evidentiary value. Is the blood sample from the suspect? Is there enough for a DNA test? Is the witness's statement verifiable? Can the witness identify a suspect?

PRACTICE TIP 2.4

Good Guide for Planning a Crime Scene Investigation

Crime Scene Investigation – A Guide for Law Enforcement

Access this Department of Justice document on-line:
   National Institute of Justice: CSI, A Guide for Law Enforcement
      http://www.ncjrs.org/pdffiles1/nij/178280.pdf
      http://www.ojp.usdoj.gov/nij/pubs-sum/178280.htm

CRIME SCENE DEBRIEFING

One of the final steps in planning the crime scene investigation process, prior to releasing and exiting the crime scene, is to plan to conduct a debriefing. The purpose of a debriefing is to ensure that a crime scene investigation is complete and to verify post-scene responsibilities. The debriefing is designed to share information between the members of the crime scene investigative team, as well as other law enforcement personnel and responders. The debriefing allows discussion and analysis of the crime scene and investigation, providing an opportunity not only to discuss how this investigation fared, but how it affects future planning and responsibilities. The debriefing also provides everyone an opportunity to make recommendations about post-crime scene needs and follow-up investigation. Finally, the debriefing puts everyone on the same page as to the status of the investigation and what is needed by those involved in it.

CSI CHECKLIST 2.9

Crime Scene Debriefing

A crime scene debriefing should be conducted by the lead investigators with all crime scene personnel and first responders. This debriefing should:

❑ Verify that the crime scene investigation is complete and that all evidence has been collected
❑ Discuss preliminary findings
❑ Identify what is needed for follow-up investigation or analysis
❑ Establish post-scene responsibilities
❑ Ensure that everyone knows what the status of the investigation is and what is needed by those involved in it

---

FINAL DOCUMENTATION OF CRIME SCENE

Part of the debriefing should ensure that all relevant reports and other documentation pertaining to the crime scene investigation have been turned over to the lead investigator, who will compile this documentation into a central *case file*. This file contains a documented record of all personnel at the scene, actions taken, and evidence collected. As the criminal investigation proceeds, more reports and documentation will be added to the case file, including follow-up investigative reports, witness and suspect interviews, and results of evidentiary testing or analysis.

CSI CHECKLIST 2.10

Final Documentation of Crime Scene

The lead investigator(s) needs to ensure that all initial reports and documentation pertaining to the crime scene investigation are collected, including:

- ❑ Initial responding officer(s) reports
- ❑ Other responders' reports and documentation (e.g., emergency medical personnel, fire department, hazardous materials team)
- ❑ Victim and witness statements
- ❑ Crime scene documentation, including videos, photographs, and sketches
- ❑ Evidence collection documentation.
- ❑ Search warrant or consent form documentation
- ❑ Additional case reports to be added when completed (e.g., forensic testing and analysis, follow-up investigative reports)

FINAL SURVEY BEFORE RELEASE OF CRIME SCENE

In planning the investigation, remember that a final survey and post-investigative walk-through of the crime scene will be needed before releasing and exiting the scene. These safeguards will help ensure that all relevant evidence has been collected, that no evidence or equipment has been left behind, and that any hazardous conditions or materials have been dealt with or reported to the proper authorities.

CSI CHECKLIST 2.11

Final Survey of Crime Scene

At the conclusion of a crime scene investigation, a final walk-through survey of the scene should be conducted to ensure that the investigation is complete, including:

- ❑ Each area identified as part of the crime scene is visually inspected
- ❑ All evidence collected at the scene is accounted for

continued

> ❑   All equipment and materials generated by the investiga-
>   tion are removed
> ❑   Any dangerous materials or conditions are reported and
>   addressed
> ❑   The crime scene is released in accordance with jurisdic-
>   tional requirements
>
> Source: U.S. Department of Justice, National Institute of Justice[4]

LEGAL CHALLENGES

One of the primary legal issues encountered in the investigation of
a crime scene is whether law enforcement officers needed a
search warrant to remain at the crime scene after the initial
response. This will be discussed in more detail in Chapter 7.

Other legal challenges involving the initial response and preliminary investigation of a crime scene generally focus on whether
proper procedures were followed to secure the scene, to maintain
safety, and to prevent contamination or destruction of evidence.

Our nation's law enforcement officers and investigators do a
remarkable job in conducting criminal investigations, but we must
never assume that they are perfect or that their investigation will be
without any errors. The nationally televised O.J. Simpson murder trial
illustrated this by successfully focusing on the mistakes made by
police at the crime scene, including taking a blanket from inside the
victim's apartment to cover the victim's body on the sidewalk outside the apartment. In the Jon Benet Ramsey murder investigation,
the responding officers did not search the entire home and allowed
several friends of the victim's family to enter and remain in the house
prior to the arrival of an investigator. The investigator later allowed
the victim's father and a family friend to search the home. The father
found his daughter's body in the basement of the home, removed a
tape from her mouth, brought the body upstairs, and placed her on the
floor near the door. The body was subsequently moved again and a
blanket placed over her.[5]

Goes to Weight of Evidence, Not Admissibility

Most courts have held that "concerns about contamination ... may
arise with respect to any forensic evidence."[6] However, legal challenges regarding procedural mistakes by law enforcement at the
crime scene or contamination of the scene go "to the weight of the
evidence and not its admissibility."[7] In challenging the way a crime
scene was handled or investigated, the defense could attack the credibility of the law enforcement witnesses or present its own

witnesses. "The potential for contamination may present an open field for cross-examination or may be addressed through testimony of defense experts at trial, as is true of other forensic evidence."[8]

SUMMARY

Typically, patrol officers from law enforcement agencies are the first to respond to a crime scene. These officers, and the crime scene investigators who are called to the scene, assess preliminary investigative considerations and procedures that are followed throughout the investigation. These considerations include providing a safe and effective initial response, establishing scene security, ensuring safety measures, providing emergency care, and creating initial documentation.

In many small departments, the patrol officer will also serve as the lead investigator unless the crime or crime scene is serious or complex enough to require specialized crime lab or investigative support. One of the most important first steps to be taken at a potential crime scene is the protection, security, and control of the scene. The proper protection and security of the crime scene will be a critical element in maintaining the legal integrity of the subsequent investigation and evidence collected. After establishing the perimeter boundary to secure a crime scene, the patrol officer or initial responding investigator needs to evaluate the scene to identify potential health or safety hazards that might endanger the crime scene or those individuals at the scene. Rendering aid to the injured is also the primary responsibility of the first responder to a crime scene. Throughout the initial response and preliminary investigation of the crime scene, the responding officers or investigators must continue to document in a clear and concise manner all actions taken and observations made.

After the initial response and preliminary investigative considerations have been dealt with by the first responders, the lead investigators of the crime scene investigation, whether patrol officers or specialized investigators, must conduct an assessment of the crime scene to determine how to proceed. An assessment of the crime scene may involve a briefing by the initial responder, another walkthrough of the scene, an assessment of the type of crime to be investigated, and planning for the level of investigation, personnel, and equipment needed to properly process the crime scene. One of the final steps in the crime scene investigation process, prior to releasing and exiting the crime scene, is to conduct a debriefing. The purpose of a debriefing is to ensure that a crime scene investigation is complete and to verify post-scene responsibilities. Part of the debriefing should ensure that all relevant reports and other documentation pertaining to the crime scene investigation have been turned over to the lead investigator, who will compile this documentation into a central *case file.* This file contains a documented record of all personnel at the scene, actions taken, and evidence collected. A final survey and post-investigative walk-through of the crime scene is needed before releasing and exiting the scene. These safeguards will help ensure that all relevant evidence has been collected, that no evidence or equipment has been left behind, and that any hazardous conditions or materials have been dealt with or reported to the proper authorities.

KEY TERMS

Chain of Custody   Theory of the Case

REVIEW QUESTIONS

1. Describe some of the preliminary investigative responsibilities in initially responding to a crime scene.

2. What is one of the most important first steps to take at a crime scene and why?

3. Explain what is meant by "ensuring scene safety."

4. What is the purpose of a "crime scene assessment" and how is this accomplished?

5. Identify and discuss the steps for a methodical process of investigating a crime scene.

6. What is the purpose of the final documentation and survey of a crime scene?

CRITICAL THINKING QUESTIONS 2.1

1. What is the importance of understanding the preliminary investigative responsibilities and techniques?

2. What public policy issues or considerations do you think might be behind some of the techniques and procedures discussed in this chapter?

3. How do the techniques and procedures discussed in this chapter influence the investigation of a crime scene?

FORENSIC RESEARCH USING THE INTERNET

1. Search the Internet for specific Web sites dealing with initial response to and planning of crime scene investigations. Discuss whether there are a sufficient number of sites that provide this information and assess at least two of these sites for substantive and relevant information.

PRACTICE SKILLS:

Practice what you have learned in the following problems:

Crime Scene Analysis 2.1

Read the following report and answer these questions:

1. What procedure was done properly in the initial response and preliminary investigation of this reported crime?

2. What procedure was done improperly?

3. How would you have handled this initial response and preliminary investigation differently?

On December 26, at approximately 5:52 a.m., police officers responded to a private residence regarding a possible kidnapping. The residents, parents of a 6-year-old girl, informed the officers that at approximately 5:45 a.m., the mother discovered that their daughter was missing from the residence. The daughter was last seen by the mother in the residence at approximately 10:00 p.m. on December 25. The daughter was last seen in her bed. Her bedroom is located on the second floor of the residence. According to officers, there were no obvious signs of forced entry into their residence.(A police sergeant later said that when he arrived at 0930 hours and entered through the rear exterior kitchen door, he saw what appeared to be a pry-mark in the door jam of this door. He said the mark was on the exterior of the house near the door knob and lock on the door, and that the damaged area appeared to have been less weathered than the surrounding surfaces on the door and door jam.) The parents stated that they believed that the house was locked when they went to bed and that it was locked when they got up.

continued

The mother told officers that she had found what appeared to be a ransom note at the bottom of the staircase leading from the first floor to the second floor. The note stated that the daughter had been kidnapped and would be decapitated if the demands of the note ($118,000 ransom) were not met. The note stated that police were not to be contacted. The author(s) of the note stated that they would phone the father between 0800–1000 hours. At approximately 0800 hours, a detective arrived at the residence, at which time the persons present included: the parents, four friends of the family (who had been called by the parents), the pastor from the family's church, and two police officers. The detective monitored incoming phone calls to the residence from approximately 0800–1300 hours. The father answered the incoming phone calls. None of the incoming calls was from the reported kidnappers.

At approximately 1300 hours, the detective asked the father and his friends to check the interior of the residence for any sign of the daughter, or anything that may have been left or taken that belonged to her. The daughter's bedroom had been sealed off by detectives at approximately 1030 hours. The father went to the basement of the house, followed by two of his friends. Within a few minutes, the detective saw the father run up the basement stairs carrying a young girl in his arms. Both arms of the girl were raised above her head. There appeared to be a string hanging from the girl's right wrist. The girl's lips were blue; she appeared to have livor mortis on the back side of her body, rigor mortis, and she was not breathing. She was dressed in a light-colored, long-sleeved turtleneck and light-colored pants (similar to pajama bottoms). The father placed the girl on the floor, inside the front door. The girl was identified by the father as his missing daughter. The girl appeared to have been dead for a period of time. The father toldthe detective that he had found his daughter in the wine cellar in the basement, underneath a blanket, with her wrists tied above her head and a piece of tape covering her mouth. The father had removed the tape from her mouth before he carried his daughter upstairs to the first floor.

WEB SITES

Crime Scene Response Guidelines from www.crime-scene-investigator.net

http://www.crime-scene-investigator.net/csi-response.html

Electronic Crime Scene Investigation: A Guide for First Responders

http://www.ojp.usdoj.gov/nij/pubs-sum/187736.htm

National Institute of Justice: *Crime Scene Investigation, A Guide for Law Enforcement*

http://www.ncjrs.org/pdffiles1/nij/178280.pdf

http://www.ojp.usdoj.gov/nij/pubs-sum/178280.htm

ENDNOTES

[1] Ibid

[2] *Crime Scene Investigation: A Guide for Law Enforcement*, National Institute of Justice, 2000

[3] Ibid

[4] Ibid

[5] For examples on this case, see the news article, *Records released in Ramsey probe,* by Christopher Anderson, Staff Writer, The Daily Camera

[6] *Oregon v. Cunningham* 197 Ore. App. 264; 105 P.3d 929 (2005)

[7] *State v. Montgomery* (Mo. App. 1976) 545 S.W.2d 655

[8] See *Oregon v. Cunningham*

CHAPTER **3**

INVESTIGATING THE CRIME SCENE: DOCUMENTING THE SCENE

"I see no more than you, but I have trained myself to notice what I see."

—Sherlock Holmes, *The Adventure of the Blanched Soldier*

"A picture is worth a thousand words."

—Napoleon Bonaparte

Chapter Outline

INTRODUCTION

In Chapter 2, we looked at how to investigate the crime scene, from the initial response and preliminary investigative steps, to the final survey and release of the scene. In this chapter, we will continue with our investigation of the crime scene, focusing on documenting the crime scene. Documenting the crime scene includes the use of notes, reports, photographs, video, and sketching in order to thoroughly record the scene and any evidence.

DOCUMENTING THE CRIME SCENE

The crime scene is documented to help provide a permanent record of what was observed, discovered, and collected at the scene, as well as the procedures followed. The objectives of documentation include:

1. To record what the crime scene looks like and what was observed at the scene
2. To record what was done at the crime scene by investigative and crime lab personnel
3. To record any evidence observed or identified at the scene and its location
4. To record the collection of evidence at the scene

Documentation provides a permanent record of the crime and crime scene for use throughout the investigation, in related investigations, and any subsequent prosecution and trial. As noted above, documentation of a crime scene is accomplished through the use of notes, reports, photography, video, and sketching.

Golden Rule of Hans Gross

In his famous text on criminalistics, *System der Kriminalistik*, written in 1893, Hans Gross wrote that an investigator should "never alter the position of, pick up, or even touch any object before it has been minutely described in an official note, and a photograph of it taken." The integrity of evidence is maintained by keeping it in its original form.

Integrity of Evidence

Hans Gross recognized a fact that is still relevant today: the integrity of evidence at the crime scene is maintained by keeping it in its original form until it has been recorded through sketching, photography, and reports.

All evidence must be protected and preserved. It should be photographed and sketched in its original position at the scene. Careful measurements must be taken. It is then collected in an appropriate manner, identified, and packaged for transfer to an evidence locker or lab. Finally, it must be held in a secure place until the case is resolved.

Investigative Notes And Reports

Investigative notes and reports are two important parts of documenting the crime scene. They can both serve as permanent records of information and must be written in a manner that furthers this purpose.

Investigative Notes

Notes are taken to describe the scene, record observations, and to collect information for later evaluation and use in reports. They are also used to document and explain evidence observed and collected at the scene, photographs taken, or diagrams and sketches made. For example, photographs may depict blood at a crime scene, but may not adequately convey the volume of blood or its relationship to other objects at the scene. Proper note-taking can supplement these photos and fill in these gaps. Notes also serve to refresh an officer's or investigator's memory when testifying in the courtroom.

Guidelines for Taking Notes

Because notes may serve as a permanent record, subject to being examined later in court, they should be written in ink, with each page identified. Notes should include the investigator's observations, recording not only what is seen, but what is heard, smelled, or any of the other senses that come into use at the scene. They should contain accurately recorded details and be written in a concise manner, with enough facts to refresh the note-taker's memory if called to testify later in court.

Notes should be entered chronologically. Common abbreviations can be used, but investigators should avoid using any personal forms of shorthand or abbreviations. Often, military time is used for consistency and to avoid any confusion about whether an entry recorded as "10" was a.m. or p.m. Notes should be entered in a loose-leaf notebook. Errors should be crossed out, not erased.

crime reports
Documentation of the initial reporting and investigation of a crime.

evidence logs
Logs that document evidence collected at the scene.

Investigative Reports

Reports are written to document the procedure followed and the progress made in a crime scene investigation. Depending on the agency and crime being investigated, there may be a variety of different reports that will need to be completed. **Crime reports** may document the initial reporting and investigation of a crime. **Evidence logs** are essential to document evidence collected at the scene. There may be officer reports from the initial responders, investigator's logs and reports, liaison agency reports, dead body reports, reports to document interviews or interrogations conducted at the scene, reports of property stolen, special actions taken, investigative follow-up reports, reports to request testing or special handling of evidence, and reports that detail the results of evidence testing.

Guidelines for Writing Reports

Reports serve as the official memory and record of an investigation and case. They include the primary documents that prepare a case for prosecution and may be read by many people, including other investigators, prosecutors, defense attorneys, judges, jurors, and the news media. Unlike notes, which may be taken under extreme circumstances in the field, the objectives of a report are to be concise, complete, clear, objective, and accurate.

One of the most important guidelines for writing complete and accurate reports is to first take and collect good notes. All of the relevant facts must be gathered and organized. The report should be thorough and accurate. Depending on the type of report being written, it should address the 5 W's and H (who, what, when, where, why, and how). An investigator should always question whether a verbal explanation would be required in addition to their report. If so, something is wrong or lacking. Reports should be reread before submission, and edited or rewritten if errors are found.

Legal Requirements

The legal requirements for any type of documentation in a crime scene investigation are that it be a true and accurate representation of whatever is being documented. Above all, any report written in a crime scene investigation should be accurate and verifiable. A report found to have errors will not render the subsequent testimony of its author inadmissible at trial. However, it may have a negative impact on the credibility of the investigator writing the report and on the investigation itself. Poorly written or inaccurate reports reflect sloppy work and the potential for improper procedures throughout the crime scene investigation.

Often, a criminal case does not come to trial for a long period of time. When the responding officer or investigator takes the stand to testify, she may not remember something that she has written or documented in her report. There are two ways to obtain this information and still have it admitted as evidence.

Present Memory Refreshed

In questioning a witness who is unable to remember something asked on the stand, it is permissible to jog or "refresh" the memory of that witness by letting the witness refer to a writing or object (her notes, a report, shopping list). After the witness's memory has been refreshed, the witness must then be able to testify independent of and without relying further on the writing. This is often called **present memory refreshed**. The key here is that the writing only serves to jog the memory of the witness and that the witness can then testify independently of the writing.

When a writing is used to refresh memory, the trial court may allow the opposing party to have the writing produced at the hearing.[1] The opposing party may inspect the writing, cross-examine the witness about it, and even introduce into evidence those portions that relate to the testimony of the witness.

Past Memory Recorded

Where the witness still has no independent recollection after attempting to "refresh" her memory, the witness will not be permitted to testify about the matter from her personal knowledge. However, the document or writing used to attempt to refresh the witness's memory may be admissible by itself and, if admitted, the witness may be asked to read the document to the jury. The document will not be shown to the jury unless the opposing party offers it. The evidence is in the reading of the document. This is called **past memory recorded.**

CRIME SCENE PHOTOGRAPHY

Crime scene photos and video are taken to provide visual documentation of the crime scene; to record it as discovered; to show the evidence and objects at the scene; and to show how the crime scene was processed. Crime scene photography is an indispensable tool to the investigator. In many crime scenes, especially those involving violence, photographs are considered an essential element to the presentation of the case in court, providing a permanent visual record of what was found and what may have happened. As evidence, photos may be preserved indefinitely and used when needed.

Today, many law enforcement agencies, particularly smaller ones, rely on patrol officers or investigators to take the photos at the crime scene. Other departments, especially larger agencies, rely on crime scene technicians or photographic specialists.

---

present memory refreshed
When the witness is permitted to refer to writing or notes in order to jog memory.

past memory recorded
When the witness is unable to refresh memory by reviewing notes or writing, the witness may not testify, but the document may be read into evidence.

Uses of Crime Scene Photography

The objectives in crime scene photography are to record the scene in a complete and accurate manner, and to photograph all stages of the crime scene processing and investigation. These photos and video are used to provide a permanent record of the original crime scene, as discovered, and to record the evidence found and collected at the scene. Another use is to record the position and condition of a victim in a death case.

Photos are used to record the location and characteristics of evidence at the scene, for example, blood splatters, trajectory of bullets, weapons, and prints. Photos also "collect" evidence that might not be otherwise retrievable, such as footprints, bullet holes, or fingerprints.

Photos help establish the elements or **corpus delicti** of a crime. (Pictures of a broken window or door to establish a "breaking" or "entry" in a burglary, for example.) Photos also show **modus operandi** evidence, or the method used to commit the crime. Photos help investigators and criminalists later in their follow-up evaluation of the crime scene and throughout the investigation of the crime.

Finally, photos are used as a visual aid at trial, especially in helping the judge and jury understand more about the crime and crime scene.

Types of Cameras Used

For years, the most common and popular type of camera used in crime scene investigation has been the *35 millimeter*, a versatile camera with an interchangable lens and a variety of different types of film available. For example, film speed, which is measured by ASA (American Standards Association), is available in 25 ASA for more light needed to 8000 ASA for taking photos without any light. Infrared film records infrared emissions rather than visible light. This special film is used in low-light surveillance, crime scene examination, and crime lab testing.

For close-up work and complex investigative photography, the *press camera* has a large 4 × 5 negative which allows for print enlargements without loss of detail and no film waste. A variation of this is the *fingerprint camera* which has lights around its close-up lens for minute detail of ridges and grooves. Many fingerprint photos and other specialized investigative photography is still done with black and white panchromatic film because it records the entire range of the visible light spectrum.

Video cameras are an essential aid to investigative photography. Most law enforcement agencies and crime labs today use some type of video to film the crime scene. With the ability to film the entire

corpus delicti
Translates to *body of the crime*, but refers to the elements that establish a crime has been committed.

modus operandi
Translates to *Method of Operation* and refers to how a crime has been committed.

crime scene and its step-by-step processing, video cameras provide a thorough visual documentation to the investigation.

Digital Cameras and Camcorders

Today, the use of digital cameras and digital camcorders is increasing in crime scene photography. Digital cameras allow crime scene investigators to quickly take and transmit pictures that they are taking at the scene back to their crime lab, to a command post, or to other law enforcement agencies that are cooperating in the investigation. For example, a fingerprint found at the crime scene could be photographed and sent to crime lab, digitized and fed into the FBI's national Automated Fingerprint Identification System (AFIS) for identification.

PRACTICE TIP 3.1

Crime Scene Photography Resources

Want to know more about crime scene photography? Check out the resources at http://www.crime-scene-investigator.net Resources for Crime Scene Photography http://www.crime-scene-investigator.net/csi-photo.html

---

Procedure in Crime Scene Photography

The key to crime scene photography is to photograph the scene as soon as possible, take photos at eye level, and take photos or video that help reconstruct the whole scene, through a pictorial sequence from the general to the specific. Photos should show all parts of the crime scene, including the entrance and exit areas, the general exterior and interior, the impact area, and all evidence. Photos should also show all stages of the crime scene investigation and the collection of evidence.

Photo Log

Before any photos are taken, a photo log must be prepared and maintained. The log should provide a record documenting all photographs taken, including who took the photo, when, where, what was photographed, and how.

Take Photos Before Moving Anything

Take photos before anything has been disturbed. If anything has been moved prior to photography, it should be noted in the report, but nothing should be reintroduced into the scene in order to take photographs. If something has been moved by anyone in the crime scene investigation, it should never be put back because it is *legally impossible* to return an object to its original position once it has been moved at the crime scene. Once moved, its original position can be noted and sketched, then photographed.

Take Photos With and Without Scale

Photograph the most fragile evidence and crime scene areas first (for example, if there is danger of evidence being destroyed by weather or traffic). In photographing evidence, first take photos of the object of evidence alone, then a larger view to show its relative size. Take a photo of the evidence in context with other objects at scene. Then, take a photo of the evidence with a marker to show scale. Photograph important evidence at least twice. A medium-distance photograph should be taken that shows the evidence and its position to other evidence. Then, a close-up photograph should be taken that includes a scale and fills the frame.

Take Photos From Different Angles

Photograph the scene from different angles to provide various perspectives that may uncover additional evidence. The overall interior crime scene should be photographed in an overlapping series using a wide-angle lens to show the entire scene and to use for reconstruction purposes. The overall exterior of the crime scene should also be photographed through a series of overlapping shots. These should include some landmarks as identifying markers. Both the overall interior and exterior should have 360 degrees of coverage. For the outside shots, the use of aerial photography should be considered to put some larger outdoor scenes in perspective.

Problems to Overcome with Crime Scene Photography

The value of crime scene photographs is described above. This includes the visual documentation and permanent record of a crime scene that photos provide. This record not only helps viewers to see what the crime scene looked like when discovered, but how it was processed and investigated. It also serves to help refresh the memory of those present at the scene. On the other hand, there may be problems to overcome in crime scene photography. Video and wide-angle photos may show irrelevant objects at the scene, along with the relevant, which may detract from the crime being investigated. Second, photos can be distorted to show inaccurate distances or relationships between objects photographed at the scene. Finally, some photos may be too graphic or gory, serving to prejudice the jury and causing a legal challenge that might exclude the visual evidence.

CSI CHECKLIST 3.1

Photographing the Crime Scene

❑ Photograph the crime scene as soon as possible
❑ Prepare a photographic log that records all photographs and a description and location of evidence
❑ Establish a progression of overall, medium, and close-up views of the crime scene
❑ Photograph from eye level to represent the normal view
❑ Photograph the most fragile areas of the crime scene first
❑ Photograph all stages of the crime scene investigation, including discoveries
❑ Photograph the condition of evidence before recovery
❑ Photograph the evidence in detail and include a scale, the photographer's initials, and the date
❑ When a scale is used, first take a photograph without the scale
❑ Photograph the interior crime scene in an overall and overlapping series using a wide-angle lens
❑ Photograph the exterior crime scene, establishing the location of the scene by a series of overall photographs, including a landmark
❑ Photographs should have 360 degrees of coverage. Consider using aerial photography
❑ Photograph entrances and exits
❑ Photograph important evidence twice (A medium-distance photograph that shows the evidence and its position to other evidence, a close-up photograph that includes a scale and fills the frame)

Source: FBI Handbook of Forensic Services

Legal Challenges to Crime Scene Photographs

To be admissible in court, each video recording or photograph must be properly identified and authenticated as being a true and accurate representation of the scene. They must be relevant and pertain to the case, and they must not be unduly prejudicial. Even though a picture is relevant in showing what happened to the victim or at the scene, it still may be excluded at trial if it is found to unduly bias the jury or prejudice the defendant. For example, photos showing a lot of blood or gore at a crime scene, or autopsy photos, might be excluded as being too inflammatory. (See Exhibit 3.1.) On the other hand, as the following case illustrates, most courts will allow "photographs that tend to shed light on, to strengthen, or to illustrate other testimony" or "photographs that show the external wounds of a deceased victim…even though the evidence is gruesome and cumulative and relates to undisputed matters."[2]

EXHIBIT 3.1 Evidentiary Rule Excluding Prejudicial Evidence

Rule 403. Exclusion of Relevant Evidence on Grounds of Prejudice, Confusion, or Waste of Time

Although relevant, evidence may be excluded if its probative value is substantially outweighed by the danger of unfair prejudice, confusion of the issues, or misleading the jury, or by considerations of undue delay, waste of time, or needless presentation of cumulative evidence.[3]

CASE

Lewis v. Mississippi

905 So.2d 729 (November, 2004)

Myers, J.

Larry Keith Lewis was involved in the shooting death of Paul Goodman. During the incident, Lewis's wife, Cynthia Lewis, suffered a gunshot wound to the neck which she miraculously survived. [After nine years of marriage, Cynthia had left her husband to seek a divorce and move in with Goodman. She later met with Lewis to discuss the terms of a divorce. The following day,] Lewis went to the apartment shared by Cynthia and Goodman and announced his presence at their front door. Goodman came to the door to see who was there and then peered out of the mini-blinds in a nearby window to obtain a better look. Upon seeing Goodman peer through the mini-blinds, Lewis fired a nine-millimeter pistol through the window, striking Goodman and injuring him. Goodman fell to the floor and was crawling for safety behind the couch when he was shot twice more by Lewis, suffering fatal wounds. After being struck initially, Goodman handed the phone to Cynthia who attempted to call 911. As she stepped behind the love seat to disconnect the computer from the Internet, she was shot in the neck, suffering momentary paralysis. A neighbor heard the shots and walked outside her apartment to see Lewis leaving the scene. Medical attention was summoned to the apartment while Lewis returned to his hotel.

…

Lewis was convicted of manslaughter and aggravated assault in the Circuit Court of Lee County and was sentenced to two consecutive twenty-year terms of imprisonment. On appeal, Lewis … contends that the trial court erred by admitting photographs of the deceased taken both at the crime scene and during the autopsy …

At trial, ten photographs were admitted which Lewis contends were irrelevant and unduly prejudicial. Nine of the photographs at issue were taken at Goodman's autopsy. These photographs illustrate the locations of Goodman's wounds. The tenth photograph depicts the location of Goodman's body at the

continued

crime scene, showing the position of the victim's body. It is Lewis's position that his participation in the crime was not at issue since he never denied firing the fatal shots, therefore making the photographs unnecessary to prove the crime. Lewis contends that the photographs only served to inflame the jury.

The issue of admissibility of crime scene and autopsy photographs is well settled in Mississippi. The Mississippi Supreme Court has held, photographs have evidentiary value in which they: 1) aid in describing the circumstances of the killing and the corpus delicti; 2) where they describe the location of the body and cause of death; and 3) where they supplement or clarify witness testimony.

....

The photographs meet all three [of these] tests ... The crime scene photograph aids in describing the circumstances surrounding the crime. This photo illustrates the contents of the apartment and the furniture which was originally in the marital home, giving the jury insight into what Lewis saw, possibly explaining his actions and arguably was taken into account in the jury's verdict of manslaughter rather than murder. The crime scene photo further clarifies the testimony for the jury regarding the positions of the victims and the layout of the apartment. The autopsy photographs clarify the testimony of the State's expert witness ... and aids the jury in understanding the location of the wounds to which he testified. By clarifying the testimony and giving the jury a visual depiction of the matters to be determined, it cannot be said that the photographs are without probative value. Therefore, the trial judge did not abuse his discretion by allowing these photographs in as evidence ...

Balancing Test

balancing test
A test that weighs probative value of evidence against its prejudicial effect.

probative value
Whether evidence submitted would tend to prove something relevant to the case.

Most courts have adopted a **balancing test** for which the **probative value** of evidence is weighed against the prejudicial effect that allowing the evidence might produce. (See Exhibit 3.2.) The court looks at whether the danger of prejudice is "unfair" and whether it "substantially" outweighs the relevance. Unfair prejudice might unduly influence or cause a jury or factfinder to reach an emotional decision, rather than one based on logic and the evidence.

The Supreme Court addressed this concept further in a criminal case, defining unfair prejudice as evidence that "speaks to the capacity of some concededly relevant evidence to lure the factfinder into declaring guilt on a ground different from proof specific to the offense charged..."[4]

EXHIBIT 3.2 Balancing Test Used in Legal Challenges

Probative Value of Evidence _____ Prejudicial Effect on Jury

CRIME SCENE SKETCHES

A sketch helps supplement the documentation and record of the crime scene by visually showing the location and size of evidence at the scene, along with the distances between evidence and other primary objects.

Crime scene investigators are taught to sketch all serious crimes or accidents that have a crime scene after photos are taken and before anything is moved. As in photography, it is always better to include too much than too little. Investigators use a rough pencil sketch format to begin with. The rough sketch is normally not drawn to scale, but should include all measurements so that a final drawn-to-scale sketch can be completed later. It is important to measure all distances and enter in appropriate location for the completed scale drawing.

Sketching Methods

There are five basic methods of sketching: the *Rectangular Coordinate, Baseline, Triangulation, Cross-projection* or *Exploded* view, and the *3-D* or *Vertical projection*. The method used typically depends on the location being sketched or the detail involved.

Rectangular Coordinate Method

rectangular coordinate method
A method of sketching that uses two adjacent walls at right angles to each other as fixed points from which straight-line distances are measured to the evidence.

The **rectangular coordinate method** of sketching uses two adjacent walls that are at right angles to each other as fixed points from which straight-line distances are measured to the evidence. (See Exhibit 3-3.) These measurements are taken at right angles, formed by the perpendicular intersection of the straight lines from each wall. This method can be used in rectangular or square areas, and is one of the most popular methods of sketching the inside of rooms and buildings.

Baseline Method

baseline method
A method of sketching commonly used outdoors that establishes an imaginary straight line from one fixed point up a certain measured distance and over at a right angle to evidence.

Another popular, easy method that can be effectively utilized both inside and outdoors, the **baseline** establishes an imaginary straight line from one fixed point up a certain measured distance and over at a right angle to evidence.

Triangulation Method

triangulation method
A method of sketching that uses triangular lines as straight line measurements from two fixed points to the evidence being sketched.

Triangulation, or the use of triangular lines, is a method of sketching that uses straight line measurements from two fixed points to the evidence being sketched. (See Exhibit 3.4.) This forms a triangle with the evidence at the point of the two converging straight lines. The triangulation method is most commonly used in outdoor crime scenes.

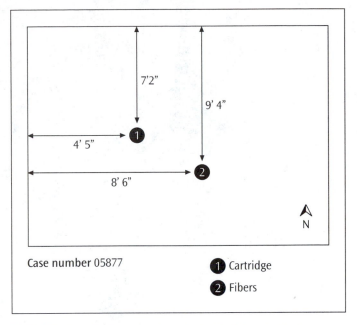

EXHIBIT 3.3   Rectangular Coordinate Sketching Method

Cross-Projection or Exploded View

cross-projection method (or exploded view)
A method of sketching that shows walls, doors, and windows as if the room had been flattened or collapsed.

The **Cross-Projection method**, also called the **Exploded View** or "blow-up," shows walls, doors, and windows as if the room had been flattened or collapsed. (See Exhibit 3.5.) This can be important when depicting blood stains or bullet holes in the walls or ceiling.

3-D or Vertical Projection

This form of finished sketch, used to show dimension and depth, shows a building as if you were standing in front. It is usually completed by a graphic artist or lab technician.

Steps in Sketching Crime Scene

There are several steps in sketching a crime scene, including planning how to organize the sketch, measuring the scene, sketching objects and evidence, and planning the elements of the sketch.

Planning

Like all other parts to the crime scene investigation, the sketch must be done in a systematic and methodical manner. The first step is proper planning. Investigators need to plan how to organize the

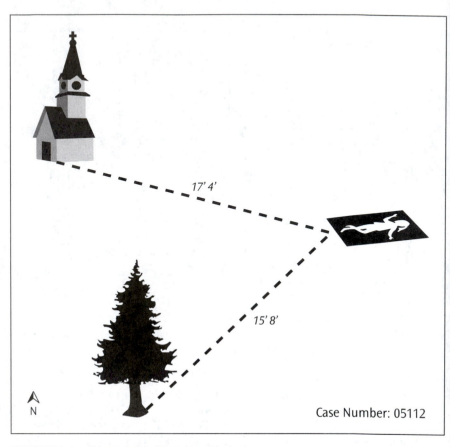

17' 4'

15' 8'

Case Number: 05112

N

EXHIBIT 3.4   Triangulation Sketching Method

sketching so that they avoid handling, contaminating, or destroying any evidence that will be collected in the search. Detailed sketching may come during this search.

After planning and deciding where to start, the proper procedure is to proceed clockwise and try to keep photos, sketch, and search in same direction to establish uniformity.

Next, plan how the sketch diagram will be drawn and organized. Be sure there is adequate space on the paper to draw all you plan to show. Do not crowd the sketch. It is better to divide a scene into sections rather than clutter the sketch. Space for margins must be allowed for—at least ½" at the top and on either side; and, a minimum of 2" or more at the bottom for symbol explanation and legend.

Plan so that all writing (numbers and letters) is horizontal with the top of the sketch sheet. This way, everything can be read without turning the paper.

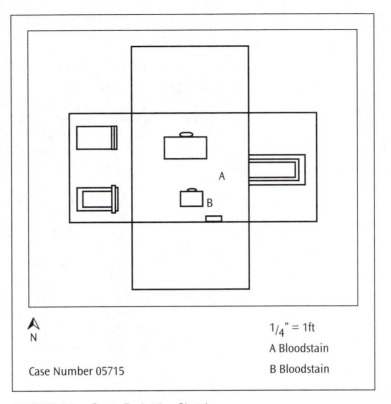

N

$1/4$" = 1ft

A Bloodstain

Case Number 05715

B Bloodstain

EXHIBIT 3.5   Cross-Projection Sketch

Measuring

All measurements in the crime scene sketch must be accurate and precise. Do not estimate distances or "walk them off." Always use a steel tape measure when measuring, so that there are no errors in distances due to the stretching of the tape.

Measure from permanent, fixed objects, and from wall to wall. Draw the outside walls of double-walled buildings first. Place outside limits using dimension lines:

|—10—|

Use broken - - - lines for measurement inside the scene. This lessens the possibility of mistaking measurement lines for a part of the scene. Be consistent in measuring from the same point on like pieces of evidence. Try measuring from the point of sharp objects or the top of the victim's head.

Don't forget to measure and sketch doors and windows, always drawing them in the position you find them (doors open, in or out, and how much). Do not include the window frame in measuring the window opening.

Sketching Objects and Evidence

To show objects, find fixed points, like wall corners, and take measurements from them. All evidence should be located by a minimum of two measurements that are at right angles of each other. Each measurement should be from a stationary point.

Opinions differ on whether to include evidence in the rough sketch. Some courts have withheld the use of a sketch until the evidence depicted has been accepted or suppressed. For example, if a rough sketch is drawn depicting 10 items of evidence found at the crime scene and the defense team is able to have some of these items suppressed from use at trial, then the whole sketch might now be prejudicial if shown to the jury with the suppressed items depicted. In the O.J. Simpson case, a sketch showing the blood stains on the Bronco might be considered prejudicial if those blood stains had been ruled inadmissible as evidence.

To help refresh memory later in the investigation or in court, the sketch team needs to take proper notes, especially of factors associated with the scene that are not sketchable, like the lighting conditions, colors, weather, times, and people present.

Elements of the Sketch

The *legend,* which identifies objects and locations in the sketch should all be in a lower corner or bottom of the sketch, outside the room or area outline. This legend should concisely explain the symbols used in the sketch and identify the objects. A *scale* is essential to a sketch and the largest, simplest scale possible should be used, usually ¼ or ½" = 1'. *Direction* must be shown, which can be done simply by showing the direction of *North* by an arrow pointing to "N." Finally, a sketch should contain the *case number* or identification, location of the crime scene, the name of the person sketching the scene, the *date,* and the time of the sketch. Before leaving the scene, the investigator should make sure that everything has been recorded in the sketch. Once the investigator has left the scene, nothing should be changed or added to the sketch.

CSI CHECKLIST 3.2

Crime Scene Sketch

A Crime Scene Sketch should include:

❑ Case identifier
❑ Date, time, and location
❑ Weather and lighting conditions
❑ Identity and assignments of personnel
❑ Dimensions of rooms, furniture, doors, and windows
❑ Distances between objects, persons, bodies, entrances, and exits
❑ Measurements showing the location of evidence (Each object should be located by two measurements from non-movable items such as doors or walls)
❑ Key, legend, compass orientation, scale, scale disclaimer, or a combination of these features

Source: FBI Handbook of Forensic Services

Finished Drawings

Finished drawings of the rough sketch can be made in ink and drawn to scale by crime lab artists. This drawing may use plastic overlays and colors to illustrate phases or evidence.

Legal Admissibility of Sketches

For evidentiary admissibility, the sketch, like all other crime scene evidence, must be preserved, kept in a secure manner, and accounted for at trial. To be admissible in court, sketches must be shown to be relevant and authenticated by the investigator who was familiar with the scene as depicted, who can then testify that the sketch is a true and accurate representation of that scene. Because most courts hold that any legal challenge over a sketch "goes to the weight of the evidence and not its admissibility,"[5] any errors in measurements or accuracy will go to the credibility of the investigator testifying. This, in turn, could cast doubts in the minds of the jury on the accuracy and credibility of the entire investigation.

SUMMARY

Processing the crime scene includes the thorough documentation through use of notes, reports, photographs, video, and sketching. It also includes the searching of the crime scene for physical evidence or clues to the crime being investigated. The crime scene is documented to help provide a permanent record of what was observed, discovered, and collected at the scene, as well as the procedures taken. Documentation provides a permanent record of the crime and crime scene for use throughout the investigation, in related investigations, and any subsequent prosecution and trial. Investigative notes and reports are two important parts of documenting the crime scene. They can both serve as permanent records of information and must be written in a manner that furthers this purpose. Crime scene photos and video are taken to provide visual documentation of the crime scene; to record it as discovered; to show the evidence and objects at the scene; and to show how the crime scene was processed. The objectives in crime scene photography are to record the scene in a complete and accurate manner, and to photograph all stages of the crime scene processing and investigation.

A sketch helps to supplement the documentation and record of the crime scene by visually showing the location and size of evidence at the scene, along with the distances between evidence and other primary objects. There are five basic methods of sketching: the *Rectangular Coordinate, Baseline, Triangulation, Cross-projection* or *Exploded* view, and the *3-D* or *Vertical projection*. The method used typically depends on the location being sketched or the detail involved. Like all other parts to the crime scene investigation, the sketching must be done in a systematic and methodical manner. To be admissible in court, photographs and sketches must be shown to be relevant, and must be authenticated by the person who took the photo or helped with the sketch and can testify that the photo or sketch is a true and accurate representation of that scene.

KEY TERMS

Balancing Test	Past Memory Recorded
Baseline Method	Present Memory Refreshed
Corpus Delicti	Probative Value
Crime Reports	Rectangular Coordinate Method
Cross-Projection Method (or Exploded View)	3-D or Vertical Projection Method
Evidence Logs	Triangulation Method
Modus Operandi	

REVIEW QUESTIONS

1. Describe how a crime scene should be documented.
2. What is the golden rule of Hans Gross and why is it important to the processing of a crime scene?

3. What are some of the advantages and disadvantages to crime scene photography?

4. Identify the crime scene sketching methods and give an example of when or where each might be used.

5. Discuss the legal requirements for admitting crime scene photographs or sketches at trial.

CRITICAL THINKING QUESTIONS 3.1

1. What is the importance of understanding the proper techniques and procedures for documenting a crime scene?

2. Why should any photographs, no matter how gory, be excluded as evidence if the photos show what really happened at a crime scene?

3. Why would it be important for the measurements in a crime scene sketch to be precise? So what if they were off a few inches here or there?

FORENSIC RESEARCH USING THE INTERNET

1. Search the Internet for specific Web sites or articles dealing with documenting a crime scene. Describe some of the techniques mentioned at these sites for photographing a crime scene.

PRACTICE SKILLS:

Practice what you have learned in the following problems:

Crime Scene Analysis 3.1

Using your classroom or a room in your home as a mock crime scene (where either a burglary has occurred or an assault, with the victim having been taken to the hospital), practice the following skills:

1. Document the scene and investigation, taking notes and photographs. (If possible, use a digital camera to see what type of photos would be taken)

continued

> 2. Use one of the sketching methods to complete a rough sketch of the scene.
>
> 3. Use one of the searching patterns to conduct a search of the scene for evidence.
>
> 4. Prepare a short report detailing the above processing of the scene and what was completed for a final survey and release of the scene.

WEB SITES

FBI Handbook of Forensic Services

    http://www.fbi.gov

Resources for Crime Scene Photography

    http://www.crime-scene-investigator.net/csi-photo.html

ENDNOTES

[1] *Federal Rules of Evidence*, Rule 612. Writing Used to Refresh Memory

[2] *Stephens v. Alabama*, 2005 Ala. Crim. App. LEXIS 139

[3] See, for example, Rule 403, *Federal Rule of Evidence*

[4] *Johnny Lynn Old Chief v. United States,* 519 U.S. 172 (1997)

[5] *State v. Montgomery (Mo. App. 1976) 545 S.W.2d 655*

INVESTIGATING THE CRIME SCENE: PROCESSING THE SCENE AND COLLECTING EVIDENCE

"The microscopic debris that covers our clothing and bodies are the mute witnesses, sure and faithful, of all our movements and all our encounters."

—Edmond Locard, "The Analysis of Dust Traces," *The American Journal of Police Science* (1930)

"For murder though it has no tongue, will speak with the most miraculous organ."

—William Shakespeare, *Hamlet*

Chapter Outline

INTRODUCTION

In Chapter 3, we learned about the proper procedures for documenting the crime scene. In this chapter, we will discover how the crime scene is searched and processed for evidence.

We will examine how evidence found during the search and processing of the scene is collected. We will look at some modern forensic equipment used to identify evidence at the crime scene, especially evidence that is not visible to the eye. We will also look at the techniques for the proper collection of this evidence, and the methods used for packaging and preserving this evidence.

PROCESSING THE CRIME SCENE

Processing the crime scene really is a "holistic" term that includes every step taken to investigate and collect evidence at the crime scene. Documentation of the crime scene, the investigation, and the evidence collected through photography and sketching is part of this methodical procedure. However, the focus of *processing* the scene is in the actual search for and collection of evidence.

CRIME SCENE SEARCHES

Crime scenes are searched in order to find and collect evidence and clues. First, the investigator must insure that the scene is secure and protected. Next, investigators must plan their search and determine the number of personnel and equipment that will be needed. Remember not to begin searching until the scene has been documented through notes, photography, and sketching.

Planning the Search

The normal procedure in planning a crime scene search is for the lead investigator or search leader to survey the scene by doing a walk-through and assign personnel to various tasks. There are several factors to consider in this planning.

Factors to Consider in Planning a Crime Scene Search

- Location of crime scene
- Type of crime and evidence sought
- Where evidence is most likely to be found
- Number of search/support personnel available
- Weather and environmental conditions
- Time available and speed desired

Search Patterns

Search patterns help ensure that a methodical approach is used to find all evidence at a crime scene. There are five established search patterns, including the *lane*, *grid*, *spiral*, *circle*, and *zone*.

Lane Search or Strip Pattern

Lane or Strip Search Pattern
A method of searching in which investigators start at one side of their search zone and walk back and forth over imaginary lanes or strips no wider than their shoulders.

In the basic **Lane or Strip Search Pattern**, investigators start at one side of their search zone and walk back and forth over imaginary lanes or strips no wider than their shoulders (or 3' at the most). (See Exhibit 4.1.) For this simple and thorough search, one searcher or many walking side-by-side may be used. Often, it is done on knees so as not to miss trace evidence.

EXHIBIT 4.1   Lane or Strip Search Pattern

Grid Search Pattern

Grid Search Pattern
A more thorough method of searching that uses two strip or lane searches over the same area but continuing again at right angles.

The **Grid Search Pattern** is a more thorough method of searching that uses two strip or lane searches over the same area but continuing again at right angles. (See Exhibit 4.2.) This search technique takes more time, but is far more thorough because it examines the same area from a different perspective.

Spiral Search Pattern

Spiral Search Pattern
A popular and adaptable method of searching in which an investigator searches in a clockwise circle, beginning at the outside of the circle and works inward sweeping in a spiral toward the impact area of the crime scene.

The **Spiral Search Pattern** is one of the most popular indoor search patterns, adaptable to any space or location. In this pattern, the investigator searches in a clockwise circle, beginning at the outside of the circle and works inward, sweeping in a spiral toward the impact area of the crime scene. (See Exhibit 4.3.) A variation of this pattern is to begin at the impact area and search outward. Caution must be exercised to avoid disturbing the scene when entering the impact area to start.

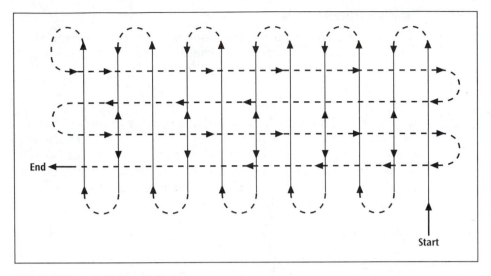

EXHIBIT 4.2   Grid Search Pattern

Circle Search Pattern
A search pattern used for outside areas, where a stake is placed in the ground, a rope tied to it, and knots tied at intervals of 3 feet. Searchers hold the rope at the knots and conduct a circular search, moving to the next knot when each circle is completed.

Circle Search Pattern

Used for outside ground areas, the **Circle Search Pattern** begins at the center of area to be searched. A wooden stake with a long rope attached is driven into the center of the area and knots are tied in the rope at intervals of about three feet. Search members hold the rope at the knots and conduct a circular search. They move to the next knot when each circle is completed until the whole area has been covered.

EXHIBIT 4.3   Spiral Search Pattern

Zone or Sector Search Pattern
Designed for large or complex crime scenes, in this method of searching the investigator divides the entire scene into square zones and uses one of the standard search patterns for each individual zone.

Zone or Sector Search

The **Zone or Sector Search Pattern** is designed for large or complex crime scenes, such as homes, buildings, and large outdoor areas. The entire scene is divided into squares, called "zones," and investigators use one of the previously described standard methods for each individual zone.

Interior Searches

Studies of crime scene investigations have found that the floors usually produce the most evidence, followed by doors, windows, and furniture. Many times, the ceiling is missed in a search and valuable evidence goes unrecovered.

Vehicle Searches

There are many places to hide things in a vehicle, including under the dash, in the wheel well, engine compartment, or trunk. The type of crime guides investigators on what evidence to look for and what area to search in a vehicle. When searching, break the vehicle into zones and search top to bottom, front to back, or side to side. Pay heed to the *Elephant in a Shoebox Theory,* which states that if you are looking for an elephant, you should not look in a shoebox.

CSI CHECKLIST 4.1

Crime Scene Search Checklist

Crime Scene Search Checklist:
- Search from the general to the specific for evidence
- Be alert for all evidence
- Search entrances and exits
- Photograph all items before collection and track them on the photographic log
- Mark evidence locations on the sketch
- Complete the evidence log with notations for each item of evidence. If feasible, have one person serve as evidence custodian
- Two persons should observe evidence in place, during recovery, and being marked for identification. If feasible, mark directly on the evidence
- Wear gloves to avoid leaving fingerprints
- Do not excessively handle the evidence after recovery

continued

> ❏ Seal all evidence packages at the crime scene
> ❏ Obtain known standards, such as fiber samples from a known carpet, for comparison
> ❏ Make a complete evaluation of the crime scene
> ❏ Constantly check paperwork, packaging, and other information for errors
>
> Source: FBI Handbook of Forensic Services

Legal Challenges to Crime Scene Searches

One of the primary issues surrounding the search of a crime scene is whether a warrant is required, and, if so, when the warrant needs to be obtained. Because of the importance of these topics, legal challenges to crime scene searches are covered extensively in Chapter 7.

WHAT ARE WE LOOKING FOR IN SEARCHING A CRIME SCENE?

physical evidence
Objects or materials that can be seen, touched, or felt, such as the murder weapon, blood stains, and fingerprints.

The focus of the crime scene search and investigation is to identify and collect **physical evidence**. Physical evidence can be seen, touched, or felt. It is often called *tangible* or *real* evidence, because it has substance and tends to either directly or indirectly prove something of issue in a case. Examples of this range from bloodstains and trace evidence such as fibers, to tool marks, fingerprints, and other impression evidence. This evidence is usually found at a crime scene, but can also be found at other locations; for example, on the suspect or in the suspect's environment.

corpus delicti
Translates to *body of the crime*, but refers to the elements that establish a crime has been committed.

WHAT IS PHYSICAL EVIDENCE USED FOR?

direct proof
Evidence that proves a disputed fact directly.

The primary purpose of physical evidence is to establish the **corpus delicti**, or "body" of the crime; that is, to show that a crime has been committed and to help prove or disprove every element of that crime. For example, a burglary may require an unlawful entry into a building with the intent to commit a crime or steal something inside. Evidence showing pry marks leading to a broken window of a closed business, and damage to an interior safe or lockbox would help to establish these elements of burglary.

circumstantial proof
Evidence that proves a disputed fact indirectly by first proving another fact. From this other fact an inference may be drawn as to the original disputed fact.

Physical evidence is sometimes used as **direct proof**, as in a recording of a robbery made by a surveillance camera. However, most physical evidence is used as **circumstantial proof**, to prove a fact in issue indirectly, by proving one fact which then gives rise to an inference in proving another fact. For example, a fingerprint found on a murder weapon is determined to belong to the defendant and is the only print found on the weapon. This evidence would not prove that the defendant was the one who actually used the weapon or even left it at the scene, It would, however, show that the defendant did handle the murder weapon, from which the jury could make inferences, along with other evidence presented, as to whether it was used by the defendant on the victim. Most criminal cases with physical evidence are proven through circumstantial evidence.

Associative Evidence

associative or linking evidence
Evidence that helps to identify a suspect and link that suspect to a crime scene.

Another primary purpose of physical evidence is to help identify and locate a suspect and to connect that suspect to the crime and the crime scene. This is called **associative or linking evidence**. A fingerprint or DNA found at a crime scene are the best examples of evidence that links a suspect to a particular object or scene. Other examples of associative evidence include blood, hair, fibers, soil, or impressions, such as footprints or tire tracks.

WHERE DO WE FIND PHYSICAL EVIDENCE?

Depending on the type of crime, physical evidence may be found in a variety of locations. Typically, evidence is collected at the crime scene, from the victim and victim's environment, and the suspect and suspect's environment.

Crime Scene

At the crime scene, evidence might be found anywhere, but special attention is given to the point of entry, points of impact or origin, and point of departure. In addition, paths leading to any of these must be searched carefully. Sometimes, like in the Scott Peterson murder case, the crime scene itself is not initially known and must be searched for and discovered. Because this case involved a boat and bodies found in the ocean, there were multiple crime scenes involved.

Victim and Victim's Environment

The victim can yield valuable evidence, especially in violent crimes. Skin scrapings, blood, hair, and fibers belonging to a suspect are among the important evidence that can be found on a victim. The victim's environment may also contain evidence from the crime, or evidence that links the suspect to the victim. For example, in a sexual assault case, the victim stated that she had first met the suspect in her apartment building parking lot, where she had given the suspect a ride to a gas station. Later that night, the suspect had entered her apartment and assaulted her. The suspect claimed that he had never met the victim. In this case, fibers, hair, and trace evidence belonging to the suspect were collected from the victim's car, supporting the victim's statement.

Suspect and Suspect's Environment

Evidence may be found on the suspect or the suspect's environment. As we learned from Chapter 1, *Locard's Exchange Theory* suggests that when criminals leave a crime scene, they take some trace evidence with them, transferred onto their bodies, clothing, or shoes when they came into contact with the crime scene. For example, suspects may have fibers, hair, dirt, or other trace materials from the crime scene or victim on them. The suspect's environment may also yield important evidence. A suspect may have used a vehicle to get to the crime scene. Sitting in the vehicle may have transferred trace evidence from the suspect's hands, clothing, or shoes. The same goes for the suspect's home, office, or any other location where the suspect has been.

CSI CHECKLIST 4.2

Sources of Physical Evidence

Physical Evidence will generally be obtained from five main sources:

❏ Crime scene
❏ Victim
❏ Victim's environment
❏ Suspect
❏ Suspect's environment

Source: U.S. Department of Justice[1]

USE OF CRIMINALISTICS IN COLLECTING PHYSICAL EVIDENCE

As we learned earlier, criminalistics is the application of science and forensic techniques to crime detection. Criminalistics is not only used in the forensic analysis of evidence at the crime lab. It is equally important to the identification and collection of evidence at the crime scene. New innovations in criminalistics and forensic science have dramatically changed the way evidence is identified and collected at crime scenes.

Forensic and Alternate Light Sources

alternate light sources
Specialized forensic lighting, such as high-intensity ultraviolet light, used to detect trace evidence at a crime scene.

Lighting is important at a crime scene to allow investigators and technicians to properly identify and collect evidence. However, much evidence cannot be seen by the naked eye, and traditional light sources are not effective in discovering it. New forensic and **alternate light sources** are now being used at crime scenes to allow the detection of this evidence. Some of these utilize high-intensity ultraviolet lights that cause some substances to fluoresce, or glow when the UV light is beamed across it. These ultraviolet lights, either alone or in combination with special dies or fluorescent powders, can detect a variety of physical evidence, including fingerprints, hair, fibers, blood, semen and other body fluids, bite marks, neck strangulation marks, bruises, and other injuries due to beatings.

Lasers can also reveal evidence invisible to the naked eye, such as fingerprints and other impression evidence, including the outline of a shoeprint in a carpet.

PRACTICE TIP 4.1

Light Source Safety

When using ultraviolet lights, lasers, and other light sources, the eyes must be protected from direct and indirect exposure. Not all laser beams are visible, and irreversible eye damage can result from exposure to direct or indirect light from reflected beams. Prolonged exposure to the skin should also be avoided. Protective eyewear appropriate for the light source should be worn by all personnel in the vicinity of the light source. Goggles must have sufficient protective material and fit snugly to prevent light from entering at any angle. The goggles must display the American National Standards Institute's (ANSI) mark denoting eye-protection compliance. Laser protective eyewear must be made of the appropriate optical density to protect against the maximum operating wavelength of the laser source.[2]

COLLECTING PHYSICAL EVIDENCE

There are several important things to remember and rules to follow when collecting evidence at a crime scene. First, before an item of evidence is collected, or even touched, don't forget to follow the *Golden Rule of Hans Gross*. As described in Chapter 3, Hans Gross wrote in his classic 1893 text on criminalistics that crime scene investigators should never "alter the position of, pick up, or even touch any object before it has been minutely described in an official note, and a photograph of it taken."

Documenting Collected Evidence

Before collecting any item of evidence, be sure to photograph and document it fully. Continue that documentation as the evidence is collected, including what the evidence is, who is collecting it, when it is being collected (including the time/date), where it is being collected, and how it is collected.

Proper Handling of Evidence

The next important rule in collecting evidence is proper handling. Evidence should never be touched or handled with bare hands. Gloves, either nitrile or latex, must be worn at all times while collecting evidence. These gloves not only protect against contamination of evidence, but also protect against many health hazards, including hepatitis and AIDS. Gloves should be changed regularly. Because of the danger of contaminating trace evidence, protective footwear or booties should also be worn while collecting evidence at a crime scene.

PRACTICE TIP 4.2

Handle with Care

Evidence at crime scenes should always be handled with care, paying attention to protecting scene integrity and protecting evidence from loss or contamination. All evidence should be appropriately packaged, labeled, and maintained in a secure, temporary manner until final packaging and submission to a secured evidence storage facility or the crime laboratory.

CSI CHECKLIST 4.3

Be Sure to Collect Proper Samples

There are many dangers and potential errors that crime scene investigators are faced with in the collection of evidence. Be sure that the following checklist has been completed:
❑   Sufficient samples

continued

> ❑ Standards of comparison samples
> ❑ Elimination samples

One of the most important elements to remember is to prevent the contamination or loss of the evidence through proper handling, collection, and packaging.

Evidence Collection Kit

An evidence collection kit (See Exhibit 4.4.), is an essential part of crime scene processing. In its research report on crime scene investigation, the U.S. Department of Justice recommended the following essential items to be included in an evidence collection kit[3]:

- Blood Collection Bindle
- Disposable scalpels
- Evidence identifiers
- Latex gloves
- Photographic ruler (ABFO scales)
- Sterile gauze
- Sterile swabs
- Test tubes/test tube rack

Excavation

- Cones/markers
- Evidence identifiers
- Metal detectors
- Shovels/trowels
- Sifting screens
- String
- Wooden/metal stakes

Fingerprint

- Brushes
- Chemical enhancement supplies
- Cyanoacrylate (super glue) wand/packets
- Flashlight
- Forensic light source
- Lift cards
- Lift tape
- Powders

Impression

- Bowls/mixing containers
- Boxes
- Dental stone (die stone)

- Permanent markers
- Snow print wax

Pattern Print Lifter

- Chemical enhancement supplies
- Electrostatic dust lifter
- Gel lifter
- Wide format lift tape

Toolmarks

- Casting materials

Trace Evidence Collection

- Acetate sheet protectors
- Bindle paper
- Clear tape/adhesive lift
- Flashlight (oblique lighting)
- Forceps/tweezers
- Glass vials
- Trace evidence vacuum with disposable collection filters

EXHIBIT 4.4   Evidence Collection Kit

CSI CHECKLIST 4.4

Prioritize Collection of Evidence

Prioritize the collection of evidence to prevent loss, destruction, or contamination:

❑ Conduct a careful and methodical evaluation considering all physical evidence possibilities (e.g., biological fluids, latent prints, trace evidence)

❑ Focus first on the easily accessible areas in open view and proceed to out-of-view locations

❑ Select a systematic search pattern for evidence collection based on the size and location of the scene(s)

❑ Select a progression of processing/collection methods so that initial techniques do not compromise subsequent processing/collections methods

❑ Concentrate on the most transient evidence and work to the least transient forms of physical evidence

❑ Move from least intrusive to most intrusive processing/collection methods

❑ Continually assess environmental and other factors that may affect the evidence

❑ Be aware of multiple scenes (e.g., victims, suspects, vehicles, locations)

❑ Recognize other methods that are available to locate, technically document, and collect evidence (e.g., alternate light source, enhancement, blood pattern documentation, projectile trajectory analysis)

Source: U.S. Department of Justice[4]

What Evidence Should be Collected at Crime Scene?

Because every crime scene is different and unique, there is no single set of rules to cover exactly what evidence should be collected at a crime scene. The general rule is to collect any evidence that may be important and that it is better to collect too much than too little. If evidence is not collected in a timely manner at the crime scene, there will likely be serious evidentiary challenges later in court.

What Type of Crime?

An important consideration in collecting evidence is to establish what type of crime was committed and look for evidence that either helps to prove or disprove this crime. Remember that one purpose of evidence is to prove the *corpus delicti* of a crime, to establish that a crime was committed, and to show how, when, and by whom it was committed.

How to Collect Physical Evidence

Most physical evidence at a crime scene will be collected by hand, using gloves, or by using a variety of hand-held collection tools, such as forceps, tweezers, or sterile gauze. However, different types of physical evidence may require different forms of packaging and collection. The following sections describe some of these different techniques and procedures.

Blood and Body Fluids

Because of the danger of contamination and degradation from bacteria, blood and body fluids should not be packaged wet. This evidence should first be allowed to air dry at room temperature in a clean, secured evidence area. It should then be refrigerated or frozen and taken to the crime lab as soon as possible. Dried blood stains need to be collected and placed in clean paper, which can then be put into a paper evidence bag, labeled, and sealed. Blood stains on small, transportable items or cloth should not be removed, but the whole item or cloth should be collected, packaged, and sent to the lab. If an object containing blood evidence is too large to be sent to the lab, scrapings of the blood should be extracted using a clean knife or forensic scraping tool. Blood stain scrapings must not be mixed. Each scraped stain must be placed into a separate evidence envelope and the tool should be cleaned after each blood stain is scraped off. Other bodily fluids, such as semen or saliva, should also be allowed to air dry. Stains found on larger objects, like bedding or clothing, should be air dried, and the whole object collected and packaged.

Locating Blood at Crime Scene

Blood evidence can be difficult to locate or identify at a crime scene. Wet blood begins clotting within a few minutes after exposure to air. A drop of blood starts drying at its outer edges and continues drying toward its center. As it dries, blood darkens in color. Older, dried blood stains can appear dark brown or black. Blood stains can be so small at a crime scene that they are not visible to the naked eye. Alternate light sources and ultraviolet light can be used to detect bloodstains that are not visible to the human eye. For example, the **luminol** chemical testing method is applied by spraying luminol over an area to search for hidden blood. After spraying, the area is viewed in darkness, using ultraviolet light. If blood is present, it will give off a bluish luminescence.

luminol
A chemical test used to detect hidden blood at a crime scene.

> ## CSI CHECKLIST 4.5
>
> **To Avoid Contamination of Evidence**
>
> ❑ Wear gloves. Change them often
> ❑ Avoid touching your face or mouth with your gloves
> ❑ Do not touch the evidence or area around it
> ❑ Avoid coughing or sneezing. Do not talk directly over the evidence
> ❑ Air dry evidence in secure, clean area before packaging
> ❑ Put evidence in paper bags. Do not use plastic
> ❑ Properly seal evidence container and maintain proper chain of custody

Trace Evidence

trace evidence
Very small amount of evidence, barely perceptible or invisible to the naked eye.

If **trace evidence** is visible at a crime scene, it is usually collected by hand, using gloves, forceps, or tweezers. Trace evidence may also be collected with a forensic vacuum, which collects it into a special paper container. Trace evidence is placed in paper bindles (for example, using a "druggist fold") which is then placed into larger envelopes, labeled, and sealed. Each collection of trace evidence must be placed into separate paper containers. Plastic bags are not use for trace evidence, because minute traces may cling to the sides. If trace evidence is still attached to some other object, such as clothing or dry blood, the whole object is collected and packaged.

Latent Prints

latent prints
Fingerprints that are not readily seen but can be developed by forensic methods.

Fingerprints left at a crime scene can be *visible* (for example, when left on blood or fresh paint), *plastic* (when an impression is left on putty or soap), or *invisible*. **Latent prints** are invisible impressions left on a surface by oils or perspiration on the ridges of fingers. Latent prints that are not visible or readily seen can be detected and visualized using forensic chemicals, powders, or alternate light sources.

Chemical Methods to Detect and Visualize Latent Prints

Chemical methods using the chemical *ninhydrin,* or the silver-based reagent called *Physical Developer* are popular for detecting and visualizing latent prints on porous surfaces. *Cyanoacrylate* or super glue is a detection and visualization method used for non-porous surfaces. This method can work especially well on plastic, leather, wet, or painted surfaces.

Powder Methods to Detect and Visualize Latent Prints

Fingerprint powders come in a variety of colors and textures. For example, on light-colored surfaces, a flat black powder can be used to detect and visualize latent prints. A lighter color of powder can be applied to darker surfaces. For ceilings, a magnetic powder might be used. The process of using fingerprint powders to detect and visualize latent prints is called **dusting**. Fluorescent fingerprint powder can also be used to visualize a luminescent print that can then be photographed and lifted.

Alternate Light Sources

As described earlier in this chapter, alternate light sources include special high-intensity lights that can cause latent prints to fluoresce, or emit visible light, allowing the detection and visualization of these hidden prints through fluorescence.

Methods Used to Collect Latent Prints

Once a latent print has been detected and visualized at a crime scene, it must be collected and properly preserved for later examination and identification. The first step in collecting a print is to photograph it. Often, a high-quality digital photograph of a fingerprint, along with digital imaging software, will assist forensic specialists in comparing and identifying prints. If the print is on a transportable object, such as a weapon or tool, the entire object is collected and sent to the crime lab. Otherwise, after the print has been carefully photographed and documented, it will be collected with the use of some type of **lifting** tool or technique. For example, when using fingerprint powder to "dust" an area for latent prints, the powder is applied with a brush using smooth, continuous strokes. Once a print becomes visible, and after it is photographed and documented, fingerprint tape or lifters are used to "lift" and collect the print. For example, if using fingerprint tape, the tape is first placed down, starting at one side of a print and smoothed over with the thumb to remove air bubbles from the tape as it is placed over the entire print. The print is then lifted and placed onto an evidence card, using the same method of smoothing it down as it is placed onto the card.

Defense attorneys and the media sometimes exaggerate the value of "dusting" for prints at crime scene, leading jurors to believe that prints are always left. Prints are not always left at a crime scene, however, investigators must try to obtain any fingerprints available, especially with the modern advances that can lift prints on everything from fabrics to gloves to human skin.

dusting
Use of fingerprint powders to detect and visualize latent prints at a crime scene.

lifting
The process of removing a latent print, discovered at a crime scene.

CSI CHECKLIST 4.6

Checklist for Collecting Evidence

❑ Document the collection of evidence by recording its location at the scene, date of collection, and who collected it.
❑ Establish chain of custody
❑ Obtain standard/reference samples from the scene
❑ Obtain control samples
❑ Consider obtaining elimination samples
❑ Immediately secure electronically recorded evidence (e.g., answering machine tapes, surveillance camera videotapes, computers) from the vicinity
❑ Identify and secure evidence in containers (e.g., label, date, initial container) at the crime scene. Different types of evidence require different containers (e.g., porous, nonporous, crushproof)
❑ Package items to avoid contamination and cross-contamination
❑ Document the condition of firearms/weapons prior to rendering them safe for transportation and submission
❑ Avoid excessive handling of evidence after it is collected
❑ Maintain evidence at the scene in a manner designed to diminish degradation or loss
❑ Transport and submit evidence items for secure storage

Source: U.S. Department of Justice[5]

MARKING PHYSICAL EVIDENCE

Investigators must mark and label each item of evidence so that they are able to identify it later. This will be especially important at trial, where a witness must be able to authenticate each item of evidence presented, including identifying the item and testifying where and when the item was collected. If a package or tag is being used for evidence identification, always include the case number and case specifics, including:

1. Name or initial of person collecting evidence and their affiliation
2. Time and date item was collected
3. Location where item was found
4. Description of item
5. Case number or victim's name

In addition to labeling each item of evidence, the outside packaging for the evidence should be labeled and the outer container sealed with evidence tape. The initials of the investigator or technician sealing the container should be written along the edges of this seal. This is all done to protect the legal integrity of the evidence and preserve the chain of custody.

Mark Evidence or Affix Evidence Tag?

In the past, most evidence was marked directly on the item somewhere. Bullets, for example, were marked on the nose or base, cartridge cases were marked inside the mouth, and firearms were marked in inconspicuous places that would not deface the weapon or interfere with its subsequent testing. Although some evidence, such as clothing and tools, may still be marked directly on the item, most crime labs recommend that the evidence be properly packaged and that the marking be placed on the container itself or on the evidence tag attached to it. This will help protect the evidence from any contamination or interference with subsequent analysis due to improper marking. On the other hand, it requires even more vigilance on the part of anyone who removes the evidence from its container and packaging to ensure that it is properly documented and placed back properly.

If the marking is made directly on the item of evidence, it should include the initials of the person marking the item and the date, be as small as possible, and in a location that will not affect the subsequent analysis or legal integrity of the evidence.

The marking and collection process should be thoroughly documented. Evidence should be marked as it is collected, but it must not be damaged or altered by the marking. Investigators use a variety of marking pens, regular pens, stylus, tapes, and tags.

PACKAGING EVIDENCE

The type of container used for packaging evidence depends on the kind of evidence collected. Some evidence needs to "breath" or dry (for example, blood or semen stains), and a paper container will be needed for that evidence. Each item of evidence must be packaged and preserved separately, so as not to contaminate or confuse. Evidence should never be mixed. All containers used must be durable to preserve integrity through the chain of custody.

Plastic or Paper?

Most evidence that is of biological origin, like blood, hair, semen, or other bodily fluids, should not be placed in plastic because of the potential for contamination with the plastic or accelerated degradation. Because plastic bags hold moisture, they may promote the growth of bacteria that could interfere with subsequent forensic analysis. Trace evidence should not be placed in plastic because it clings to the sides and is hard to remove. On the other hand, certain drugs and controlled substances, such as a quantity of pills, might be better placed in a plastic evidence bag. So might other evidence, such as certain small weapons or tools, household items, or other objects. Many crime lab technicians prefer plastic evidence bags because they are easy to seal and the evidence inside is clearly visible to lab personnel. Often, evidence is individually placed in packages made of paper, boxes, or tubes, then placed in a plastic evidence bag.

Evidence Submission Form

A copy of an *Evidence Submission Form* (See Exhibit 4.5.) should be attached to the outside of the evidence container. This form lets the crime lab know what type of evidence is inside and where it needs to go (for example, chemistry section, impression evidence section), without the need for breaking the seal on the evidence container.

PRACTICE TIP 4.3

Evidence Collection Guidelines

Want to read more about evidence collection guidelines? Try one of these sites:

   Evidence Collection Guidelines from www.crime-scene-investigator.net
   http://www.crime-scene-investigator.net/csi-collection.html
   DNA Evidence Collection and Preservation
   http://www.ncjrs.org/nij/DNAbro/evi.html
   Trace Evidence Recovery Guidelines
   http://www.fbi.gov/hq/lab/fsc/backissu/oct1999/trace.htm

EXHIBIT 4.5   Evidence Submission Form

CRIME LABORATORY

Date _____

EVIDENCE RECEIPT

Lab Case _____

Agency Case _____

Investigating Officer _____ Phone: _____

Agency _____ Address: _____

Suspect(s) _____ Victim(s) _____

Offense _____ Date of _____ County _____

☐ New Case ☐ Additional Evidence ☐ Resubmission ☐ Investigative Lead

SUMMARY OF

CIRCUMSTANCES:

_____

EVIDENCE SUBMITTED: Indicate the examination(s) requested for *each* item.

ITEM	DESCRIPTION (Physically describe items, sources, who/where taken	EXAM

NOTES:

CHAIN OF CUSTODY:

ITEM #	RECEIVED FROM	RECEIVED BY	LOCATION	DATE	TIME

NOTES:

The CRIME REPORT must accompany this form.   Page _____ Of _____

FINAL SURVEY AND RELEASE OF PROCESSED SCENE

As described in Chapter 2, a final survey of the crime scene is needed before releasing and exiting the scene. This survey is a safeguard to ensure that all relevant evidence has been collected, that no evidence or equipment has been left behind, and that any hazardous conditions or materials have been dealt with or reported to the proper authorities.

The final survey should include a review of all aspects of the search. All personnel involved in the search and processing of the crime scene should be checked with to ensure that all documentation is accurate and complete, and that all evidence has been properly collected and secured. The scene should be photographed to show the final condition prior to release. Documentation should include the time and date of release of the scene, the investigator releasing the scene, and the name of the person to whom the scene was released. Investigators should understand that once the scene has been released, reentry may require a search warrant, if one has not already been obtained.

CHAIN OF CUSTODY

chain of custody
The proper preservation and protection of crime scene evidence in order to insure its physical and legal integrity.

Chain of custody is the preservation and protection of crime scene evidence to insure its physical and legal integrity. The chain of custody is a method of authentication for physical evidence. It generally involves the preservation, safekeeping, and documentation of physical evidence from its collection through the resolution of the case. Documentation should include everyone who handled the evidence, everywhere the evidence went, and anything done to the evidence. Although a break in the chain of custody will not automatically result in the exclusion of physical evidence at trial, most courts require that "proof of a chain of custody is necessary to establish that the evidence recovered by the police is the same as that tested by the laboratory" or collected at the crime scene.[6] Generally, the chain of custody must show "with reasonable certainty that the item [has] not been altered, substituted, or contaminated prior to analysis . . .."[7]

LEGAL CHALLENGES

Legal challenges involving the collection of evidence from the crime scene generally fall into two areas: the way evidence was collected or the way evidence was preserved. Challenges involving collection techniques generally attack the manner in which evidence was collected. This could range from alleged contamination of the evidence when collected, or sloppy or improper collection techniques or equipment used. Challenges to improper preservation procedures attack the legal integrity or authenticity of the evidence due to some contamination or misuse of the evidence during preservation or a break in the chain of custody.

SUMMARY

Crime scenes are searched to find and collect evidence and clues. Search patterns help to ensure that a methodical approach is used to find all evidence at a crime scene. There are five established search patterns, including the *lane (or strip)*, *grid*, *spiral*, *circle*, and *zone*. One of the primary issues surrounding the search of a crime scene is whether a warrant is required, and, if so, when the warrant needs to be obtained.

Depending on the type of crime, physical evidence may be found in a variety of locations. Typically, evidence is collected at the crime scene, from the victim and victim's environment, and the suspect and suspect's environment. New innovations in criminalistics and forensic science have dramatically changed the way evidence is identified and collected at crime scenes. For example, new forensic technology and alternate lighting sources are now being used at crime scenes that allow the detection of trace evidence. Lasers can also reveal evidence invisible to the naked eye, such as fingerprints and other impression evidence.

Because every crime scene is unique, there is no single set of rules to cover exactly what evidence should be collected at a crime scene. The general rule is to collect any evidence that may be important and that it is better to collect too much than too little. Before collecting any item of evidence, be sure to photograph and document it fully. Continue that documentation as the evidence is collected, including what the evidence is, who is collecting it, when it is being collected (including the time/date), where it is being collected, and how it is collected.

Investigators must mark and label each item of evidence so that they are able to identify it later. This will be especially important at trial, where a witness must be able to authenticate each item of evidence presented, including identifying the item, and testifying where and when the item was collected. Different types of physical evidence require different forms of packaging and collection.

Chain of custody is the preservation and protection of crime scene evidence in order to insure its physical and legal integrity. It generally involves the preservation, safekeeping, and documentation of physical evidence from its collection through the resolution of the case. Documentation should include everyone who handled the evidence, everywhere the evidence went, and anything done to the evidence. Legal challenges involving the collection of evidence from the crime scene generally fall into two categories: the way evidence was collected or the way evidence was preserved. Challenges involving collection techniques generally attack the manner in which evidence was collected. Challenges to improper preservation procedures attack the legal integrity or authenticity of the evidence due to some contamination or misuse of the evidence during preservation or a break in the chain of custody.

KEY TERMS

Alternate Light Sources

Associative or Linking Evidence

Chain of Custody

Circle Search Pattern

Circumstantial Proof

Corpus Delicti

Direct Proof

Dusting

Grid Search Pattern

Lane or Strip Search Pattern

Latent Prints

Lifting

Luminol

Modus Operandi

Motive

Physical Evidence

Spiral Search Pattern

Trace Evidence

Zone or Sector Search Pattern

REVIEW QUESTIONS

1. Name the four primary crime scene search methods and give an example of when or where each might be used.

2. Discuss what physical evidence is and what it is used for.

3. Identify the general areas where we might find physical evidence at a crime scene

4. Describe how criminalistics and forensic equipment is used in collecting evidence at a crime scene.

5. Explain how and why physical evidence is marked.

6. Assess some of the issues surrounding the packaging of evidence. Give examples.

7. Describe how to collect wet versus dried blood found at a crime scene.

8. Define chain of custody and its importance in the collection of evidence.

9. Discuss some of the legal challenges involved in the collection of evidence.

CRITICAL THINKING QUESTIONS 4.1

1. Why is it important to follow one of the methods described in this chapter for searching a crime scene? What might influence the use of one or more of these methods?
2. What is the importance of understanding the proper techniques and procedures for collecting evidence at a crime scene? What are the consequences of not following these procedures?
3. How do the techniques and procedures discussed in this chapter influence the collection of evidence at a crime scene?

FORENSIC RESEARCH USING THE INTERNET

Search the Internet for specific Web sites or articles dealing with searching a crime scene or collecting physical evidence at a crime scene. Identify some of the new techniques listed or newer forensic tools used to help identify and collect evidence.

PRACTICE SKILLS:

Practice what you have learned in the following crime scene problems:

Crime Scene Analysis 4.1

A note is found lying on a painted desktop at a crime scene. There are dry bloodstains on the desktop, along with several drops of blood that are still wet. Describe what evidence you would collect, how you would collect it, and what type of container you would place it in. Explain why for each step.

Crime Scene Analysis 4.2

Form teams and set up a small crime scene area for each team. Have someone from each team place the following evidence at one of the other team's crime scene, so that each team has

continued

matching items of evidence. Each team collects the evidence at their crime scene using proper procedures.

Latent print on a soda can or clear glass

Hair or Fiber

Simulated blood stain (red food coloring or ketchup): both wet and dry

WEB SITES

Evidence Collection Guidelines from www.crime-scene-investigator.net

http://www.crime-scene-investigator.net/csi-collection.html

DNA Evidence Collection and Preservation

http://www.ncjrs.org/nij/DNAbro/evi.html

Trace Evidence Recovery Guidelines

http://www.fbi.gov/hq/lab/fsc/backissu/oct1999/trace.htm

ENDNOTES

[1] U.S. Department of Justice, Crime Scene Investigation: A Guide for Law Enforcement, 2000

[2] FBI, *Handbook of Forensic Services*, 2003

[3] U.S. Department of Justice, *Crime Scene Investigation: A Guide for Law Enforcement*, 2000

[4] U.S. Department of Justice, *Crime Scene Investigation: A Guide for Law Enforcement*, 2000

[5] U.S. Department of Justice, *Crime Scene Investigation: A Guide for Law Enforcement*, 2000

[6] *Robertson v. Commonwealth*, 12 Va. App. 854, 857, 406 S.E. 2d 417, 419 (1991)

[7] *Washington v. Commonwealth*, 228 Va. 535, 550, 323 S.E. 2d 577, 587 (1984)

INVESTIGATIVE CONSIDERATIONS AND SPECIAL CRIME SCENES

"To gather facts, prepare a case,
Always heed this vow -
Ask the Who and What and Why
And Where and When and How."

—Buckles' Law

"Whenever you have excluded the impossible, whatever remains,
however improbable, must be the truth."

—Sherlock Holmes, in Sir Arthur Conan Doyle's *The Adventures of the Beryl Coronet*

Chapter Outline

INTRODUCTION

In previous chapters on investigating the crime scene, we learned how to document and process a crime scene, and how to identify, collect, and preserve physical evidence. In this chapter, we will look at the special investigative issues and considerations that may come up during this processing of a crime scene.

METHODICAL INVESTIGATIVE PROCESS

As we have learned, a crime scene investigation is a specialized part of a criminal investigation and requires a methodical process that carefully (and thoroughly) identifies, documents, collects, preserves, and evaluates information at a crime scene. This methodical process is essential for answering questions necessary for solving the crime.

5 Ws & H

The importance of the quote at the beginning of this chapter cannot be overstated. *Who, what, when, where, why*, and *how* must be at the core of any methodical approach to crime scene investigation and evidence. These questions are the heart and soul of any investigation. Some of the important questions to ask at any crime scene include the ones designed to answer:

- Who was the victim?
- What happened?
- When did it happen?
- Where did it happen?
- Why did it happen to this particular victim or property?
- How was the crime committed?
- Who committed the crime?
- Why was this crime committed?
- Why this victim or property?
- Who could benefit from this particular act? How?
- What could be gained or lost?
- If stolen property, where could it be sold?
- If missing, where could the property be, why and how?
- What is unusual or different about this crime scene? What is out-of-place?

Many questions need to be answered to prove or disprove a case.

Every crime scene tells a story and it is up to the investigators and crime scene personnel to be able to find the answers to the above questions through their methodical investigation of the scene.

M.O.M

Motive, opportunity, and means to commit a particular crime.

motive

Reason a crime was committed.

M.O.M.

To help answer these questions, investigators should look for evidence that will help identify or exclude someone who had *M.O.M*—the *Motive*, *Opportunity*, and *Means* to commit this particular crime.

Motive

Motive is the reason a crime was committed. There are many reasons people commit crimes, including financial gain, revenge, or just for the "thrill." In some crimes, like a killing in the heat of passion, there may not be any particular motive other than some form of retaliation from anger or rage. Although motive is not legally required to be proven in a criminal prosecution, most juries want to know the "why" of the crime. In the murder of Lacy Peterson and her fetus, for example, the husband, Scott, was portrayed at first by the media as a loving husband, distraught over his wife's disappearance. Later, evidence was discovered that he was having an affair and had told another woman that he would soon be free of his wife. At his murder trial, prosecutors said that the motive was a combination of the affair, the financial gain from the life insurance, and the freedom from having to pay child support if his son were to be born and his marriage ended in divorce.

Motive can also be important in crimes involving financial gain, especially in arsons, embezzlement, or crimes for which someone is found to financially benefit from the criminal act. In these cases, crime scene evidence may include an insurance policy, bills, or financial records. For example, at one crime scene, the body of the homeowner, a divorced mother of a teenage son, was found in the hallway near the front door of the home. A glass pane in the front door had been broken, and the house ransacked, with cash apparently taken. The victim had been stabbed with a large, serrated knife. The crime appeared to be a burglary in which the victim had surprised the burglar and was attacked. The body was discovered during the noon hour by the postal mail carrier who delivered mail each day around the midday. While the crime scene was being investigated, police contacted the son, who was attending classes at his high school. Upon hearing the news, the son became distraught and had to be consoled by friends and school officials. The search of the crime scene revealed a life insurance policy on the mother naming the son as sole beneficiary. The search also uncovered illegal drugs in the son's bedroom, as well as credit card receipts from the mother's credit card for cash advances totaling several hundred dollars. The mother's signature on the credit card receipts turned out to be forged.

Opportunity

opportunity
Time and availability to be able to commit a particular crime.

Opportunity is the time and availability for someone to be able to commit a particular crime. Who had the *opportunity* to commit this crime? Usually, evidence to support this is found during the follow-up investigation and interview of witnesses. For example, evidence in the form of employer time records or witness statements that a suspect was not at work during the time the crime was committed. In the Lacy Peterson murder, Scott Peterson gave police a statement that he had been fishing and later witness statements placed him in the area where the body of his wife was later found.

Evidence may also be found at a crime scene to help show opportunity. A broken clock found at a crime scene may suggest that the crime was committed at a particular time. The body of a homicide victim may yield evidence as to time of death. In the above case involving the murder of the mother in her home, the examination of the body determined the time of death to be around 7 a.m. The teenage son did not show up at his school until 9 a.m.

Means

means
Ability to commit a particular crime.

Means is the *ability* to commit a particular crime. This may be physical, mental, or some form of equipment or expertise. For example, the Washington, D.C. sniper killings required a rifle and some expertise in the shooting of a rifle. Lacy Peterson's body and the body of her unborn son had been found washed ashore in the San Francisco Bay area. The bodies were found a few miles from where Scott Peterson claimed he been fishing in his recently purchased boat the day Lacy was reported missing. In the murder of the mother in her home case, the murder weapon was a large, serrated knife. The teenage son was known to carry a large knife with a "saw-tooth" blade. The stabbing wounds were found to be from forceful, downward thrusts, concentrated in the victim's neck and upper back area, and inflicted by an assailant who was left-handed and who was over 6 feet tall. The teenage son was left handed and stood 6 feet 2 inches.

MO—Modus Operandi

modus operandi
Method of operation. How a criminal commits a crime.

A crime scene investigation is often aided by looking for the *MO*, or **modus operandi**—*method of operation*—of that particular crime. The method of operation includes all aspects of how the crime was committed and what happened at the crime scene, including time, date, and point of entry, tools or weapons used, how they were used, what was taken or damaged, techniques employed, special knowledge or skills needed to carry out the crime, type of victim involved, how attacked, means of attack, object of attack, and any peculiarities displayed by the offender at scene.

Modus operandi can be very important to a crime scene investigation, especially serial crimes or gang killings, in which the criminal may tend to use a similar MO each time he or she commits a crime. An example of this may be in a burglary, where the burglar usually enters a building using the same method (e.g., pry bar on rear window) and only takes money or weapons. Another example is in a serial killing, in which all of the victims have been bound with duct tape, tortured, and killed in a particular manner. On the other hand, the method for how some crimes are committed may change with the particular circumstances or evolve with the criminal. If a burglar sees another window open on the way to the rear window, the method of entry may differ. A serial killer may evolve in his method of binding or torturing his victims, or seek to confuse the police.

Signature

signature
An action or ritual that some serial criminals perform at a crime scene in effect leaving a form of psychological "calling card."

A **signature** is an action or ritual that some serial criminals perform at a crime scene, in effect leaving a form of psychological "calling card." Some investigators believe that it is left at the crime scene by an offender who is compelled to fulfill some behavioral need left unsatisfied by the crime itself.[1] Others believe that it is done to garner publicity or merely taunt the police. The signature is different from a **trophy**, an item that some serial criminals take from the victim or crime scene as a form of memento or souvenir of the crime.

trophy
Item that some serial criminals take from the victim or crime scene as a form of memento or souvenir of the crime.

The signature aspect is not required to complete a crime. It goes beyond the MO and is accomplished by performing some additional action or ritual at the crime scene. In some burglaries, for example, an offender may defecate on the floor of the crime scene or take something from the refrigerator to eat. Serial killers or rapists may use some unique form of ligature or knot in binding their victims. Sexual assaults or murders may involve some form of sadistic torture or ritual, like placing an object on or into the body of a victim, or posing the body.

Staging

staging
Intentional altering of a crime scene to mislead the investigation.

Staging is the intentional altering of a crime scene to mislead the investigation. This is typically done by the offender to *redirect* the focus of the investigation or to *mask* the actual crime being committed.

Redirecting

redirecting
Altering a crime scene in order to shift focus from offender or protect the family.

Redirecting the focus is often done by an offender who knows the victim and wants to shift the focus away from himself, or by a family member or friend who is trying to protect the family. In the Lacy Peterson murder, the husband, Scott Peterson, tried to redirect the investigation by claiming that he discovered his wife missing when he returned from a fishing trip on Christmas Eve. He said that when he last saw his wife that morning, she was going to walk their dog. A neighbor had found the dog, leash attached, on the street where the victim lived. Scott Peterson later joined the search organized by police to look for his wife where she was supposed to be walking the dog.

Another form of redirecting is when a family member or friend attempts to alter the crime scene to redirect an investigation in order to protect the family. An example of this is when someone finds the victim of a suicide and tries to make it look like an accident or homicide in order to protect the family from embarrassment or to ensure that the family will be covered by the victim's life insurance.

Masking

masking
Attempt to cover up or conceal a crime with another crime.

Masking is most often accomplished by an offender who does not know the victim. An example of this is when a burglar or murderer sets fire to the premises in order to mask the crime and destroy evidence. In the murder of the mother in her home, the crime was masked to make it appear as if the mother was killed during the commission of a burglary. The crime scene investigation revealed that the glass on the door had been broken from the inside and that numerous items of value were left intact, including jewelry, stereo equipment, prescription drugs, a coin collection, and more cash from a jar on the kitchen counter.

SPECIAL CRIME SCENES

Every crime scene is different. In addition to standard procedures covered in the previous chapters, some crime scenes might require additional investigative considerations.

Burglary

point of entry (POE)
Areas at crime scene where offender entered to commit a crime.

Burglary is generally defined as the unlawful entry into a building with the intent to steal or commit a felony. Some definitions may add a "breaking" element to the entry. In proving that a burglary did occur, the crime scene investigation should look carefully for a **point of entry**, or **POE**. Where did the burglar enter the premises? How was entry accomplished? Was the entry forcible? The POE is an important area to locate and search for tool marks, footprints, fingerprints, and trace evidence. (It is also important, along with *what* was stolen, in establishing the modus operandi.) Impression or trace evidence may also be found at the **point of departure**, or **POD**. In addition, any **point of impact (POI)**, the areas around the crime scene where ransacking occurred or objects were moved or disturbed, need to be searched.

point of departure (POD)
Areas at crime scene where offender exited crime scene.

point of impact (POI)
Areas at crime scene where ransacking occurred or objects were moved or disturbed.

Robbery

A robbery is generally defined as the taking of money or personal property from the person of another with force or threats of force. One of the immediate investigative considerations at a robbery is the securing of the scene. Most robberies occur at some type of business, where customers come and go. It is very important for this scene to be "frozen" and movement stopped until investigators can determine whether there may be physical evidence. Generally, robbery scenes do not yield much physical evidence. Robberies are more often solved by witnesses and informants. However, sometimes a robber may touch something at the scene, leave footprints (especially if the weather outside is rainy or snowy), or some fiber or other trace evidence. (See Exhibit 5.1.) A holdup note may inadvertently be left. The possibility of some form of physical evidence being left behind requires that the robbery crime scene be quickly secured and methodically assessed.

EXHIBIT 5.1   Suspect Touching Counter at Robbery Scene

Arson

Arson is the intentional burning of a building or structure. In many states, the definition of arson also covers vehicles and other forms of property. Motives for arson are generally centered on financial gain, especially from insurance or bankruptcy schemes. However, arsons can also be motivated by everything from extortion or intimidation to spite, pyromania, or terrorism. As mentioned above, arson can also be committed to mask or conceal another crime. Because arson is such a specialized type of crime scene, it can involve additional investigative considerations.

Video Record Crowd

An initial investigative consideration is in what needs to be documented in the approaching of an arson crime scene. Sometimes, the offender who set the fire will remain or return to the scene to watch his or her handiwork. It is important, therefore, to video record the crowd and all cars at or near an arson scene, so that investigators can go over this video later to supplement their investigation.

Document Smoke and Flames

Another investigative consideration is in documenting (through notes, photography, and video recordings) the color, location, direction, and extent of the smoke and flames observed at the crime scene. Smoke contains traces of the fuel being burned and the color of the smoke may help identify the type of fuel. Black smoke generally indicates a carbon-based fuel like gasoline or oil. White or gray smoke may indicate wood or paper.

Observing and documenting the flames can also be important to an arson crime scene investigation. The color of flames can help identify the type of fuel used. For example, an orange and yellow flame indicates wood fuel, red indicates some type of petroleum, and a blue flame indicates natural gas or propane. The direction of the flames should also be documented. Fires tend to burn up and away from their source. Documenting the location and direction of the flames can help to identify the **point of origin (POO)**, or where the fire was started.

point of origin (POO)
The location at a scene where the fire was started.

accelerant
A catalyst in the starting and spreading of a fire.

alligatoring
A charring of wood that is checked and resembles the pattern of an alligator's scales.

Searching the Arson Crime Scene

In searching the arson crime scene, an important investigative consideration is finding and documenting the *point of origin*. As stated above, this is where the fire was started. Because of the use of an **accelerant**, a catalyst in the starting and spreading of a fire, the POO will typically be an area with the deepest charring. Often, any wood there will show an **alligatoring** effect, a charring that is checked and resembles the pattern of an alligator's scales. (See Exhibit 5.2.) An arson scene will often have more than one point of origin, especially a large structure where the arsonist is attempting to quickly spread the fire to envelop the whole structure.

EXHIBIT 5.2 Alligatoring Effect in Arson Fire

Another important investigative consideration in the search of an arson scene is to look for accelerants, their containers, and any type of kindling material. Gasoline or some other flammable liquid is the most commonly used accelerant in arsons. Often, an arsonist will pour the flammable liquid in a line throughout parts of the structure to cause the fire to spread from one area to the next. This is known as a **trailer**. Evidence of trailers can be observed in the charring that follows this line, or in areas along the line that show heavier burning. In looking for evidence of accelerants, investigators also need to look for **igniters**, or something used to start the fire. Matches, cigarettes, and candles are commonly used igniters. However, some arsonists may use explosives, or some form of sophisticated device made from electrical or chemical sources.

trailer
Flammable liquid or materials placed along a line to spread a fire from one area to another.

igniters
Something used to start a fire, like matches or candles.

Crimes Against Children

Crimes against children involve forms of abuse, neglect, or exploitation. These can be physical, emotional, or sexual. Often, these crimes have occurred over a period of time, or are being reported some time after their occurrence. This presents problems in ascertaining a "crime scene" to investigate. Although for the criminal investigation the interviewing of the victim will be very important, for crime scene investigative purposes, the focus will be on the proper examination and documentation of injuries to the victim. For example, an examination of the victim of physical abuse will document current injuries, but also look for evidence of older, age-dated injuries, broken bones, and bruising that might indicate a pattern of abuse. Bruises that appear to "wrap-around" the victim's arm, leg, back, or buttocks area might indicate the use of a cord or belt. All injuries to the victim will need to be photographed and documented.

Sexual Assault

An important investigative consideration in a sexual assault is the proper collection of physical evidence, both from the crime scene and from the victim. The crime scene investigation will be conducted using the methodical procedures discussed in previous chapters. The other investigative consideration will be collecting evidence from and documenting injuries to the victim. Most hospitals carry sexual assault "kits" that contain materials and instructions to properly collect and preserve physical evidence from the victim. (See Exhibit 5.3.) In addition, all injuries to the victim must be photographed and any clothing worn at the time of the assault collected.

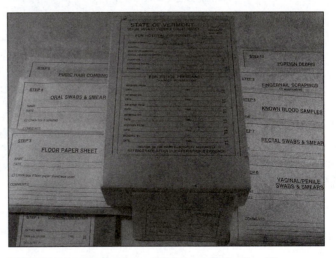

EXHIBIT 5.3   Sexual Assault Evidence Collection Kit
Source: State of Vermont and Sirchie Labs

Death Investigation

The need for a thorough and methodical crime scene investigation is essential when a death scene is encountered. The securing of the crime scene and the proper search for and collection of physical evidence will be especially important. Special investigative considerations are required to establish the time and cause of death.

Types of Death

Death scenes are classified into four types: natural, accidental, suicide, and homicide. Natural death can be a result of old age, disease, or a heart attack. Accidental deaths can result from a variety of factors, including drowning, vehicle or workplace accidents, and accidental shootings. Suicide is the taking of one's own life.

Homicide is the killing of one person by another person. Homicide can either be noncriminal or criminal. Noncriminal would include excusable and justifiable homicide. An example of excusable homicide is the accidental killing of a person by another, as in an automobile accident. Justifiable homicide occurs when a killing is justified by law, as in the police using deadly force to prevent a violent felony, or in self-defense. Criminal homicide is broken down into murder and manslaughter.

Cause of Death

Establishing the cause of death will be important to identifying the type of death scene and whether there will be a need for a criminal investigation. The medical examiner will determine the official cause of death. However, every death scene should be treated initially as a potential homicide until a different cause of death has been established. Even when the death appears to be from natural or accidental causes, the scene should be secured and protected until the cause of death has been confirmed through investigation and all possibilities have been eliminated. This will involve identifying the victim, inspecting the scene for any suspicious circumstances, signs of struggle, or anything that looks out of place. If a natural death is being considered, the victim's doctor needs to be contacted and medical history needs to be obtained.

If a suicide is suspected, the scene should be treated as a crime scene for documentation purposes. This should include sketching and photographing the scene, and searching the scene for evidence that will verify suicide as cause of death. In particular, the search should look for notes left by the victim and evidence of a motive.

If the cause of death is by gunshot wound, in a suicide look for a contact wound and tattooing (powder burns around the wound), which would indicate that the weapon was held against the skin when fired. Generally, a person commits suicide with a firearm by firing into the mouth or the same side of the temple as the gun hand. The firearm will be at the scene, usually near the hand. In a murder, the firearm will usually not be found at the scene and there will be no contact wound or tattooing (usually fired from a longer distance—even if a few inches). (See Exhibit 5.4.) When a knife is used in a suicide, look for cutting type wounds and *hesitation* marks—smaller initial cuts made by the victim.

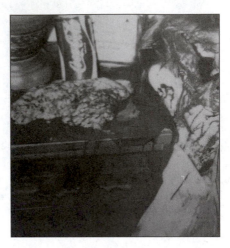

EXHIBIT 5.4 Death by Firearm
Note the unusual positioning of the soda can on top of the brain matter.

Establishing Time of Death

Establishing the time of death is important, especially in narrowing or eliminating suspects. The medical examiner will make the official determination on the time of death, but the crime scene investigators can help with this through observations and documentation. A body goes through certain changes after death. One of these changes is the loss of body heat as the body cools to reach the temperature of its environment. The normal body temperature is 98.6 degrees Fahrenheit. A body will lose a couple of degrees the first hour, then lose approximately 1 ½ degrees each hour for the next 18 hours.

Another change is the stiffening of certain muscle fibers in the body due to the breakdown of enzymes. This is called **rigor mortis** and, although certain factors, such as strenuous exercise, can affect the timing, it usually begins in the jaw and face within 4 hours after death. Over the next 12–16 hours, rigor moves down to affect the whole body and remains for another 12–16 hours. The timing of rigor is generally accurate within 4–8 hours.

A **cadaveric spasm**, often called a "death grip," is an immediate stiffening of a particular group of muscles, usually a hand or arm, caused by a sudden, violent death. This effect can sometimes be found in suicide or other sudden violent death where the victim is gripping something (like a gun) at the time of death.

Another investigative consideration in death scene investigation is **postmortem lividity**. After death, circulation in the body ceases and gravity causes blood to settle to the lowest levels of the body. For example, if a body is on its back, blood would settle in the lower levels of the arms, legs, and back. This settling of blood is

rigor mortis
Stiffening of body after death.

cadaveric spasm
Called a "death grip," an immediate stiffening of a hand or arm upon sudden, violent death.

postmortem lividity
Settling of blood in the body after death.

called *postmortem lividity* and has the appearance of a purplish and dark blue discoloration. Lividity generally starts as soon as circulation stops. It can be seen in the body within 1–3 hours and generally reaches full lividity within 12 hours. Lividity does not shift with the moving of a body. Therefore, the location of a body in relation to the position the body was in when found can help determine whether the body was moved after death. For example, in one crime scene made to look like a suicide, the victim was found lying on his back with a gun near his right hand. However, signs of lividity were observed only along the left side of the victim's body, indicating that the body had been moved after death.

Dead Body Searches

States have different rules concerning the search of a dead body at the scene of a crime. Some areas require that only the coroner's or medical examiner's investigators can search the body at the crime scene. Other states require the body to be searched later at the morgue. Still other states have requirements about who must be notified of a dead body at the crime scene and who must be present to certify the death.

In dead body searches, investigators need to insure that trace evidence is protected on and around the body. One technique for insuring this after photos, notes, and sketching is done is to tie paper bags securely on the victim's hands so that the fingers and nails can later be examined at the medical examiner's office and that fingerprints can be taken. Also, clothing and inventory contents should be searched. Finally, be sure to search around the immediate area of the body and under the body. Make sure the body is placed in a body bag so that no trace evidence is lost from the body or clothes during transport to the medical examiner's office.

CSI CHECKLIST 5.1

Special Investigative Considerations: Photographing a Dead Body

Upon arrival at the scene, and prior to moving the body or evidence, the investigator should:

❑ Photograph the body and immediate scene (including the decedent as initially found)
❑ Photograph the decedent's face

continued

❑ Take additional photographs after removal of objects/items that interfere with photographic documentation of the decedent (e.g., body removed from car)

❑ Photograph the decedent with and without measurements (as appropriate)

❑ Photograph the surface beneath the body (after the body has been removed, as appropriate)

❑ Never clean face, do not change condition

❑ Take multiple shots if possible

Source: National Institute of Justice, *Death Investigation*

PRACTICE TIP 5.1

Death Scene Investigation

For an excellent guide to death scene investigation, check out the following Department of Justice publication:
Death Investigation: A Guide for the Scene Investigator
http://www.ojp.usdoj.gov/nij/pubs-sum/167568.htm

SOLVABILITY FACTORS

solvability factors
Factors at a crime scene that law enforcement officials have no control over, but that may affect the solving of the crime.

Sometimes, there are factors at a crime scene that law enforcement officials have no control over, but that may affect the solving of the crime or the later prosecution or defense of the person charged with committing the crime. These are called **solvability factors**. For example, if a rape victim bathes before reporting the crime or a burglary victim cleans up the messy house before law enforcement arrives, vital evidence may be lost or destroyed.

Most of a crime scene investigation involves factors that law enforcement officials *do* have control over, including the passage of time. The general rule is that the probability of success in an investigation decreases with time. The quicker a crime scene is responded to, protected, and investigated, the better the chances of solving the case.

Factors that Influence Solvability at Crime Scene

Factors that may influence this are called "time-critical" factors. They may include:

- Escape of suspect from scene of crime.
- Destruction or removal of evidence from the scene.

- Contamination of scene by witness or victim.
- Contamination of scene by law enforcement officers.
- Loss of evidence due to failure to identify or collect.
- Improper handling or collection of evidence.

CRIME SCENE RECONSTRUCTION

crime scene reconstruction
Recreation of a crime scene, or parts of it, in order to prepare a case for trial, verify information from the original scene, or to continue an investigation.

Crime Scene Reconstruction is the recreation of a crime scene, or parts of it, in order to prepare a case for trial, verify information from the original scene, or to continue an investigation. The Association for Crime Scene Reconstruction defines it as:

"The use of scientific methods, physical evidence, deductive reasoning, and their interrelationships to gain explicit knowledge of the series of events that surround the commission of a crime."[2]

Many investigators and legal personnel will not have an opportunity to be present at an initial crime scene when everything is freshly searched and processed. These investigators and legal personnel may come into the case much later, when the case has to be reviewed or reopened. In most criminal cases, there are investigators and legal personnel whose jobs include responsibilities for case preparation and verification prior to trial. For major, violent criminal cases and property crimes, investigators may need to recreate the crime scene, or parts of it, in order to conduct or continue their investigation.

Steps in Crime Scene Reconstruction

There are six basic steps in the reconstruction of a crime scene, with the focus on carefully reading through all documentation, re-interviewing relevant individuals, and verifying information.

1. Obtain Documentation

The first step in reconstructing a crime scene is to obtain all documentation, including reports, sketches, photographs, and video. Be sure to include supplemental reports, including autopsy findings and any lab testing or analysis.

2. Read and Re-Read

Next, read through the initial crime report and look over the sketches and photographs to get a "feel" for the crime scene. If the crime scene was videotaped, watch the video.

Carefully read and re-read each report. Try to obtain and read any notes taken by personnel who responded to the crime scene, especially the first responders and the investigative personnel who searched and processed the scene.

3. Interview

Interview each individual who was at the crime scene, including victims, witnesses, first responders, and investigative or crime lab personnel. Verify information on any statements given or reports made by these individuals. Try to find out if anyone has remembered something new or different from their original observations.

4. Visit Crime Scene

Visit the crime scene. Use the above documentation and interviews to try to visualize how this scene must have appeared to investigators and whether the documentation fits the scene.

5. Recreate Crime Scene

Using the information gathered, reconstruct or recreate the crime scene. If possible, use the original crime scene for reconstruction. If not, find a suitable area to be used. Measure and mark off this area. Try to recreate it using similar furniture and objects. If these cannot be found, use simulated objects and mock-ups.

6. Verify

Check with witnesses and have them look over and verify that the reconstruction is an accurate representation of the crime scene. Does viewing this scene jog the memory of any witness? Go through reports and documentation again, and using the reconstructed scene, try to verify that all procedures were followed and that the evidence could have been collected as stated. If necessary, re-interview using what was discovered in the reconstruction assessment.

PRACTICE TIP 5.2

Association for Crime Scene Reconstruction

For more information on crime scene reconstruction, visit:
Association for Crime Scene Reconstruction
http://www.acsr.org/

LEGAL CHALLENGES

As noted in earlier chapters, an important legal issue in the investigation of a crime scene is whether investigators need a search warrant to search and process the scene. Because of its importance, this topic will be discussed in more detail in Chapter 7.

Other legal challenges involving the investigative considerations and special crime scenes discussed in this chapter generally focus on whether proper procedures were followed at the scene. Since the televised O.J. Simpson murder trial, where errors at the crime scene by both police and lab personnel were targeted by defense, attorneys look closely at whether proper procedure was used at the crime scene. Often, defense attorneys use former crime scene investigators or criminalists as expert witnesses. In a North Carolina murder trial, where the defendant was prosecuted for bludgeoning his wife to death (the defendant claimed that his wife fell down the stairs), defense called a director of a Connecticut crime lab to testify. The criminalist called the murder scene investigation a "study in errors."[3] In some crime scene investigations, blankets have inadvertently been used by officers to cover up the bodies before the scenes were processed.[4] In a Pittsburgh shooting death investigation, the county coroner criticized police for making inadvertent mistakes that included calling in the fire department to wash away blood from the street before the coroner's office had an opportunity to investigate the scene.[5]

Legal Challenges to Credibility

Legal challenges about improper or sloppy procedures at a crime scene are said to go "to the weight of the evidence and not its admissibility."[6] This means that the legal challenge attacks the credibility of the law enforcement or crime lab witness, and it will be up to the jury to decide how much "weight" will be given to the testimony and evidence presented. The attack on the credibility of a law enforcement witness may be done by the defense on "cross-examination or may be addressed through testimony of defense experts at trial, as is true of other forensic evidence."[7] In the North Carolina murder trial mentioned above, the jury decided that the weight of all evidence presented was stronger than any mistakes made at the crime scene. The defendant was found guilty of murder.

SUMMARY

A crime scene investigation is a specialized part of a criminal investigation and requires a methodical process that carefully (and thoroughly) identifies, documents, collects, preserves, and evaluates information at a crime scene. *Who, what, when, where, why*, and *how* must be at the core of any methodical approach to crime scene investigation and evidence. These questions are the heart and soul of any investigation. Why this victim or property? Who could benefit from this particular act? How? What is unusual or different about this crime scene? What is out-of-place? Many questions need to be answered to prove or disprove a case. Every crime scene tells a story and it is up to the investigators and crime scene personnel to be able to find the answers to the above questions through their methodical investigation of the scene. To help answer these questions, investigators should look for evidence that will help to identify or exclude someone who had *M.O.M*—the *Motive*, *Opportunity*, and *Means* to commit this particular crime. A crime scene investigation is often aided by looking for the *MO*, or modus operandi (*method of operation*), of that particular crime. The method of operation includes all aspects of how the crime was committed and what happened at the crime scene. A signature is the way some criminals may leave their own unique mark or "signature" on their crime, usually associated with serial crimes. Staging is the intentional altering of a crime scene to mislead the investigation. This is typically done by the offender to *redirect* the focus of the investigation or to *mask* the actual crime being committed.

Every crime scene is different. In addition to standard procedures, some crime scenes might require additional investigative considerations. For example, in a burglary, the focus of a crime scene search may be on the point of entry and points of impact. In an arson, the point of origin is important and the scene must be searched for evidence of *igniters* and *accelerants*. Investigative considerations in child abuse may include age-dated injuries and wrap-around bruises. In death investigations, special investigative considerations will be in establishing the time and cause of death. Sometimes there are factors at a crime scene that law enforcement officials have no control over, but that may affect the solving of the crime or the later prosecution or defense of the person charged with committing the crime. These are called *solvability factors*.

Crime scene reconstruction is the recreation of a crime scene, or parts of it, in order to prepare a case for trial, verify information from the original scene, or to continue an investigation. There are six basic steps in the reconstruction of a crime scene, with the focus on carefully reading through all documentation, re-interviewing relevant individuals, and verifying information.

Legal challenges involving the investigative considerations and special crime scenes discussed in this chapter generally focus on whether proper procedures were followed at the scene and whether evidence collected was properly maintained.

KEY TERMS

Accelerant	Cadaveric Spasm
Alligatoring	Crime Scene Reconstruction

Igniters

Masking

Means

Modus Operandi (MO)

M.O.M

Motive

Opportunity

Masking

Point of Departure (POD)

Point of Entry (POE)

Point of Impact (POI)

Point of Origin (POO)

Postmortem Lividity

Redirecting

Rigor Mortis

Signature

Solvability Factors

Staging

Trailer

Trophy

REVIEW QUESTIONS

1. Define the terms *modus operandi*, *5 Ws and H*, and *M.O.M*, and describe how these terms are used in crime scene investigation.

2. Explain what a *signature* is at a crime scene.

3. Define *staging* at a crime scene and identify the two ways this can be attempted.

4. Distinguish between *POE*, *POD*, *POI*, and *POO*, and discuss their importance in crime scene investigation.

5. Describe some of the investigative considerations for an arson scene.

6. Describe some of the investigative considerations in a death investigation.

7. Identify some of the "solvability factors" and how they might affect a crime scene investigation.

8. Discuss the steps in reconstructing a crime scene.

CRITICAL THINKING QUESTIONS 5.1

1. What is the importance of understanding modus operandi in a crime scene investigation?

2. Why would an offender leave a "signature" at a crime scene and how can identifying this be used to further a crime scene investigation?

3. How would someone "stage" a crime scene and why? Give examples.

4. What is the importance of understanding how to reconstruct a crime scene?

FORENSIC RESEARCH USING THE INTERNET

1. Search the Internet for specific articles dealing with special crime scenes involving arson or death investigations. Assess the special investigative considerations discussed in the article.

PRACTICE SKILLS:

Practice what you have learned in the following problems:

Crime Scene Analysis 5.1

Terms:

Motive	Opportunity	Means
Modus Operandi	Signature	Staging
Point of Origin	Point of Impact	Point of Entry

Directions: Match one of the above terms for each of the following:

1. Employer record showing suspect was not at work on day of crime
2. Where fire was started in arson
3. Insurance policy found at death scene
4. Serial killer draws a target on each victim's forehead
5. A broken window where burglar went into home
6. Area of room where assault occurred
7. Receipt showing suspect purchased gasoline on day of arson
8. Family friend moves gun from suicide victim's hand to make it appear that death was homicide
9. Serial burglar enters homes by prying rear window, always leaves through a rear door

Crime Scene Analysis 5.2

Formulate and discuss some theories of how the soda can in Figure 5-4, page 98, might have ended up under the victim's brain. Describe how these theories might be tested and verified.

WEB SITES

Association for Crime Scene Reconstruction: http://www.acsr.org/

Death Investigation: A Guide for the Scene Investigator
http://www.ojp.usdoj.gov/nij/pubs-sum/167568.htm

ENDNOTES

[1] An excellent resource for this can be found in FBI Special Agent and Profiler John Douglas and Corinne Munn's article in the FBI Law Enforcement Bulletin, February 1992: *Violent Crime Scene Analysis: Modus Operandi, Signature, and Staging*

[2] Association for Crime Scene Reconstruction, http://www.acsr.org/

[3] See the article by Matt Bean, *Defense focuses on crime scene integrity*, Court TV (Sept 23, 2003)

[4] For example, this happened in both the Jon Benet Ramsey and the Nicole Simpson murders

[5] See the article by David Conti, *Crime scene tainted*, Pittsburgh Tribune-Review (May 13, 2003)

[6] *State v. Montgomery* (Mo. App. 1976) 545 S.W.2d 655

[7] See *Oregon v. Cunningham*

CHAPTER **6**

SOURCES OF LAWS GOVERNING CRIME SCENE INVESTIGATIONS

"Evidence which tends to establish some fact material to the case, or which tends to make a fact at issue more or less probable, is relevant."

—Commonwealth v. Scott, 480 Pa. 50 (1978)

"The law is reason, free from passion."

—Aristotle

Chapter Outline

- Sources of Laws Governing Crime Scene Investigations
- Constitution
- Case Law
- Statutory Law
- Substantive Law
- Elements of a Crime
- Prima Facie Case
- Procedural Law
- Rules of Criminal Procedure
- Rules of Evidence
- How Evidence Law Influences Crime Scene Investigative Process
- Types of Evidence
- Forms of Evidence
- Relevancy
- Exculpatory Evidence
- Evidence versus Proof
- Burden of Proof

INTRODUCTION

As we learned in the previous chapters, it is important for anyone involved in the investigation, prosecution, or defense of a crime to understand the proper procedures of crime scene investigation. However, it is also *essential* that these people know the *laws* governing crime scene investigation. This chapter will present an overview of the sources of these laws and where to find them. Chapter 7 will focus on the specific laws and court decisions governing crime scene searches. Subsequent chapters will cover the laws determining the admissibility of forensic evidence found at the crime scene and will examine the laws that govern crime scene witnesses and evidence in court.

SOURCES OF LAWS GOVERNING CRIME SCENE INVESTIGATIONS

Laws that govern criminal investigations can be found in three primary sources: the Constitution, case law, and statutory law.

Constitution

Constitution
The United States's founding document that establishes framework of government and laws. Supreme law of the land.

Laws governing crime scene investigations have their foundation in the **Constitution**, both the federal constitution and individual state constitutions. A constitution is a country's or state's founding document that establishes both the framework of government and laws. Our United States Constitution, ratified in 1787 and the "supreme law of the land,"[1] contains fundamental principles and procedures that must be followed in any crime scene investigation. For example, the Fourth Amendment to the Constitution governs safeguards and procedures for searching a crime scene and the seizure of evidence. (This is the most important area of law in a crime scene investigation and will be examined fully in Chapter 7.) The Fifth Amendment contains protections and procedures for the identification and interrogation of suspects found at the crime scene. The Sixth Amendment establishes principles for ensuring the right to counsel and fair trial procedures for a criminal defendant. The Fourteenth Amendment provides **due process** protection. Laws and legal rules dealing with crime scene investigations must satisfy the protections and limitations established by the Constitution or risk being overturned by the courts who have the power to interpret the Constitution and say what the law is.[2]

due process
Constitutional protections extended to suspects and defendants in a criminal investigation.

Case Law

The courts are responsible for interpreting our Constitution and determining whether statutory laws are constitutional. A court's decision may change an existing statutory law or rule dealing with crime scene investigation, or may even establish new law. If a statutory law is found by the court to violate a constitutional provision, the court may overturn the statute. The decision of a court is called **case law** or **common law**. A ruling of an appellate court that must be followed by all lower courts is called a **precedent**.

Case law is important because it not only guides our courts, but it also dictates the policies and procedures that *must* be followed by all law enforcement and investigative personnel. Cases decided years ago, like *Mapp v. Ohio*[3] or *Miranda v. Arizona*[4] still control how crime scene searches are conducted and suspects interrogated. Most of the legal standards and tests used today in determining whether a crime scene investigation was conducted properly are the result of court decisions establishing case law. Knowing how to find and understand the significance of these court decisions pertaining to crime scene investigations is essential for investigators and those preparing for a criminal prosecution.

Statutory Law

Statutory law is law that has been legislated. Statutes can be found in local ordinances, and in state and federal codes. Statutory law is important because the definitions for most crimes can be found in criminal codes and statutes.

Statutory laws are either **substantive law** or **procedural law**. That is, they either provide us with a definition and elements of a particular law or they provide us with rules to tell us how to enforce the law. For crime scene investigators, both of these areas are equally important.

Substantive Criminal Law

Substantive laws are those that define a crime and list the elements for the crime and the punishment that could be received upon conviction. These are found in a written statute or code. For example, Title 18 of the United States Code contains the definitions and elements for most of the federal criminal laws. Each state has its own set of criminal laws. These are usually called Penal Codes,[5] Criminal Codes,[6] or Statutes.[7]

case law
Judge-made law based on court decisions. Term is used today interchangeably with common law.

common law
Case law. A uniform set of laws for a state or country based on court decisions.

precedent
A court decision that serves as a rule of law or standard to be looked at in deciding subsequent cases.

statutory law
Laws passed by legislature.

substantive law
Defines the law, providing elements and sanctions.

procedural law
Rules that set forth legal process and tell us how to enforce the law.

Elements of a Crime

elements of a crime
Essential parts from the definition of a crime that must each be established in order to prove that a crime has been committed.

The definition of a crime found in these statutes or clarified in case decisions includes the **elements** of that crime. It is essential that crime scene investigators know the *elements* for crimes in order to ascertain whether a crime has in fact been committed and, if so, what crime has been committed.

How do you know that a crime has been committed (or which crime it is) if you do not know the definition and elements of that crime? A mini-mart that reports a robbery may actually be reporting a burglary or petty larceny. Looking for evidence to prove the wrong elements at a crime scene may result in the loss of the entire case. This becomes critical in a crime scene investigation because *all* elements *must* be proven for a conviction. In order to know which crime has been committed and what elements must be proven for that particular crime, all investigators should have a solid grounding in substantive criminal law.

Prima Facie Case

prima facie
Translates to "at first sight" and means that at first sight, all of the elements for a particular crime have been established.

By knowing the elements (definitions) of crimes, and then by applying proper crime scene investigative techniques, you are able to establish a **prima facie** case. A prima facie case is one in which all of the elements of a particular crime have been established in order to prove that on the face of the evidence or facts obtained, a crime has or has not been committed. For example, the common law definition of a burglary is defined as requiring a "breaking and entering." To establish these elements, evidence at the crime scene of a broken lock or window might help to prove a "breaking," whereas fingerprints or footprints inside the building would help to establish "entering."

PRACTICE TIP 6.1

Establishing a Prima Facie Case

In order to establish a prima facie case when investigating a crime scene, always consider the definition of the crime that was committed. Break down the definition into the elements that will need to be established and proven. Look for the evidence that will establish each element and satisfy this proof. Be prepared to identify and collect evidence that will prove every element needed to establish the action.

Procedural Law

Procedural laws are sets of rules or procedures that tell *how* the law is to be enforced or investigated in a specific area. In this area of procedural law, crime scene investigations are mostly governed by *rules of criminal procedure* and *rules of evidence*.

Rules of Criminal Procedure

rules of criminal procedure
Statutory laws and approved court rules governing procedural aspects of criminal investigations, and search and seizure.

Rules of criminal procedure govern procedural aspects of criminal investigations, mainly dealing with search and seizure and arrest. These rules can generally be found in a state or federal government's statutes or court rules. For example, there are *Federal Rules of Criminal Procedure* and each state has its own set of criminal procedure rules.

In crime scene investigation, *rules of criminal procedure* can detail when a search warrant is required to search a crime scene, how a warrant can be obtained, time limits and specifications in executing the warrant, and when a warrantless search or arrest can be conducted. (See Exhibit 6.1.) These rules can also govern other procedures that might relate to an investigation, such as how to obtain comparison samples from a suspect to match with evidence obtained at the crime scene.

EXHIBIT 6.1   Non-Testimonial Identification Order

Need a blood sample from a possible suspect to try to match DNA with blood found at a crime scene, but you're not sure what you need to get this? Some states require that a court order be secured to gather this evidence. Here's an example from the *Vermont Rules of Criminal Procedure*, (VRCrP) Rule 41.1 (c):

RULE 41.1 NON-TESTIMONIAL IDENTIFICATION

    (c) **Basis for Order**

An order shall issue only on an affidavit or affidavits sworn to before the judicial officer and establishing the following grounds for the order:

    (1) that there is probable cause to believe that an offense has been committed;

    (2) that there are reasonable grounds, that need not amount to probable cause to arrest, to suspect that the person named or described in the affidavit committed the offense; and

    (3) that the results of specific nontestimonial identification procedures will be of material aid in determining whether the person named in the affidavit committed the offense.

PRACTICE TIP 6.2

Finding Rules of Criminal Procedure
Visit this Web site to find your state's Rules of Criminal Procedure:
    http://www.law.cornell.edu/topics/state_statutes2. html#criminal_procedure

EVIDENCE LAW

evidence
Anything that tends to prove or disprove a fact at issue in a criminal action.

evidence law
Body of rules that help to govern conduct and determine what will be admissible in criminal proceedings and trials.

Evidence is anything that tends to prove or disprove a fact at issue in a criminal action. Evidence can include almost anything submitted to the jury or trier of fact for consideration. It can be offered in many forms, from witness testimony to physical objects, including weapons or bloodstains, crime scene sketches, diagrams, photographs, and documents.

Evidence law is a body of rules that helps to govern conduct and determines what will be admissible in certain legal proceedings and trials. This law can generally be found in *Rules of Evidence*[8] or an *Evidence Code*.[9]

How Evidence Law Influences Crime Scene Investigative Process

Evidence law influences the crime scene investigative process. Rules of evidence affect how crime scenes are investigated and how a case is presented through evidence and witnesses in the criminal trial process. These rules and laws also establish how much evidence is required to prove a criminal case. The gathering of information and evidence at a crime scene must focus on establishing the elements to the crime being investigated and meeting the burden in proving that crime at trial. There are rules that govern the admissibility of any evidence gathered. These rules also determine which evidence will not be admissible. For example, information will be excluded as evidence when it does not pertain to something at issue in the case. Even when it is important to the case, information may be excluded if it is unreliable, confusing, or prejudicial. Information will not be admissible as evidence if it violates some public policy that protects a special relationship or communication, such as an attorney and client, or husband and wife. The importance is in understanding that evidence law and rules form a framework that guide what information should be gathered and how that information must be obtained.

> ## PRACTICE TIP 6.3
>
> ### Researching Evidence Laws on the Internet
>
> *Want some help in finding and researching your state or federal evidence laws? Try visiting one of the following Web sites:*
>
> ### Finding State Evidence Codes
>
> *An excellent resource for laws, court decisions, and legal resources of all kinds is the Legal Information Institute (LII), Cornell Law School.*
>
>   *http://www.law.cornell.edu/states/listing.html*
>
>   *FindLaw is another excellent legal resource for state and federal laws and cases.*
>
>   *http://guide.lp.findlaw.com/casecode/*
>
> ### Finding Federal Rules of Evidence
>
> *Most Web sites will refer you to the LII (Legal Information Institute) for its searchable copy of the Federal Rules of Evidence:*
>
>   *http://www.law.cornell.edu/rules/fre/overview.html*

Types of Evidence

To effectively gather evidence to be presented at trial, we need to first understand what constitutes evidence and what needs to be looked for in obtaining information. We know that evidence is defined as something that tends to prove or disprove a fact or matter at issue. Evidence is classified by type and form. There are two basic types of evidence, *direct evidence* and *circumstantial evidence*.

Direct Evidence

direct evidence
Evidence that proves a disputed fact directly, through an eyewitness, for example.

Direct evidence proves a disputed fact *directly* through the testimony of a witness who saw or heard the dispute in question. An eyewitness is the best and most common example of direct evidence. Direct evidence relies on the senses and perception of the eyewitness and does not require any intervening or indirect fact to be proven first. There are no inferences that need to be drawn from direct evidence. For example, a witness at a crime scene saw the defendant stab the victim with a knife. If the witness testifies as to what she saw, this would be direct evidence.

Circumstantial Evidence

circumstantial evidence
Proves a disputed fact indirectly by first proving another fact. From this other fact an inference may be drawn as to the original disputed fact.

inference
A deduction of fact that may logically be drawn from another fact.

Circumstantial evidence proves a disputed fact indirectly by first proving another fact. From this other fact, an **inference** may be drawn as to the original disputed fact. We have often heard it said on television, "You can't prove anything! All you have is *circumstantial* evidence!" In reality, most cases are proven with circumstantial evidence. This type of evidence can be much more credible than eyewitness testimony. For example, a victim is found at a crime scene, dead from multiple stab wounds, the bloody knife still in victim's chest. If the defendant's fingerprints were found on the bloody knife, this is an example of circumstantial evidence.

Other examples of circumstantial evidence in this case include matching the blood on the knife to that of the victim, finding victim's bloodstains on the clothing of the defendant, and other physical evidence, like DNA, fibers, and footprints, all linking the defendant to the crime scene and victim. There is no direct evidence that could be offered to prove that the defendant actually stabbed the victim, but there can be an inference drawn as to this fact. By offering all of the circumstantial evidence, a trier of fact might *infer* that the defendant stabbed the victim.

CSI CHECKLIST 6.1

Types of Evidence

Types of Evidence:	Example:
❑ Direct	Eyewitness
❑ Circumstantial	Fingerprint

Forms Of Evidence

In addition to the two basic types of evidence, there are four basic forms of evidence: testimonial, physical, documentary, and demonstrative.

1. Testimonial Evidence

testimonial evidence
Oral or "spoken" evidence presented by witnesses who come into court to give their testimony under oath.

Testimonial evidence is oral or "spoken" evidence presented by witnesses who come into court to give their testimony under oath. This is the most common form of evidence, and it is also used to illustrate, or is used as a foundation for, most of the other forms of evidence. For example, in a violent assault, you may have a victim, or other people, at the crime scene who actually witnessed the assault. You may also have people who heard the commotion and saw the defendant run from the scene. These people would all be called as witnesses to *testify* as to what they saw or heard.

In addition to these witnesses, you might have evidence from the crime scene (bloody clothing, fingerprints, weapon) that helps to prove the crime or link the defendant to it. To be admitted as legal evidence, these objects must be authenticated through the *testimony* of someone who will testify that he or she was at the crime scene or that the crime scene evidence in question is what it purports to be.

2. Physical Evidence

physical evidence
Something that can be seen, touched, or felt, and can be identified by its own nature.

Physical evidence, one of the most important forms of evidence sought at the crime scene, is something that can be seen, touched, or felt, and can be identified by its own nature. Physical evidence is said to "speak for itself" and therefore is considered more reliable than other forms of evidence. Examples of physical evidence include the weapon found at the crime scene, fingerprints, bloodstains, semen, hair, fibers, and many other items. In order for physical evidence to be admitted into court, a proper foundation must be presented through a witness who can testify as to the authenticity of the evidence.

3. Documentary Evidence

documentary evidence
Evidence in the form of writings or records, including letters, notes, contracts, printings, pictures, or recordings.

Documentary evidence is sometimes called "writings" and consists of letters, notes, insurance policies, pictures, and similar materials found at the crime scene or through the criminal investigation. Like physical evidence, a proper foundation must be presented through a witness who can testify as to the document's identity and its authenticity.

4. Demonstrative Evidence

demonstrative evidence
Demonstrates, illustrates, or recreates evidence that has already been presented or a point or matter that needs further explanation.

Demonstrative evidence "demonstrates," illustrates, or recreates evidence that has already been presented or a point or matter that needs further explanation. This demonstration is usually done in conjunction with the investigation of the crime scene and includes evidence such as crime scene photographs, sketches, displays, mock-ups, and diagrams.

CSI CHECKLIST 6.2

Forms of Evidence

Forms of Evidence:	Example:
❑ Testimonial	Witness
❑ Physical	Fingerprint
❑ Documentary	Insurance policy
❑ Demonstrative	Sketch or photos of crime scene

Relevancy

relevancy
A basic requirement for the admissibility of evidence is that it tends to prove or disprove a fact in issue.

probative
Tends to prove something.

A basic requirement for the admissibility of evidence is that it must tend to prove or disprove a fact in question. This is called **relevancy**. In order to satisfy this relevance requirement, evidence must be **probative**; that is, it must *tend* to prove something. However, it does not *have* to actually prove anything. It must simply tend to be more probable than not in proving or disproving something at issue in a case. As a Pennsylvania court noted, "Evidence which tends to establish some fact material to the case, or which tends to make a fact at issue more or less probable, is relevant."[10] Even the slightest tendency is sufficient. If we are trying to prove that the defendant forged a document found at a crime scene using a red pen, the fact that the defendant owned a red pen does not alone prove that this same red pen was used in the forgery or that the defendant actually forged the document. It may, however, be relevant because it tends to shed some light on and add another piece to the puzzle of who forged the document.

CSI CHECKLIST 6.3

Types and Forms of Evidence

Types of Evidence	Forms of Evidence
❑ Direct	❑ Testimonial
❑ Circumstantial	❑ Physical
	❑ Documentary
	❑ Demonstrative

logical relevance
When evidence tends to prove or disprove a fact in issue.

legal relevance
Even when relevant, evidence is not admissible if it violates any other evidence rule or law.

hearsay
A statement made out of court and offered in court as evidence to prove the truth of the assertion made in the statement.

Logical and Legal Relevancy

The concept of relevance includes **logical relevance** and **legal relevance**, both of which are necessary for evidence to be admissible. Logical relevance is established if evidence tends to prove or disprove a fact in issue. The evidence must logically pertain to the case and must tend to prove or disprove something related to the determination of the case. This is really the normal definition of relevance. Legal relevance, on the other hand, pertains to the legal admissibility of relevant evidence. Legal relevance requires that evidence not violate any other evidence rule or law. For example, there are evidentiary rules that exclude **hearsay** or prejudicial evidence, even when relevant to a case.

Relevant Evidence Is Generally Admissible; Irrelevant Evidence Is Inadmissible

A fundamental rule of evidence is that relevant evidence is admissible and evidence that is not relevant is not admissible.[11] This rule makes it clear that, unless otherwise limited or prohibited, all relevant evidence is admissible. However, the concept of *legal relevance* is also found within this rule and modifies this principle by setting out the sources that may result in relevant evidence being excluded. There may be constitutional provisions, statutes, or other laws that provide for the exclusion of even relevant evidence. The Constitution, for example, may limit or exclude evidence seized in violation of the Fourth Amendment protection against unreasonable search or a confession obtained in violation of the Fifth Amendment protection against self-incrimination. The rules of evidence themselves provide exclusions against the admission of certain evidence, even when relevant. Examples of this may include evidence that wastes time, is confusing, or is prejudicial. Other examples include hearsay, privileged communications, and exclusions of evidence that do not meet other evidence rule or legal limitations.

Exclusion of Relevant Evidence on Grounds of Prejudice

Even when relevant, evidence may still be excluded if its probative value is substantially outweighed by the danger of unfair prejudice to the trier of fact. This can present a difficult decision for the trial judge, who must rule on what constitutes prejudice. Evidence is generally presented in a case to try to persuade or influence the trier of fact. This evidence, if relevant to the matter at issue, will often have an adverse and prejudicial effect on an opponent's case. The key, then, is whether the prejudice is *unfair*. Evidence would not be unfairly prejudicial unless "its primary purpose or effect is to appeal to a jury's sympathies or to provoke horror or a desire to punish."[12] An example of this would be the introduction of particularly graphic or gruesome crime scene photos. The Supreme Court addressed this concept further, defining unfair prejudice as evidence that "speaks to the capacity of some concededly relevant evidence to lure the factfinder into declaring guilt on a ground different from proof specific to the offense charged... ."[13] An example of this might be evidence of prior bad acts or crimes committed by a defendant. This evidence might be relevant to prove that the defendant had a history of committing similar crimes, but this fact might also unfairly prejudice the jury into believing that if the defendant did it once, he or she would do it again. (See Exhibits 6.2 and 6.3.)

EXHIBIT 6.2   Exclusion of Relevant Evidence on Grounds of Prejudice, Confusion, or Waste of Time

---

Wyoming Rules of Evidence

Rule 403. Although relevant, evidence may be excluded if its probative value is substantially outweighed by the danger of unfair prejudice, confusion of the issues, or misleading the jury, or by considerations of undue delay, waste of time, or needless presentation of cumulative evidence.

EXHIBIT 6.3   Court Order in Motion to Admit Crime Scene Photos

---

SUPERIOR COURT OF THE STATE OF CALIFORNIA IN AND FOR THE COUNTY OF LOS ANGELES

Date: 30 May 1995

    Department 103, Hon. Lance A. Ito, Judge

    People v. Orenthal James Simpson

    Case: BA097211

The Court has read and considered the prosecution's motion to admit various autopsy and crime scene photos, the response in opposition filed by the defense, the letter briefs filed by the prosecution ..., as well as the letter brief filed by the defense ... The court conducted an informal, hour long conference with counsel for the parties, and heard the argument of counsel on the record ... The court has spent 10 hours in chambers examining the photos in question.

    ....

The court must make two basic determinations as to each photograph: 1) Is the information offered by the photo relevant to the issues in the case? Evidence Code Section 350; 2) Is the probative value of the photo substantially outweighed by the probability that its admission will (a) necessitate undue consumption of time or (b) create substantial danger of undue prejudice, of confusing the issues, or misleading the jury. Evidence Code Section 352...

continued

EXHIBIT 6.3   Court Order in Motion to Admit Crime Scene Photos   *Continued*

....

CS11 is a close up of the body of NBS at the bottom of the stairs. It shows blood spatters on the right back and smears on the right outside thigh. It is similar but not identical to People's Exhibit 43 (c), 54 (4), and 220. Of interest is what appears to be a patterned shoeprint in the large amount of blood on the walkway approximately one foot to the east of the left hand. The prosecution proffer is that the large amount of blood and the patterned shoeprints in the blood explain the presence of the victim's blood in the carpeting of the defendant's Bronco automobile. The court finds the probative value to outweigh the prejudicial impact.

....

G 51 and 53 both depict several injuries to the left ear, neck and throat area. G 53 depicts a blood clot behind the left ear; however the photographer's scale obscures the severe injury to the left neck. G 51 clearly depicts the severe wound to the left neck; however, it does not depict the blood clot. These photos are clearly relevant to the nature of the struggle between RLG and his assailant. In a more perfect world ... a single photo would have included all the injuries in this area. These are graphic and disturbing photos; however, the court finds that their probative value outweighs the prejudicial impact.

IT IS SO ORDERED...

Balancing Test

balancing test
Weighs probative value of evidence against its prejudicial effect.

Most courts have adopted a **balancing test** whereby the probative value of evidence is weighed against the prejudicial effect that allowing the evidence might produce. The court looks at whether the danger of prejudice is "unfair" and whether it "substantially" outweighs the relevance. Unfair prejudice might unduly influence or cause a jury or factfinder to reach an emotional decision, rather than one based on logic and the evidence.

CSI CHECKLIST 6.4

What is Probative Value of Evidence?

❑   Does it Substantially Outweigh Prejudicial Effect on Jury?

Exculpatory Evidence

exculpatory evidence
Evidence that tends to clear a party of blame or guilt.

Brady Motion
A motion to dismiss a case because evidence favorable to the accused has been suppressed by the state, either willfully or inadvertently, resulting in prejudice to the defendant.

When conducting a crime scene investigation, evidence may be found that tends to clear a party of blame or guilt. This is called **exculpatory evidence**. In criminal actions, the law requires the prosecution to reveal any exculpatory evidence gathered to the defense. A violation of this may result in what is known as a **Brady Motion**. A Brady Motion is a request for a judge to dismiss a case because evidence favorable to the accused has been suppressed by the state, either willfully or inadvertently, resulting in prejudice to the defendant. It is named after a 1963 Supreme Court case that held the "suppression by the prosecution of evidence favorable to an accused upon request violates due process where the evidence is material either to guilt or to punishment, irrespective of the good faith or bad faith of the prosecution."[14]

This becomes especially important to the defense gathering evidence in a criminal action. However, it can be even more important for the law enforcement and prosecution investigators. Since the Brady decision, other Supreme Court cases have held that the duty to disclose exculpatory evidence is applicable even though there has been no request by the accused.[15] The Court has further held that the rule encompasses evidence even when "known only to police investigators and not to the prosecutor."[16] Finally, the Court has held that a "prosecutor has a duty to learn of any favorable evidence known to the others acting on the government's behalf in this case, including the police."[17]

Evidence versus Proof

onus probandi
Burden of proof.

Although often confused with each other, these terms have different meanings. Evidence involves the *means* by which some fact is offered to prove or disprove an issue in dispute, whereas proof is the *effect* that the evidence has on the trier of fact and the *conclusion* drawn from the evidence that has been submitted. Proof is inferred from the evidence submitted. Evidenced is classified by its types, forms, and functions, whereas proof is viewed in terms of its **onus probandi**, or "burden" of proving or establishing the requisite degree of belief in the mind of the trier of fact regarding the evidence submitted.

Burden of Proof

burden of proof
The duty to meet a certain standard or establish the requisite degree of belief in the mind of the trier of fact regarding the evidence submitted.

Burden of proof is the duty to meet a certain standard or establish the requisite degree of belief in the mind of the trier of fact regarding the evidence submitted. Under our adversary system, the prosecution bringing a criminal action has the burden of proving their case by proving every element of the crime being prosecuted.

Standards or Degrees of Certainty in Burdens of Proof

It is not necessary in the law to prove beyond *any* doubt to be successful in proving a criminal case. The standard of proof will depend on the type of legal action. Each type of legal action has a specific standard or degree of certainty that must be proven in order to meet that particular burden of proof and persuasion. There are two primary standards or degrees of certainty for burdens of proof. *Beyond a reasonable doubt* is the standard required to convict a defendant in a criminal action. **Preponderance of evidence** is the standard required in a civil action. There are also two other standards of proof that may be used in crime scene investigation, *reasonable suspicion* and *probable cause*.

preponderance of evidence
Burden of proof in a civil action. Plaintiff must produce sufficient evidence to persuade the trier of fact that what the plaintiff claims is more likely true than not.

Beyond a Reasonable Doubt

Beyond a reasonable doubt is the standard for the burden of proof required to convict a defendant in a criminal action. This standard requires something to be "almost certainly true." Although the evidence does not have to be proved beyond any doubt, it must lead the trier of fact to a near certainty of the truth of the facts asserted.

beyond a reasonable doubt
Burden of proof in criminal action. Requires trier of fact to believe something to be almost certainly true, leaving no reasonable doubt.

What Is Reasonable Doubt?

There is no universal definition for reasonable doubt and, as a result, courts have long struggled to define it in a way to pass constitutional muster. One of the most famous definitions was an 1850 Massachusetts court decision that described reasonable doubt as a "term often used, probably pretty well understood, but not easily defined." The court went on to define it as "not a mere possible doubt" but one that "leaves the minds of jurors in that condition that they cannot say they feel an abiding conviction, to a moral certainty, of the truth of the charge."[18]

In an 1895 case, a trial court told the jury, "I will not undertake to define a reasonable doubt further than to say that a reasonable doubt is not an unreasonable doubt—that is to say, by a reasonable doubt you are not to understand that all doubt is to be excluded; it is impossible in the determination of these questions to be absolutely certain. You are required to decide the question submitted to you upon the strong probabilities of the case, and the probabilities must be so strong as, not to exclude all doubt or possibility of error, but as to exclude reasonable doubt."[19]

Reasonable Suspicion

reasonable suspicion
Standard of proof required for a law enforcement officer to stop and question a person. Based on the officer's reasonable suspicion that the person has committed a crime, is committing a crime, or is about to commit a crime.

Reasonable suspicion is a term in criminal law to justify a law enforcement officer's actions to stop and question a person based on suspicion that a person has committed a crime, is committing a crime, or is about to commit a crime. This type of certainty may be enough to justify an investigative stop, but would be less than the probable cause required to arrest. For example, a police officer sees two people in a vehicle with its lights out and engine running, parked by a closed business late at night in a high-crime area. The officer would have reason to stop and question the occupants of the vehicle, but, without more evidence, would lack legal cause to make an arrest.

Probable Cause

probable cause
Standard of proof required for search warrants and arrests in criminal actions. Requires that evidence be considered "more probable than not" in proving what is alleged.

Probable cause requires more certainty than reasonable suspicion. It is the standard of proof required for a warrant or arrest, and is something that would be considered "more probable than not." It includes facts that would warrant a reasonable person to believe that a crime had been committed and that the accused had committed it.

SUMMARY

Laws that govern criminal investigation can be found in three primary sources: the Constitution, case law, and statutory law. Our United States Constitution is the "supreme law of the land," and contains important provisions, such as the Fourth Amendment protection against unreasonable search or seizure, that can directly affect how a crime scene is investigated. Laws and legal rules dealing with crime scene investigations must satisfy the protections and limitations established by the Constitution or risk being overturned by the courts who have the power to interpret the Constitution and say what the law is.[20] Case law is important because it not only guides our courts, but dictates the policies and procedures that *must* be followed by all law enforcement and investigative personnel. Cases decided years ago, such as *Mapp v. Ohio*[21] or *Miranda v. Arizona*[22] still control how criminal scene searches are conducted or suspects interrogated. Most of the legal standards and tests used today in determining whether a crime scene investigation was conducted properly are the result of court decisions establishing case law. Knowing how to find and understand the significance of these court decisions pertaining to crime scene investigations is essential for investigators and those preparing for a criminal prosecution. Statutory law is important because the definitions for most crimes can be found in criminal codes and statutes. These definitions include the elements for a crime, each of which must be proven in order to establish that a crime has been committed and that a particular person committed that crime. Statutory law also contains rules of criminal procedure that govern how a criminal investigation is conducted, usually pertaining to procedures dealing with search and seizure, or interrogation.

Evidence law is also important because it contains rules that help to determine what will be admissible in criminal proceedings and influences the crime scene investigative process. Rules of evidence affect how crime scenes are investigated and how a case is presented through evidence and witnesses in the criminal trial process. These rules establish how much evidence is required to prove a criminal case. The gathering of information and evidence at a crime scene must focus on establishing the elements to the crime being investigated and meeting the burden in proving that crime at trial. There are rules that govern the admissibility of any evidence gathered. These rules also determine which evidence will not be admissible. Understanding these evidence and criminal laws, and procedure, is important in knowing how a crime scene can be investigated, what evidence can be collected, and how that evidence can be legally obtained.

KEY TERMS

Balancing Test	Evidence
Beyond a Reasonable Doubt	Evidence Law
Brady Motion	Exculpatory Evidence
Burden of Proof	Hearsay
Case Law	Inference
Circumstantial Evidence	Legal Relevance
Common Law	Logical Relevance
Constitution	Onus Probandi
Demonstrative Evidence	Physical Evidence
Direct Evidence	Precedent
Documentary Evidence	Preponderance of Evidence
Due Process	Prima Facie
Elements of a Crime	Probable Cause

Probative

Statutory Law

Procedural Law

Substantive Law

Reasonable Suspicion

Testimonial Evidence

Relevancy

REVIEW QUESTIONS

1. Describe the three primary sources of laws governing crime scene investigations and give an example of each.

2. Explain what is meant by establishing a *prima facie* case.

3. What is the difference between substantive and procedural law?

4. What are the rules of evidence?

5. Identify the two types and four forms of evidence and give an example of each.

6. Distinguish evidence from proof.

7. What is the burden of proof in a criminal prosecution?

CRITICAL THINKING QUESTIONS 6.1

1. What is the importance of each of the sources of law to crime scene investigation?

2. What is the importance of the rules of evidence to crime scene investigation?

3. How do laws influence the gathering of crime scene evidence or the investigation of a crime scene?

FORENSIC RESEARCH USING THE INTERNET

Find and assess the Internet site for each of the following sources of law that covers your state:

1. Criminal Law (criminal codes or statutes)

2. Rules of Criminal Procedure

3. Rules of Evidence

4. State Supreme Court Decisions

PRACTICE SKILLS:

Practice what you have learned in the following problems:

Crime Scene Analysis 6.1

Identify the form of evidence for each of the following:

1. A diagram of an intersection where two vehicles collided
2. A will
3. A forensic specialist explaining in court how she took photos at a crime scene
4. The bloody glove found at a crime scene

Crime Scene Analysis 6.2

For each of the following case problems, apply the definitions of crimes below and determine which crime has been committed, or what has to be further investigated in order to ascertain this:

1. A student returns to the classroom after a break to find her books missing from her desk. She yells, "Help, I've been robbed!" The police are called to the scene to investigate.

2. A man takes a case of beer from a mini-mart cooler and begins to walk out with it. The clerk, behind the counter, says, "Excuse me, you need to pay for that beer." The man replies, "Don't try to stop me or I'll hurt you" and walks out the door. The clerk calls the police.

3. Two teens, knowing that a neighbor is planning to hold a garage sale, enter the garage early in the morning to steal things of value. As they are leaving, a customer for the garage sale walks in and the teens knock the customer down and flee.

continued

Definitions of Crimes

Robbery is the illegal taking of property from the person of another by using force or the threat of immediate force.

Burglary is the unlawful entering of a building or structure with the intent to commit a felony or theft therein.

Larceny is the stealing (unlawful taking and carrying away) of personal property of another with the intent to permanently deprive the owner of possession.

WEB SITES

Federal Rules of Evidence:

http://www.law.cornell.edu/rules/fre/overview.html

FindLaw Cases and Codes

http://guide.lp.findlaw.com/casecode/

Legal Information Institute (LII), Cornell Law School.

http://www.law.cornell.edu/states/listing.html

State Statutes dealing with Criminal Procedure

http://www.law.cornell.edu/topics/state_statutes2.html#criminal_procedure

ENDNOTES

[1] Article VI, United States Constitution

[2] See the landmark U.S. Supreme Court case establishing Judicial Review, *Marbury v. Madison*, 5 U.S. 137 (1803).

[3] 367 U.S. 643 (1961)

[4] 384 U.S. 436 (1966)

[5] For example, see California Penal Code.

[6] For example, see Chapter 61 of the *West Virginia Code* covering *Crimes and Their Punishment*.

[7] For example, in Vermont, the criminal code is found in *Title 13* of the *Vermont Statutes Annotated*.

[8] For example, see the *Federal Rules of Evidence*. Most states have rules of evidence modeled after these federal rules (e.g., *Vermont Rules of Evidence*.

[9] See, for example, the *California Evidence Code*.

[10] *Commonwealth v. Scott*, 480 Pa. 50 (1978)

[11] See *Federal Rule of Evidence,* Rule 402.

[12] *State v. Jones,* No. 92521 (Vt. Sup. Ct, 1993)

[13] *Johnny Lynn Old Chief v. United States,* 519 U.S. 172 (1997)

[14] *Brady v. Maryland*, 373 U. S. 83 (1963)

[15] *United States v. Agurs* , 427 U.S. 97 (1976)

[16] *Kyles v. Whitley*, 514 U. S. 419 (1995)

[17] Ibid

[18] *Commonwealth v. Webster*, 59 Mass. 295 (1850)

[19] *Dunbar v. United States*, 156 U.S. 185 (1895)

[20] See the landmark U.S. Supreme Court case establishing Judicial Review, *Marbury v. Madison*, 5 U.S. 137 (1803).

[21] 367 U.S. 643 (1961)

[22] 384 U.S. 436 (1966)

LAWS OF CRIME SCENE SEARCHES

"With recent advances in evidence detection technology and forensic analysis, crime scene searches have become possibly the most important component in many criminal investigations... To lawfully conduct a crime scene search, however, investigators must be extremely careful to follow the dictates of the Fourth Amendment."

—Special Agent Kimberly Crawford, J.D., Legal Instructor at FBI Academy

"A warrantless search must be strictly circumscribed by the exigencies which justify its initiation."

—Terry v. Ohio, 392 U.S., at 25-26

Chapter Outline

- What are the Sources of Laws Governing Crime Scene Searches?
- What is the Fourth Amendment Search Warrant Requirement?
- Can Police Search a Crime Scene Without a Warrant?
- Is There a Crime Scene Exception to the Search Warrant Requirement?
- What is the Importance of *Mincey v. Arizona*?
- What are the Exceptions to the Search Warrant Requirement?
- What is an Exigency and How Does it Apply to Crime Scene Searches?
- What is a Consent Search and Why Important to Crime Scene Searches?
- What is a Protective Sweep?
- What is the Plain View Doctrine and How is it Used in Crime Scene Searches?
- What are the Three Tests Used by the Courts in Assessing Legality of Searches?
- What are Some of the Legal Challenges to Crime Scene Searches?
- What is the Exclusionary Rule?
- What are the Fruits of the Poisonous Tree Doctrine?
- What is a Motion to Suppress and How is it Used?

INTRODUCTION

In previous chapters, we looked at how a crime scene is investigated, documented, and processed. Included in this processing is the searching for evidence. Numerous cases over the past years, including the World Trade Center bombings and the Scott Peterson trial have dramatized the need for all investigators, whether they be law enforcement charged with initially investigating the crime, or investigators for the prosecution or defense, to know and understand the legal issues and requirements involved in crime scene searches. In this chapter, we will examine the laws governing these crime scene searches. We will look at the constitutional basis for requiring a search warrant, the exceptions to the search warrant requirement that can be used in crime scene searches, and the legal challenges to these warrantless searches.

SOURCES OF LAWS GOVERNING CRIME SCENE SEARCHES

Laws governing the search of a crime scene are found in three primary sources: statutory laws or rules of criminal procedure, case law, and the U.S. Constitution.

Rules of Criminal Procedure

Rules of Criminal Procedure
Statutory laws and approved court rules governing procedural aspects of criminal investigations, and search and seizure

Many laws dealing with search and seizure can be found in a state's statutory criminal code and in court rules of criminal procedure. Every state has its own set of rules, usually listed under that state's name, followed by **Rules of Criminal Procedure** (for example, *Vermont Rules of Criminal Procedure*). The federal government also has rules governing criminal procedure that can be found in the *United States Code* and in the *Federal Rules of Criminal Procedure*.

Rules of criminal procedure can provide valuable information detailing when a search warrant is required, how a warrant can be obtained, time limits and specifications in executing the warrant, and when a warrantless search or arrest can be conducted. Quite often, however, these rules fall short of addressing specific questions and issues pertaining to crime scene searches. For these rules, we need to look at *case law*.

> ## PRACTICE TIP 7.1
>
> ### Finding Search & Seizure Laws
>
> *Search and seizure is generally covered in a state's rules or statutes dealing with criminal procedure. You can check to see what specific rules are covered in your state's statutes by going to:*
>
> *State Statutes dealing with Criminal Procedure http://www.law.cornell.edu/topics/statues2.html#criminal_procedure*

Case Law

case law
Judge-made law based on court decisions.

Case law is judge-made law based on court decisions. In case law, courts rule on the constitutionality of criminal procedure statutes and search or seizure issues. These rulings are extremely important because they can interpret, define, revise, or even overturn a particular procedural rule or element of that rule. Most of the legal standards and tests used today in determining whether a crime scene search was conducted properly are the result of court decisions establishing case law. Knowing how to find and understand the significance of these court decisions pertaining to crime scene search is essential for investigators and those preparing for a criminal prosecution.

Constitution

due process
Constitutional protections extended to suspects and defendant in a criminal investigation.

Laws governing crime scene searches have their foundation in the Constitution, both the federal constitution and the individual state constitutions. The U.S. Constitution is the "supreme law of the land."[1] The Constitution provides protections and limitations that are part of the **due process** requirements for the criminal justice system. Laws and legal rules dealing with crime scene searches must satisfy the protections and limitations established by the Constitution or risk being overturned by the courts who have the power to interpret the Constitution and say what the law is.[2]

Fourth Amendment and Crime Scene Searches

Fourth Amendment
Constitutional
Amendment establishing
standard for search war-
rant and protections
against unreasonable
search and seizure.

Central to these constitutional limitations is the **Fourth Amendment**. The basic legal requirement governing the search of a crime scene is that authorities must comply with the Fourth Amendment to the U.S. Constitution. The Fourth Amendment provides protection against *unreasonable searches or seizure* by government agents and law enforcement officers who then attempt to use that evidence in a criminal prosecution. (See Exhibit 7.1.)

EXHIBIT 7.1   Fourth Amendment

Amendment IV, U.S. Constitution
The right of the people to be secure in their persons, houses, papers, and effects, against unreasonable searches and seizures, shall not be violated, and no warrants shall issue, but upon probable cause, supported by oath or affirmation, and particularly describing the place to be searched, and the persons or things to be seized.

FOURTH AMENDMENT SEARCH WARRANT REQUIREMENT

The Fourth Amendment protects against unreasonable searches. The courts have long held that "searches conducted outside the judicial process, without prior approval by judge or magistrate, are per se unreasonable under the Fourth Amendment — subject only to a few specifically established and well-delineated exceptions."[3] Searches conducted with a warrant are presumed to be reasonable. The general rule in Fourth Amendment analysis of a crime scene search is that a warrant is required unless there is an established legal exception.

probable cause
Standard of proof needed
to obtain search warrant,
requiring that evidence
be considered "more prob-
able than not" in proving
what is alleged.

To obtain a warrant, the Fourth Amendment sets forth two essential requirements. First, officers must establish **probable cause** to believe that the location to be searched contains evidence of a crime. Second, officers must support this probable cause with some type of sworn affidavit "particularly describing the place to be searched, and the persons or things to be seized."[4]

The *probable cause* requirement of the Fourth Amendment can generally be easily met when a crime scene is involved because the very existence of a crime provides officers with sufficient cause to believe that evidence will be found at the crime scene. In addition, the *particularity* requirement of the Fourth Amendment can also be met by listing the types of evidence normally associated with the type of crime being investigated. Crime scene technicians and forensic personnel can also help meet this requirement.

CSI CHECKLIST 7.1

Requirements for Search Warrant

❑ Probable cause to believe that the location to be searched contains evidence of a crime

❑ Supported by oath or affirmation (usually through supporting affidavit)

❑ Particularly describing the place to be searched, and the evidence to be seized

---

Can Police Search a Crime Scene Without a Warrant?

When law enforcement officers first respond to the report of a potential crime, there is no time and no legal reason to obtain a warrant. The officers would first need to verify that a crime has been committed and that there is a crime scene with the likelihood of evidence present. The questions then become, can the officers initially enter the crime scene without a warrant? What can they do at the crime scene and for how long? Whether law enforcement investigators need a warrant to search a crime scene depends on many factors. One of the first factors to consider is whether the crime scene is in a public place or on private premises.

Public Place

The general rule is that police may enter a public place at any proper time. If a crime has occurred in a public place, there is generally no requirement that a warrant be obtained. However, even this could change depending on where exactly the crime took place and what is being searched.

Private Premises

reasonable expectation of privacy
Standard set by *Katz v. United States*, 389 U.S. 347 (1967) and still used today to determine validity of searches under the Fourth Amendment.

For private property, the courts look at whether the search was conducted in a home or somewhere else. The courts also look at whether there was a **reasonable expectation to privacy** on the property and whether this was waived through consent or emergency circumstances. This standard of Fourth Amendment analysis was established in the 1967 Supreme Court case of *Katz v. United States.*[5]

Is There a Crime Scene Exception to Search Warrant Requirement?

Law enforcement officers respond to reports of crimes as an *exigency* or emergency, and can generally enter a crime scene to verify that a crime has been committed, and to check for victims or suspects. However, once inside, how long can the officers remain and what can they investigate without having to obtain a search warrant? For years, many courts allowed crime scene investigations to be fully conducted under a "murder scene" or "crime scene" exception based on this emergency exception to the warrant requirement. In a 1968 case, the U.S. Supreme Court held that a warrantless search must be "strictly circumscribed by the exigencies which justify its initiation."[6]

Then, 10 years later in 1978, the U.S. Supreme Court addressed the "crime scene exception" in the landmark decision, *Mincey v. Arizona*. This major case rejected this exception and set the standard for crime scene searches, which is still used today.

CASE

Mincey v. Arizona

United States Supreme Court

437 U.S. 385 (June, 1978)

Crime Scene Investigation

During a narcotics raid by police on Mincey's apartment, an undercover officer was shot and killed. After the shooting, the narcotics agents looked about quickly for other victims, but refrained from further investigation and secured the scene to wait for detectives. Within 10 minutes, homicide detectives arrived, took charge of the investigation, and began to search the crime scene for evidence. Their search lasted four days, during which period the entire apartment was searched, photographed, and diagramed. The officers opened drawers, closets, and cupboards, and inspected their contents; they emptied clothing pockets; they dug bullet fragments out of the walls and floors; they pulled up sections of the carpet and removed them for examination. Every item in the apartment was closely examined and inventoried, and 200 to 300 objects were seized. No warrant was ever obtained. Mincey's pretrial motion to suppress the fruits of this warrantless crime scene search was denied. Much of the evidence introduced against him at trial (including photographs and diagrams, bullets and shell casings, guns, narcotics, and narcotics paraphernalia) was the product of the four-day search of his apartment.

Legal Issue

Is there a *crime scene* or *murder scene exception* to the search warrant requirement of the Fourth Amendment? Mincey was convicted of murder and appealed, arguing that the warrantless search

continued

was unconstitutional. The Arizona Supreme Court affirmed the conviction, holding that there was a "murder scene exception" to the Fourth Amendment's search warrant requirement and therefore the warrantless search of a homicide crime scene is constitutionally permissible...

Holding of the Court

The United States Supreme Court disagreed with Arizona and overturned their decision. The Court reasoned that the Fourth Amendment proscribes all unreasonable searches and seizures, and that "searches conducted outside the judicial process, without prior approval by a judge or magistrate, are per se unreasonable under the Fourth Amendment—subject only to a few specifically established and well-delineated exceptions." The Court rejected the existence of any crime scene or murder scene exception to the search warrant requirement, stating:

"We do not question the right of the police to respond to emergency situations. Numerous state and federal cases have recognized that the Fourth Amendment does not bar police officers from making warrantless entries and searches when they reasonably believe that a person within is in need of immediate aid. Similarly, when the police come upon the scene of a homicide they may make a prompt warrantless search of the area to see if there are other victims or if a killer is still on the premises...The need to protect or preserve life or avoid serious injury is justification for what would be otherwise illegal absent an exigency or emergency and the police may seize any evidence that is in plain view during the course of their legitimate emergency activities.

But a warrantless search must be "strictly circumscribed by the exigencies which justify its initiation...

The point of the Fourth Amendment, which often is not grasped by zealous officers, is not that it denies law enforcement the support of the usual inferences which reasonable men draw from evidence. Its protection consists in requiring that those inferences be drawn by a neutral and detached magistrate instead of being judged by the officer engaged in the often competitive enterprise of ferreting out crime."

In sum, we hold that the "murder scene exception" created by the Arizona Supreme Court is inconsistent with the Fourth and Fourteenth Amendments—that the warrantless search of Mincey's apartment was not constitutionally permissible simply because a homicide had recently occurred there."

Importance of Mincey

In *Mincey*, the U.S. Supreme Court rejected any crime scene or murder exception to the search warrant requirement. The Court held that the "seriousness of the offense under investigation itself" does NOT create "exigent circumstances of the kind that under the Fourth Amendment justify a warrantless search." The Court reasoned that when the police come upon the scene of a homicide they may make a prompt warrantless search of the area to see if there are other victims or if a killer is still on the premises. But, the ruling stated that a warrantless search must be "strictly circumscribed by the exigencies which justify its initiation." Here, the officers stayed several days and searched the entire premises. The Court said this was not justified by the exigency.

Can 2 Hour "General Exploratory Search for Evidence" be conducted after Initial Crime Scene Entry?

The following U.S. Supreme Court case affirmed *Mincey*, but addressed the issue of whether investigators could conduct a 2-hour "general exploratory search for evidence" shortly after the initial crime scene entry.

CASE

Thompson v. Louisiana

Supreme Court of the United States

469 U.S. 17 (1984)

Crime Scene Investigation

Responding to a call from Thompson's daughter of a homicide, deputies from the Jefferson Parish Sheriff's Department entered Thompson's home and discovered Thompson's husband dead of a gunshot wound in a bedroom and Thompson lying unconscious in another bedroom due to an apparent drug overdose. According to Thompson's daughter, Thompson had shot her husband, then ingested a quantity of pills in a suicide attempt, and then, changing her mind, called her daughter, informed her of the situation, and requested help. The daughter then contacted the police. Upon their arrival, the daughter admitted them into the house and directed them to the rooms containing the Thompson and the victim. The deputies immediately transported the then-unconscious Thompson to a hospital and secured the scene. Thirty-five minutes later, two members of the homicide unit of the Jefferson Parish Sheriff's Office arrived and conducted a follow-up investigation of the homicide and attempted suicide. The homicide investigators entered the residence and commenced what they described at the motion to suppress hearing as a 'general exploratory search for evidence of a crime.' They did not obtain a search warrant and during their search, which lasted approximately two hours, the detectives examined each room of the house and discovered a pistol, a torn-up note and another letter, alleged to be a suicide note. This evidence was later used against Thompson at trial.

continued

Legal Issue

Can crime scene investigators conduct a shorter search than was conducted in *Mincey*, if it is a "general exploratory search for evidence?" Thompson was convicted of the second-degree murder of her husband. On appeal, the Louisiana Supreme Court affirmed the conviction, holding all of the evidence seized to be admissible, distinguishing the case from *Mincey* on the basis of a shorter time period used for the search.

Holding of the Court

The United States Supreme Court disagreed with Louisiana and overturned their decision, stating: "The Louisiana Supreme Court attempted to distinguish *Mincey* in several ways. The court noted that *Mincey* involved a 4-day search of the premises, while the search in this case took only two hours and was conducted on the same day as the murder. Although we agree that the scope of the intrusion was certainly greater in *Mincey* than here, nothing in *Mincey* turned on the length of time taken in the search or the date on which it was conducted. A 2-hour general search remains a significant intrusion on petitioner's privacy and therefore may only be conducted subject to the constraints—including the warrant requirement—of the Fourth Amendment. The Louisiana Supreme Court also believed that petitioner had a "diminished" expectation of privacy in her home, thus validating a search that otherwise would have been unconstitutional. The court noted that petitioner telephoned her daughter to request assistance. The daughter then called the police and let them in the residence. These facts, according to the court, demonstrated a diminished expectation of privacy in petitioner's dwelling and therefore legitimated the warrantless search.

Petitioner's attempt to get medical assistance does not evidence a diminished expectation of privacy on her part. To be sure, this action would have justified the authorities in seizing evidence under the plain-view doctrine while they were in petitioner's house to offer her assistance. In addition, the same doctrine may justify seizure of evidence obtained in the limited "victim-or-suspect" search discussed in *Mincey*. However, the evidence at issue here was not discovered in plain view while the police were assisting petitioner to the hospital, nor was it discovered during the "victim-or-suspect" search that had been completed by the time the homicide investigators arrived. Petitioner's call for help can hardly be seen as an invitation to the general public that would have converted her home into the sort of public place for which no warrant to search would be necessary. Therefore, the Louisiana Supreme Court's diminished-expectation-of-privacy argument fails to distinguish this case from *Mincey*.

...For the reasons stated above... the judgment of the Louisiana Supreme Court is reversed, and the cause is remanded for further proceedings not inconsistent with this opinion."

Mincey Remains Standard Today

In the 1999 case of *Flippo v. West Virginia*[7], the U.S. Supreme Court again affirmed the standard set in *Mincey* and rejected any type of "homicide scene exception" to the search warrant requirement. This remains the standard today governing crime scene searches.

CASE

Flippo v. West Virginia

United States Supreme Court

528 U.S. 11 (1999)

Crime Scene Investigation

One night, Flippo and his wife were vacationing at a cabin in a state park. Flippo called 911 to report that they had been attacked and the police arrived to find Flippo waiting outside the cabin, with injuries to his head and legs. After questioning him, an officer entered the building and found the body of Flippo's wife, with fatal head wounds. The officers closed off the area, took Flippo to the hospital, and searched the exterior and environs of the cabin for footprints or signs of forced entry. When a police photographer arrived at about 5:30 a.m., the officers reentered the building and proceeded to "process the crime scene." For over 16 hours, they took photographs, collected evidence, and searched through the contents of the cabin. According to the trial court, "at the crime scene, the investigating officers found on a table in Cabin 13, among other things, a briefcase, which they, in the ordinary course of investigating a homicide, opened, wherein they found and seized various photographs and negatives." The photographs included several taken of a man who appears to be taking off his jeans. He was later identified as a friend of Flippo and a member of the congregation of which Flippo was the minister. At trial, the prosecution introduced the photographs as evidence of Flippo's relationship with this friend and argued that the victim's displeasure with this relationship was one of the reasons that Flippo may have been motivated to kill her.

Legal Issue

At his trial for the murder of his wife, Flippo moved to suppress the photographs and negatives discovered in an envelope in the closed briefcase during the search. He argued that the police had obtained no warrant, and that no exception to the warrant requirement justified the search and seizure. His motion to suppress evidence seized in a warrantless search of a "homicide crime scene" was denied by the trial court on the ground that the police were entitled to make a thorough search of any crime scene and the objects found there.

Holding of the Court

The U.S. Supreme Court reversed the West Virginia court's decision. They held that a "warrantless search by the police is invalid unless it falls within one of the narrow and well-delineated exceptions to the warrant requirement, none of which the trial court invoked here. It simply found that after the homicide crime scene was secured for investigation, a search of "anything and everything found within the crime scene area" was "within the law." This position squarely conflicts with *Mincey v. Arizona*, where we rejected the contention that there is a "murder scene exception" to the Warrant Clause of the Fourth Amendment. We noted that police may make warrantless entries onto premises if they reasonably believe a person is in need of immediate aid and may make prompt warrantless searches of a homicide scene for possible other victims or a killer on the premises, but we rejected any general "murder scene exception" as "inconsistent with the Fourth and Fourteenth Amendments...

The... the judgment of the Circuit Court of West Virginia, Fayette County, is reversed, and the case is remanded for further proceedings not inconsistent with this opinion."

> ## PRACTICE TIP 7.3
>
> ### Researching State and Federal Laws
>
> *Want some help in researching your state or federal laws and cases on crime scene investigations? Try visiting one of the following Web sites and typing in key words like crime scene in their search feature:*
>
> > *Legal Information Institute (LII), Cornell Law School.*
> > *http://www.law.cornell.edu/states/listing.html*
> > *FindLaw*
> > *http://guide.lp.findlaw.com/casecode/*

EXCEPTIONS TO SEARCH WARRANT REQUIREMENT

exigency
Emergency. The initial response to a crime scene is considered to be an exigent or emergency circumstance.

consent
Permission by a person who has authority to grant it authorizing officers to enter and conduct an initial investigation of a crime scene.

There are two major exceptions to the search warrant requirement that pertain to crime scene investigation: **exigency** and **consent**. An *exigency* is an emergency situation. Most crime scenes initially create exigent circumstances for an officer to enter and check for victims or suspects. *Consent* is permission by a person who has authority to grant it authorizing officers to enter and conduct an initial investigation of a crime scene. The general rule is that warrants are generally required to search a person's home or his person unless there is consent or "the exigencies of the situation" make the needs of law enforcement so compelling that the warrantless search is objectively reasonable under the Fourth Amendment.[8]

Courts have consistently held that law enforcement officers may enter private premises when they "reasonably believe that a crime is taking place or has just taken place, for the limited purposes of rendering aid to a possible victim of the crime or seeking or apprehending the perpetrators or taking any necessary steps to secure the premises."[9] Law enforcement officers typically respond to a crime scene as a result of a reported crime, an emergency call, or at the request of the person in lawful possession or control over the property. Under these circumstances, officers have a legitimate reason and authority to be on the premises, and can enter the crime scene to establish that a crime has been committed, to check for victims or suspects, to prevent the loss of evidence, and to secure the scene.

Exigency

As noted above, one of the primary exceptions to the search warrant requirement for crime scene investigators is *exigent* or emergency circumstance. If the law enforcement officers who initially responded to the crime scene have reason to believe that a person within a private home is in need of immediate aid or that a life-threatening situation exists, they are permitted to enter the premises. Again, once inside, they are permitted to conduct a reasonable investigation as to the nature and scope of the exigency and, if circumstances warrant, conduct a search for victims or a *protective sweep* for suspects.

Protective Sweep

protective sweep
A brief search of a crime scene, limited in scope to checking for suspects.

A **protective sweep** is a brief search of a crime scene, limited in scope to checking for suspects. It was first established by a 1990 U.S. Supreme Court case.[10] Since then, courts have restricted its use at a crime scene to a check for suspects. As a Pennsylvania court held, "It cannot be used as a pretext for an evidentiary search. It cannot be lengthy or unduly disruptive. It must be swift and target only those areas where a person could reasonably be expected to hide. Above all, it must be supported by articulable facts and inferences giving rise to reasonable suspicion that the area to be swept harbors an individual posing a danger to the police."[11] Even though it is limited in scope to checking for suspects, whatever is observed in *plain view* can be seized.

Three Different Tests Used by Courts

reasonable person test
This test asks what a "reasonable person" would have done given the circumstances.

totality of the circumstances test
This test looks at all of the facts in a particular situation in trying to determine if an action was warranted.

balancing test
This test balances the intrusiveness of the search and defendant's reasonable expectation of privacy with the nature of the emergency.

In order to determine what is a legitimate emergency for this important exception to the search warrant requirement, the courts have used several tests. One test looks at whether the actions were reasonable under the circumstances and would have satisfied the **reasonable person test**, which asks what a "reasonable person" would have done given the circumstances. Another test looks at the search by considering the **totality of the circumstances**, or all of the facts in a particular situation. The **balancing test** tries to look at the intrusiveness of the search, along with the nature of the emergency and balance it with the reasonable expectation of privacy on the part of the defendant.

What Constitutes an Exigency?

An exigency is an emergency. The courts have held that emergencies can include life-threatening situations, "hot" pursuit, the imminent loss or destruction of evidence, and the fighting of fires, among other examples. Most crime scenes establish an initial exigency due to the possibility of suspects or victims being on the premises.

How Long can Authorities Remain after Exigency?

The following U.S. Supreme Court case was decided just a few weeks before *Mincey*. In this major case decision, the issue before the Court was how long authorities could remain at a fire scene after the fire had been extinguished and fire personnel had left. The Court also addressed the question of whether fire department personnel were bound by Fourth Amendment restrictions.

CASE

Michigan v. Tyler

United States Supreme Court

436 U.S. 499 (May, 1978)

Crime Scene Investigation

Tyler was convicted of conspiracy to burn his furniture store. Firefighters had responded and had begun fighting the fire at the store shortly after midnight on January 22. Finding two plastic containers of flammable liquid at the scene, a fire department official and a police detective attempted to take pictures and to look through the fire scene to determine the cause, but had to abandon their efforts because of the smoke and steam. They departed around 4 a.m. and returned after daylight to continue their investigation. By that time, the fire had been extinguished and the building was empty. According to the detective's testimony, they discovered suspicious "burn marks in the carpet," which could not be seen earlier that morning, "because of the heat, steam, and the darkness." They also found "pieces of tape, with burn marks, on the stairway." There was neither consent nor a warrant for these entries and seizures.

On February 16, without consent or a warrant, a Sergeant from the Michigan State Police Arson Section visited the fire scene to take photographs and investigate the scene. The Sergeant secured physical evidence and formed opinions that played a substantial role at trial in establishing arson as the cause of the fire and in refuting the respondents' testimony about what furniture had been lost.

Legal Issue

How long can officials remain at an arson crime scene to investigate? Both at trial and on appeal, Tyler objected to the evidence obtained from the different searches conducted. The evidence was admitted and Tyler was convicted.... The Michigan Supreme Court reversed, holding that "[Once] the blaze [has been] extinguished and the firefighters have left the premises, a warrant is required to reenter and search the premises, unless there is consent or the premises have been abandoned." Applying this principle, the court ruled that the series of warrantless entries that began after the blaze had been extinguished on January 22 violated the Fourth and Fourteenth Amendments.

Holding of the Court

The United States Supreme Court disagreed with Michigan and held that the evidence collected on January 22 was all admissible. The Court acknowledged that the Fourth Amendment protected against intrusions by government officials, whether they be "health, fire, or building inspectors..." and

continued

said that "there is no diminution in a person's reasonable expectation of privacy nor in the protection of the Fourth Amendment simply because the official conducting the search wears the uniform of a firefighter rather than a policeman, or because his purpose is to ascertain the cause of a fire rather than to look for evidence of a crime, or because the fire might have been started deliberately. Searches for administrative purposes, like searches for evidence of crime, are encompassed by the Fourth Amendment." However, the Court also "recognized that ... A burning building clearly presents an exigency of sufficient proportions to render a warrantless entry" reasonable..."And once in a building for this purpose, firefighters may seize evidence of arson that is in plain view." The Court stated that "Fire officials are charged not only with extinguishing fires, but with finding their causes. Prompt determination of the fire's origin may be necessary to prevent its recurrence, as through the detection of continuing dangers such as faulty wiring or a defective furnace. Immediate investigation may also be necessary to preserve evidence from intentional or accidental destruction. And, of course, the sooner the officials complete their duties, the less will be their subsequent interference with the privacy and the recovery efforts of the victims. For these reasons, officials need no warrant to remain in a building for a reasonable time to investigate the cause of a blaze after it has been extinguished. And ...the warrantless seizure of evidence while inspecting the premises for these purposes also is constitutional. The circumstances of particular fires and the role of firemen and investigating officials will vary widely. ... In determining what constitutes a "reasonable time to investigate," appropriate recognition must be given to the exigencies that confront officials serving under these conditions, as well as to individuals' reasonable expectations of privacy.

... On the facts of this case, we do not believe that a warrant was necessary for the early morning re-entries on January 22. As the fire was being extinguished, [fire officials] began their investigation, but visibility was severely hindered by darkness, steam, and smoke. Thus they departed at 4 a. m. and returned shortly after daylight to continue their investigation. Little purpose would have been served by their remaining in the building, except to remove any doubt about the legality of the warrantless search and seizure later that same morning. Under these circumstances, we find that the morning entries were no more than an actual continuation of the first, and the lack of a warrant thus did not invalidate the resulting seizure of evidence.

The entries occurring after January 22, however, were clearly detached from the initial exigency and warrantless entry. Since all of these searches were conducted without valid warrants and without consent, they were invalid under the Fourth and Fourteenth Amendments, and any evidence obtained as a result of those entries must, therefore, be excluded at the respondents' retrial.

In summation, we hold that an entry to fight a fire requires no warrant, and that once in the building, officials may remain there for a reasonable time to investigate the cause of the blaze. Thereafter, additional entries to investigate the cause of the fire must be made pursuant to the warrant procedures governing administrative searches... Evidence of arson discovered in the course of such investigations is admissible at trial, but if the investigating officials find probable cause to believe that arson has occurred and require further access to gather evidence for a possible prosecution, they may obtain a warrant only upon a traditional showing of probable cause applicable to searches for evidence of crime."

Importance of Michigan v. Tyler

The importance of this case is the statement of the Court that once officials are inside the crime scene under exigency circumstances, they may "remain there for a reasonable time to investigate" and that evidence "discovered in the course of such investigation is admissible at trial." This ruling seems to be in opposition to the standard set a few weeks later by the Court in *Mincey*, which held that a warrantless search must be "strictly circumscribed by the exigencies which justify its initiation." This variation in the two rulings has come back over the years in different state court opinions that have interpreted *Michigan v. Tyler* as allowing officers to remain at a crime scene without a warrant in order to have "reasonable time to investigate."

Although *Michigan v. Tyler* held this, it is important to note that the Court did set limits on it and upheld the exclusion of evidence after the day of the fire, saying that these were "clearly detached from the initial exigency and warrantless entry. The Court also keyed in on the nature of this crime as a "fire." The Court said that whether officials could remain at a fire scene for a "reasonable time to investigate" depended on the "circumstances of particular fires and the role of firemen and investigating officials," which the Court said "vary widely." Finally, the Court balanced the "exigencies that confront officials serving under these conditions" with the "individuals' reasonable expectations of privacy."

Does Odor of Decay Constitute Exigency?

Sometimes, law enforcement officers are called to a location to investigate odd or suspicious circumstances that may not seem at first to support a crime scene exigency. To further complicate matters, these requests may not come from an occupant of the premises or someone who can give consent. In the following case, the Indiana Court determines whether the odor of decay constitutes an exigency that would allow officers to enter a private home.

CASE

Smock v. Indiana

Court Of Appeals of Indiana, First District

766 N.E.2d 401 (2002)

Crime Scene Investigation

Police officers went to Smock's apartment late in the evening on March 22, following a neighbor's report of a strong odor. Upon arriving at the apartment building, the neighbor indicated that there was a strong odor in the air, which the officers could smell, and that he had not seen Smock in some time. The officers went to Smock's apartment and when they received no answer upon knocking, they entered the apartment to see if someone inside needed help. Once inside, the four officers conducted a search of the apartment using their flashlights to see if anyone was inside. The final place searched

continued

was a closet underneath the stairs, wherein the body of Tim Miller was found in a pile of clothes and bags which had been covered with paint, bleach, and other cleaners. After finding the body, the officers secured the scene and waited for detectives and the coroner to arrive. Upon the arrival of detectives and the coroner, the officers re-entered Smock's apartment and from the kitchen gathered items of evidence, which were covered in dried blood. The items included a claw hammer, a lock-blade knife, and a box cutter. The items were collected and packaged at approximately 4:15 a.m. on March 23, and later removed from the apartment. Around 8 a.m., a search warrant was obtained, after which officers conducted a further search of Smock's apartment, locating a knife in a drawer. The knife had also apparently been used in the attack up on Miller.

Legal Issue

The issue in this case is whether the odor of decay constitutes an exigency that would allow officers to enter a private home.

Holding of the Court

The Indiana Court held that the "Fourth Amendment to the Constitution of the United States requires a warrant be issued before a search of a home is conducted in order to protect against unreasonable searches and seizures. However, there are exceptions to the warrant requirement...A well-recognized exception to the warrant requirement is when exigent circumstances exist. Under the exigent circumstances exception, police may enter a residence if the situation suggests a reasonable belief that someone inside the residence is in need of aid. The facts and circumstances of each warrantless search and seizure determine its validity. Smock asserts that the officers violated his Fourth Amendment right ... because they entered his apartment and seized items without a warrant. The State counters that the officers could enter Smock's apartment under the exigent circumstances doctrine because of the odor present in the apartment building, the report that Smock had not been seen in some time, and the acknowledgement by neighbors that many people had come and gone from the apartment. The State reasons that these circumstances created the reasonable belief that someone may be in the apartment in need of aid. Smock contends that the odor of decay precluded the officers from possessing any belief that someone was in need of aid in the apartment. Rather, Smock contends that the facts show that a fatality had already occurred; therefore, no exigent circumstances existed, and the police should have obtained a warrant before entering the apartment.

No Indiana case has directly addressed the issue of whether the presence of a strong odor of decay may form the basis for the exigent circumstance exception to the warrant requirement. However, ...the Fourth Circuit Court of Appeals upheld a warrantless entry of a home when the defendant's landlady had not seen him in some time and an unusual odor was emanating from his room. Likewise, ...the North Carolina Supreme Court upheld a warrantless search of a crawl space under a house and the subsequent entry of the residence when a police officer noticed green flies and the smell of rotting flesh coming from the crawl space. Several other cases have similarly found that there was no violation of the warrant requirement when officers smelled the odor of decaying flesh and had further fears that someone may have been in the residence in need of aid.

While we do not address whether the presence of the odor of decaying flesh in and of itself is enough to trigger the exigent circumstances exception to the warrant requirement, we hold that in this situation the officers did have a reasonable belief that someone may have been in need of immediate assistance. Just as in the above cited cases, the officers could smell the odor of decaying flesh. They were unable to make contact with anyone in the apartment through knocking. They had information that Smock had not been seen in some time. They were also told that many people had come and

continued

gone from the apartment, leading them to believe that someone could still be inside of the apartment alive but severely injured, or that someone may have been hiding in the apartment. Based upon the reasonableness of the officers' beliefs, no warrant was needed for the initial entry and search of Smock's apartment, which resulted in the discovery of Miller's body.

....

The judgment of the trial court is affirmed."

CSI CHECKLIST 7.2

Determining Whether Exigency Exists

❑ Is there reasonable belief that a crime is taking place or has just taken place?

❑ Is there reasonable belief that victims or suspects may be found at the scene?

❑ Is there an immediate need to prevent the loss or destruction of evidence?

❑ Is there an immediate need to take necessary steps to secure the premises?

Scope of Exigent Search

Under exigent circumstances, the scope of a warrantless crime scene search can include verifying that a crime has been committed, checking for victims and rendering aid to any injured victims found, conducting a protective sweep of the premises for suspects, and ensuring that no evidence is in danger of being imminently lost or destroyed. If a crime scene involves a dead body, the medical examiner can usually be allowed to enter, examine and remove the body if still within the exigency. Officers may also document the crime scene through sketches and photos or videotaping. Securing the crime scene and ensuring that people at the scene are not contaminating evidence is allowed. However, officers must take care to do only what is reasonably necessary to deal with the exigency. Once the exigency has been dealt with and the scene secured, a warrant is required in order for officers to remain on the premises and continue to search.

plain view doctrine
Officers may seize any evidence observed in plain view while lawfully on premises.

Plain View Doctrine

While legally on the premises conducting their initial crime scene investigation, law enforcement officers may investigate or seize anything observed in **plain view** that is evidence of a crime or illegal contraband. Evidence in plain view is not subject to the Fourth

Amendment search warrant requirements, as long as the law enforcement officers were lawfully in the place where the plain view evidence was observed.

Can Officers Re-Enter Crime Scene to Collect Evidence Observed in Plain View During Initial Entry?

In the following Michigan case, the Court addressed the issue of officers re-entering a crime scene, after it had been initially entered and secured, in order to collect only evidence been observed in plain view during the initial entry.

CASE

People v. Martin

Court of Appeals of Michigan

2003 Mich. App. LEXIS 2451 (2003)

Crime Scene Investigation

On the afternoon of March 29, 1998, Roscommon County Sheriff's Deputy Jack Sheppard responded to a report of a shooting at defendant's residence. After Deputy Sheppard arrived, he ordered the occupants of the residence to come outside. Defendant crawled out of the home, visibly wounded, and told Deputy Sheppard, "She just fired again." Deputy Sheppard then entered the home and saw defendant's wife, Dawn, lying on the living room floor. He saw a rifle on the floor next to her and noticed six spent shell casings, various bullet holes, and a large amount of blood in the vicinity. Paramedics were called to the scene, and they took the defendant and his wife to the hospital. Dawn Martin died from the wounds she sustained in the altercation. At trial, the prosecution alleged that defendant shot and killed Dawn. Defendant claimed, however, that Dawn had committed suicide.

After defendant and his wife were taken to the hospital, Deputy Sheppard requested that crime lab personnel come process the scene. [Two forensic scientists arrived around 4 p.m. The third arrived around 6:25 p.m. They testified that they only photographed and collected evidence observed by Deputy Sheppard and did not conduct any search or collection of evidence beyond this until a search warrant was issued around midnight.]

Legal Issue

Can crime scene personnel re-enter a crime scene, after it had been initially entered and secured, in order to collect only that evidence which had been observed in plain view during the initial entry? Defendant argued that the scientists' entry into the home and collection of evidence without prior authorization of a search warrant constituted an illegal search. The prosecution opposed the motion, arguing that the evidence was admissible because Deputy Sheppard, who lawfully entered the premises, could have seized the evidence that was in his plain view...

continued

Holding of the Court

The Michigan Court held that this "case is clearly distinguishable from *Mincey* and *Thompson* because no generalized search of premises occurred. On the contrary, as defendant stipulated, "all material evidence examined and seized" during the second entry into defendant's home was seen in Deputy Sheppard's plain view when he was lawfully present in the home. Neither *Mincey* nor *Thompson* addresses the situation presented in this case. As a substantial number of other jurisdictions have decided...we conclude that when police officers enter a private residence pursuant to exigent circumstances and observe evidence in plain view but do not seize the evidence, a subsequent warrantless entry shortly after the first entry to process evidence that could have legally been seized by the officer who first viewed the evidence does not violate the Fourth Amendment. The "second entry" in this case, "restricted in nature and scope to securing the evidence observed in plain view" by Deputy Sheppard, constitutes a permissible continuation of Deputy Sheppard's search...

... Deputy Sheppard was not equipped to seize forensic evidence upon his initial entry into defendant's residence. His first responsibility was to assist the victims of the shooting and secure the premises. It would have made little sense to require him to remain in the residence until crime lab personnel arrived to assist him in seizing the evidence. We borrow from and apply here the words of the Court in *Taylor, supra, quoting Smith v State, 419 So . 2d 563, 572* (Miss, 1982):

"The actions of the [forensic scientists] (after the re-entry of the [mobile home]) were merely to effectuate the physical seizure of articles in plain view which [Deputy Sheppard] would have been able to seize had not the circumstances been so "exigent." There was no unwarranted delay in time, nor was there any expansion of the scope of the search. The fact that the actual physical taking of the items into the custody of the police was effectuated by [forensic scientists] who [were] trained to preserve the evidentiary value of the objects, rather than by the first officers to view the objects, is not significant."

Affirmed.

CSI CHECKLIST 7.3

Checklist for Plain View

❏   Was the officer lawfully on the premises?
❏   Was the evidence observed in plain view?

Consent

The other major exception to the search warrant requirement for a crime scene is when the law enforcement officers have **consent** to enter the premises. Generally, when a person who owns or is in possession of a property calls the police for help or calls to report a crime on their property, the police are being given consent to enter the premises. While on that property, they may conduct a reasonable investigation to ascertain if a crime has been committed, render aid to injured victims, and, depending on the nature of the crime reported, conduct a *protective sweep* of the premises to search for suspects and to insure the safety of victims and witnesses. Any evidence in plain view while conducting this initial investigation may be seized.

How Long Does Consent Last?

The following Texas case examines the question of how long consent, once given, lasts and whether officers can exceed the scope of the consent given.

CASE

Scaggs v. Texas

Court of Appeals of Texas, Third District, Austin

18 S.W.3d 277 (Texas, 2000)

Crime Scene Investigation

... Appellant's wife, Penny Scaggs, was murdered in her West Austin home on March 6, 1996. She had been beaten to death with a pipe and then stabbed several times. The appellant, who was chief executive officer of an Austin company, claimed that he had dinner with her that evening then returned to work at 7:00 p.m. He said he then discovered her body upon returning home from work shortly after 9:00 p.m.... Appellant gave written consent for a search of his house and agreed to an interview with Sergeant David Carter.... After interviewing the appellant on the night of the murder, Sergeant Carter realized he had to confirm or eliminate the appellant as a suspect. Therefore, the next day, Sergeant Carter arranged to have the dumpsters behind the appellant's place of business picked up and searched. The search yielded discovery of a one and one-half inch galvanized pipe, a kitchen knife, several latex gloves, and some missing jewelry belonging to the victim. The evidence was taken to the DPS crime lab for blood and fingerprint analysis. It was determined that four fingerprints left in the talcum powder inside the latex gloves matched those of the appellant. DNA analysis showed that blood found on the knife, gloves, and pipe belonged to the victim. The blood analysis showed that the victim's blood was on the outside finger of one glove; the appellant's fingerprint was found on the inside of the same finger of the glove....

Legal Issue

The issue here is how long consent, once given, lasts and whether officers can exceed the scope of the consent given.

Holding of the Court

The Texas Court stated, "... [A]ppellant complains that the "trial court erred in denying appellant's motion to suppress evidence illegally seized from his home." Appellant alleges that police officers

continued

unlawfully seized and took from his home a butcher block and a photograph of the victim. Evidence was admitted to show that a knife allegedly used to attack the victim was the knife missing from the butcher block. The photograph seized was used to identify the victim's jewelry found in the dumpster. Appellant, who was not under arrest or in custody, "having been informed of his constitutional right not to have a search made," gave police officers written consent to "conduct a complete search" of his home and authorized the officers "to take any papers, materials or any other property which they may desire, upon giving receipt for the same." This consent form was signed by appellant at 10:05 p.m. on March 6, 1996, soon after the discovery of his wife's body. Officers were in the home until the early morning hours on March 7. The house was then "sealed" for the continuing investigation. The officers returned to the house later on March 7 and again on March 8...[A]ppellant ... claims that the officer's continued search of the house on March 7 and 8 exceeded the scope of his consent to the search. When appellant gave his written consent to the search of his home he was not under arrest or in custody. Appellant's consent to search could have been withdrawn at any time, but it was not. Appellant's written consent was not limited in scope or time; it authorized a "complete search."

....

...In this case, appellant was not in custody and was in frequent contact with the police officers during the time they were in control of his house, and during this time appellant assured the officers of his complete cooperation. He did not, although he had the opportunity to do so, withdraw his consent to a "complete search" of his house or the taking of any of his property. The record fully supports the trial court's finding that appellant voluntarily consented to the search and that the search did not exceed the scope of appellant's consent. Based on the totality of the circumstances presented by the record, we independently find that appellant voluntarily consented to the search and that the search did not exceed the scope of appellant's consent. The trial court did not abuse its discretion and did not err in denying appellant's motion to suppress. ....The judgment of the trial court is affirmed."

CSI CHECKLIST 7.4

Checklist for Consent

- ❏ Did the person consenting have the authority to do so?
- ❏ Was the consent voluntary?
- ❏ Was the consent in writing or worded specifically enough to withstand legal challenges?

Implied Consent?

Is there an *implied consent* for officers to conduct a search at a crime scene? In other words, does the act of calling 911 or reporting a crime to the police "imply" consent to have officers then respond and initially enter the premises? Most courts believe there is ... to a limited extent. In one Texas case, the defendant called police and reported having discovered his wife dead in the garage. Upon arriving, police searched the detached garage and the home, based upon the information provided by appellant. The Texas Court of Criminal Appeals held:

"...when a crime is reported to the police by an individual who owns or controls the premises to which the police are summoned, and that individual either states or suggests that it was committed by a third person, he or she implicitly consents to a search of the premises reasonably related to the routine investigation of the offense and the identification of the perpetrator. As long as the individual is not a suspect in the case or does nothing to revoke his consent, the police may search the premises for these purposes, and evidence obtained thereby is admissible. This implied consent is valid only for the initial investigation conducted at the scene and does not carry over to future visits to the scene."[12]

In an Arizona case, the defendant reported to police that his wife had been killed in their restaurant. The Court held that the defendant, who was not a suspect at the time, implicitly consented to the search of the restaurant and authorized the subsequent investigation.[13]

In a Pennsylvania case, the Court found that a call to 911 for help established implied consent. The Court held that "where police are conducting a valid search pursuant to a defendant's implied consent, the initial investigation in its entirety is permissible." The Court went on to say that "all evidence observed in plain view during the initial protective sweep is admissible."[14]

When *West Virginia v. Flippo* was remanded from the U.S. Supreme Court back to the state court, the West Virginia Supreme Court of Appeals decided it based on the theory of implied consent:

"We have recognized that consent is one of the exceptions to the warrant requirement. In doing so, this Court has stated that "'the general rule is that the voluntary consent of a person who owns or controls premises to a search of such premises is sufficient to authorize such search without a search warrant, and that a search of such premises, without a warrant, when consented to, does not violate the constitutional prohibition against unreasonable searches and seizures.'" This Court has observed that "whether a consent to a search is in fact voluntary or is the product of duress or coercion, express or implied, is a question of fact to be determined from the totality of all the circumstances." However, our cases have cautioned that "mere submission to colorable authority of police officers is insufficient to validate a 'consent' search or to legitimatize the fruits of the search, and evidence so obtained is incompetent against an accused." We have also indicated that "the State must prove the voluntariness of the consent by a preponderance of the evidence."

...

... consent to search may be implied by the circumstances surrounding the search, by the person's prior actions or agreements, or by the person's failure to object to the search. Thus, a search may be lawful even if the person giving consent does not recite the talismanic phrase: "You have my permission to search." The implied consent exception is undoubtedly a rational and practical rule to be applied when the police are summoned by the owner or occupier of a dwelling and told that a crime has occurred in his/her dwelling. Indeed, 'one can hardly expect the police to get a search warrant for a house or building when the owner is obviously cooperative and gives every appearance of being the victim, rather than the perpetrator, of a crime.'

...

Therefore, we hold that when a person summons the police to a dwelling he/she owns, possesses, or controls, and that person states that a crime was committed against him/her or others by a third person at the premises, he/she implicitly consents to a search of the premises reasonably related to the routine investigation of the offense and the identification of the perpetrator, absent a contrary limitation imposed by the person summoning the police. As long as the person summoning the police is not a suspect in the case or does not affirmatively revoke his/her implied consent, the police may search the premises without a warrant for the purposes of investigating the reported offense and identifying the perpetrator, and evidence obtained thereby is admissible. If the person affirmatively revokes his/her implied consent or becomes a suspect during the investigation, the police must stop the search and obtain a warrant for the purpose of continuing the search...The implied consent exception is valid only for the initial investigation conducted at the scene, and does not extend to future visits to the scene."[15]

Scope of Consent Search

In order for a consent search to comply with Fourth Amendment requirements, it must be given voluntarily by a person who has lawful authority to give consent. To gain a valid consent that will survive subsequent legal challenges, officers should either obtain the consent in writing or ask specific questions that clearly establish that the person giving the consent is authorized to do so, that the consent is voluntarily given, and that there are no limitations to the consent.

As noted in several cases above, the scope of a consent search should be limited to the initial crime scene search. If officers have left the scene or if suspicion falls on the person who gave the consent, a search warrant should be obtained.

LEGAL CHALLENGES TO CRIME SCENE SEARCHES

The primary legal challenges to crime scene searches are that they violated the Fourth Amendment protections against unreasonable search or requirement of a search warrant. If so, any evidence obtained as a result of the search can be excluded from trial through a court created legal rule called the *Exclusionary Rule*. To enforce this rule, defense attorneys will file a *motion to suppress*.

Exclusionary Rule

Exclusionary Rule
A legal rule, established by case law, that prohibits the admission of illegally obtained evidence in a criminal action.

The **Exclusionary Rule** prohibits the admission in a criminal trial of any evidence obtained illegally or in violation of the Fourth Amendment. This rule was created by the U.S. Supreme Court in a 1914 case that held "in a federal prosecution the Fourth Amendment barred the use of evidence secured through an illegal search and seizure."[16] In a 1961 landmark case, the Court extended this rule to the states[17], holding that all courts in this country are governed by Fourth Amendment requirements and limitations.

Fruits of Poisonous Tree Doctrine

Fruits of the Poisonous Tree Doctrine
Derivitive Evidence Rule
From the *Exclusionary Rule*. Any evidence obtained as a result of the original search being unlawful is also unlawful.

Additional significance to unreasonable search or seizures is that any evidence obtained as a result of the original unlawful search is also unlawful under the **Fruits of the Poisonous Tree Doctrine** or what is known as the **Derivative Evidence Rule**. Therefore, if the original crime scene search was unlawful, then all evidence found as a result of that search, whether it was at the crime scene or elsewhere, will be inadmissible in court.

Motion to Suppress

motion to suppress
A legal motion filed before trial that seeks to suppress or exclude certain evidence from being admitted.

Evidence obtained in violation of the Fourth Amendment through an unreasonable search will be inadmissible at trial if a **motion to suppress** is filed in pre-trial hearings or in the form of objections at trial.

SUMMARY

Laws governing crime scene searches are found in three primary sources: statutory and court rules of criminal procedure, case law, and the Constitution. At the heart of the constitutional limitations are the Fourth Amendment protections against unreasonable searches and seizures. This has been interpreted by the courts to require a search warrant as a general rule. However, there are exceptions to this warrant requirement. Exceptions include exigency, or emergency situations, and consent. Most crime scenes involve an initial exigency that allows officers to conduct a brief investigation to determine if a crime has been committed, whether there are victims or suspects at the scene, whether evidence needs to be immediately protected against loss or destruction, and whether the crime scene itself needs to be secured. However, once this initial exigency has been resolved and the scene secured, the officer must obtain a search warrant to remain on the scene and continue the search. Since its major decision in *Mincey v. Arizona,* the U.S. Supreme Court has consistently held that there is no "crime scene" or "murder" exception to the search warrant requirement at a crime scene.

In order for a consent search to comply with Fourth Amendment requirements, it must be given voluntarily by a person who has lawful authority to give consent. The scope of a consent search should be limited to the initial crime scene search. If officers have left the scene or if suspicion falls on the person who gave the consent, a search warrant should be obtained. While conducting a crime search or protective sweep for suspects under either exigent circumstances or consent, any evidence in plain view may be seized by officers.

The primary legal challenges to crime scene searches are that they violate the Fourth Amendment protections against unreasonable search or requirement of a search warrant. If so, any evidence obtained as a result of the search can be excluded from trial through a court-created legal rule called the *Exclusionary Rule.* To enforce this rule, defense attorneys will file a *motion to suppress*.

KEY TERMS

Balancing Test	Exigency
Case Law	Fourth Amendment
Consent	Fruits of the Poisonous Tree Doctrine
Derivative Evidence Rule	
Due Process	Motion to Suppress
Exclusionary Rule	Plain View Doctrine

Probable Cause

Protective Sweep

Reasonable Expectation of Privacy

Reasonable Person Test

Rules of Criminal Procedure

Totality of the Circumstances Test

REVIEW QUESTIONS

1. Identify the three primary sources of laws governing crime scene searches.
2. What is the general rule established by the Fourth Amendment regarding a search warrant?
3. Can the police search a crime scene without a warrant? If so, when?
4. What did *Mincey v. Arizona* hold and what is its importance to crime scene searches?
5. What did *Michigan v. Tyler* hold and what is its importance to crime scene searches?
6. What is an exigency and when does it constitute an exception to the search warrant requirement?
7. What constitutes a consent search?
8. What is a *Protective Sweep* search?
9. What is the *Plain View Doctrine* and how is it used in a crime scene search?
10. What are the legal challenges to crime scene searches?

CRITICAL THINKING QUESTIONS 7.1

1. Why do we have laws that govern the search of a crime scene?
2. Do you believe that the current laws provide adequate safeguards for this process?
3. What public policy issues or considerations do you think might be behind these laws?
4. If it were up to you, would you keep these laws as they are, or delete, narrow, or expand them? Explain your reasoning.
5. How do these laws influence the gathering of crime scene evidence or investigation of a crime scene?

FORENSIC RESEARCH USING THE INTERNET

1. Find your state's rules of criminal procedure and look for any specific rules that pertain to the search of a crime scene. Compare and contrast them with some of the rules and court tests listed in this chapter.

2. Find out if your state appellate court posts their case decisions on the Internet. If so, find a case that illustrates an issue discussed in this chapter dealing with the search of a crime scene. If your state decisions are not on the Internet, go to the Web site for the U.S. Circuit Court of Appeals in your circuit, or search the U.S. Supreme Court decisions.

PRACTICE SKILLS:

Practice what you have learned in the following crime scene problems:

Crime Scene Analysis 7.1

In the case of *Smock v. Indiana*[18], after finding the body, the officers secured the scene and waited for detectives and the coroner to arrive. Upon the arrival of detectives and the coroner, the officers re-entered the defendant's apartment and from the kitchen gathered items of evidence, which were covered in dried blood. The items included a claw hammer, a lock-blade knife, and a box cutter. The items were collected and packaged at approximately 4:15 a.m. on March 23, and later removed from the apartment. Around 8 a.m., a search warrant was obtained, after which officers conducted a further search of the defendant's apartment, locating a knife in a drawer. The knife had also apparently been used in the attack upon the victim.

For the above described crime scene, answer the following questions:

1. Did the police need a search warrant when they "re-entered the defendant's apartment and from the kitchen gathered items of evidence, which were covered in dried blood"? Why or why not?

2. Would the knife found in the drawer during the 8 a.m. search pursuant to a search warrant, be admissible?

continued

Crime Scene Analysis 7.2

At about 4:40 am, a police officer responded to a call that some-one discovered a dead body in a cabin. One of the cabin occu-pants met the officer at a highway turnoff and brought the officer to a cabin that he shared with his brother and defendant. The officer observed the dead body on the floor in the cabin. The officer instructed the occupants of the cabin to wait out-side with him while he summoned his supervising officer. When the supervisor arrived at the scene, the two officers went back inside the cabin, made further brief observations of the body and its surroundings, and concluded that death had resulted from natural causes, possibly bleeding ulcers. After the officers exited the cabin, the other brother told them that he thought he saw a knife. The officers entered the cabin again and discovered a puncture wound on the body. They sum-moned criminal investigators, who arrived one at a time, the first around 6:00 a.m. The investigators remained at the scene for about five hours and seized numerous items of physical evidence. No search warrant was ever obtained.[19]

For the above described crime scene, answer the follow-ing questions:

1. Do the police need a search warrant to search the above crime scene? Why or why not?

2. How would you investigate this crime scene?

3. What search patterns would you consider using at this crime scene? Sketching methods?

Crime Scene Analysis 7.3

Police patrol officers were flagged down by a citizen who said he just witnessed a man breaking into his neighbor's garage and leaving with a cardboard box. The witness pointed out a man walking down the street carrying a cardboard box. Officers detained the man and went to the house where the garage that was allegedly broken into was located. Officers walked around the adjoining house and knocked on the door, but no one answered, and officers could find no sign of forced entry to the house. Officers then went to the garage where they observed that a door panel to the garage had been forc-ibly broken and was open. Officers then entered the garage

continued

in search of additional suspects. Although they did not find any additional suspects, the officers observed a large number ofcarparts from what appeared to be newer model cars. There were no cars in the garage. An officer observed the Vehicle Identification Numbers (VINs) for several of the car parts and, without moving the parts, wrote down the number and called it in to his dispatcher, who ran the numbers through NCIC. The parts came back as reported stolen. Upon getting the results, the officers secured the garage as a crime scene and obtained a search warrant based on the information that he had gained from his entry into the building.[20]

For the above described crime scene, answer the following questions:

1. Did the police need a search warrant to enter and search the above crime scene?

2. Did the police need a warrant to inspect and write down the VINs from the auto parts?

3. How would you investigate this crime scene?

Explain your answers.

WEB SITES

Crime-Scene-Investigator.Net

    http://www.crime-scene-investigator.net/index.html

FindLaw Cases and Codes

    http://guide.lp.findlaw.com/casecode/

FindLaw U.S. Supreme Court Decisions

    http://www.findlaw.com/casecode/supreme.html

Legal Information Institute (LII), Cornell Law School.

    http://www.law.cornell.edu/states/listing.html

State Statutes dealing with Criminal Procedure

    http://www.law.cornell.edu/topics/state_statutes2.html#criminal_procedure

Supreme Court Collection of Cornell Law School

    http://supct.law.cornell.edu/supct/

U.S. Supreme Court

    http://www.supremecourtus.gov/

ENDNOTES

[1] Article VI, United States Constitution

[2] See the landmark U.S. Supreme Court case establishing Judicial Review, *Marbury v. Madison*, 5 U.S. 137 (1803)

[3] *Katz v. United States*, 389 U.S. 347 (1967)

[4] *Amendment IV*, U.S. Constitution

[5] *Katz v. United States*, 389 U.S. 347 (1967)

[6] *Terry v. Ohio*, 392 U.S. 1 (1968)

[7] *Flippo v. West Virginia*, 528 U.S. 11 (1999)

[8] *McDonald v. United States*, 335 U.S. 451

[9] *New Jersey v. Faretra*, 330 N.J. Super. 527 (2000)

[10] *Maryland v. Buie*, 494 U.S. 325 (1990)

[11] *Commonwealth v. Crouse*, 729 A.2d 588 (Pa. Super. 1999)

[12] *Brown v. Texas*, 856 S.W.2d 177 (Tex. Crim. App. 1993)

[13] *State v. Fleischman*, 157 Ariz. 1 (Ariz. Ct. App. 1988)

[14] *Commonwealth v. Witman*, 2000 Pa Super 92 (2000)

[15] *West Virginia v. Flippo*, 212 W.Va 560 (2002)

[16] *Weeks v. United States*, 232 U.S. 383 (1914)

[17] *Mapp v. Ohio*, 367 U.S. 643 (1961)

[18] *Smock v. Indiana*, 766 N.E. 2d 401 (2002)

[19] *Phillips v. State*, 625 P.2d 816 (Alaska, 1980)

[20] *State v. Faretra*, 750 A.2d 155 (New Jersey, 2000)

CRIME LAB AND CRIMINALISTICS

"Like all other arts, the Science of Deduction and Analysis is one which can only be acquired through long and patient study."

—Sherlock Holmes, in Sir Arthur Conan Doyle's *"The Book of Life"*

"Criminalistics is the science of individualization."

—James W. Osterburg, Journal of Criminal Law & Criminology[1]

Chapter Outline

INTRODUCTION

In prior chapters, we learned the importance of using proper procedures to collect, package, and preserve evidence from the crime scene. In this chapter, we will examine where that evidence goes once it is collected. We will look at the *crime lab*, how it is set up, staffed, and the services it provides to law enforcement agencies and criminal investigations. We will also look at the personnel of the crime lab, the *criminalists*, and the science of *criminalistics* that is used in their detection of crime and analysis of evidence. Finally, we will look at the legal challenges facing the crime lab and lab personnel at trial.

FROM CRIME SCENE TO CRIME LAB

Physical evidence that is collected from the crime scene is transported to either a secure evidence area, usually at a law enforcement facility, for storage until trial, or taken to the crime lab for analysis and testing. As noted before, proper documentation must be maintained throughout the transport and handling of this evidence in order to preserve the *chain of custody*. This includes documenting (with dates and times) every place the evidence went, who handled it, and why.

Evidence Control Units

Evidence that is maintained at a law enforcement facility is usually kept in a specially built or equipped evidence room or locker. Due to the length of time from collection of evidence to trial (which can be years) and appeal, evidence from criminal cases can pile up. Agencies need to have a comprehensive evidence control and management policy in effect, and have a space where evidence can be stored safely and securely. Many law enforcement agencies have an **Evidence Control Unit** or section with specially trained personnel who manage the receipt, handling, packaging, transfer, and storage of evidence. For example, the FBI established an Evidence Control Unit in 2003 to handle the administrative processing and management of evidence from receipt to disposition. The administrative personnel working in this unit use a computer-based **Laboratory Information Management System (LIMS)**, an automated evidence-tracking system. LIMS provides a paperless process for evidence tracking, quality and inventory control, casework documentation, and direct administrative reporting.

When evidence needs to be analyzed or tested, it is sent to the crime lab. This might be done directly from the crime scene or

Evidence Control Unit
Specially trained personnel who manage the receipt, handling, packaging, transfer, and storage of evidence.

Laboratory Information Management System (LIMS)
Automated evidence-tracking system.

later from the evidence storage and control areas at a law enforcement agency. The ability of a crime lab to provide scientific analysis is largely dependent on the proper techniques employed to recognize, document, collect, and preserve evidence at the crime scene.

CRIME LAB

crime lab
Forensics analysis and testing laboratory serving law enforcement agencies in a particular area.

The **crime lab** is the forensics analysis and testing laboratory serving law enforcement agencies in a particular area. Crime labs provide a variety of essential services to crime scene investigations, including the processing of the crime scene, collection and analysis of evidence, and providing expert witnesses and courtroom testimony.

Crime labs are typically under the general operations of law enforcement agencies, although there are some non-law–enforcement state and regional government labs, as well as private labs. Historically, crime labs were staffed by law enforcement officers, but today, with the need for specialized scientific analysis and testing, most crime labs are staffed by civilian technicians and criminalists.

History of Crime Labs

The first official crime laboratory was established in 1910 at Lyon, France, by Edmond Locard. In 1923, August Vollmer started the first crime lab in the United States, at the Los Angeles Police Department. In 1932, the first federal crime lab was created in the Southern Railway Building in Washington, D.C., by the United States Bureau of Investigation (USBOI), under the directorship of J. Edgar Hoover. In 1935, this agency was later renamed the Federal Bureau of Investigation (FBI). After several moves in its history (including the Department of Justice building and the J. Edgar Hoover building), a new FBI crime lab was opened at Quantico, Virginia, in 2003. The last state to establish its own crime lab was Alaska, which established the Alaska Scientific Crime Detection Laboratory in 1986. (See Exhibit 8.1.)

EXHIBIT 8.1 Early History of Crime Labs

1910: Edmond Locard founded the first official police crime laboratory in Lyon, France
1923: First American crime laboratory established at Los Angeles Police Department, under direction of August Vollmer
1932: What is now called the FBI National Crime Lab is created under the leadership of J. Edgar Hoover

Modern Crime Labs

Today, there are almost 400 crime labs throughout the United States employing over 10,000 personnel. There are forensic laboratories at every level from federal crime labs to state labs, county labs, and labs in many city police departments. There are also private and military labs. According to a census of crime labs taken by the Bureau of Justice Statistics, a typical laboratory operation has about 18 FTE employees, including 2 managers, 2 secretaries/clerks, 12 analysts, and 2 technicians.[2]

An example of a city crime lab is the Mesa, Arizona, Police Department Crime Laboratory. Established in 1980 as a one-person operation, the only service that was initially offered was the analysis of controlled substances. As the city grew, the crime lab also increased in the forensic services required to meet the city's needs. Today, there are over 22 personnel working in the crime lab, providing services that include forensic analysis and testing of evidence, crime scene processing, and expert testimony in court.[3]

An example of a regional crime lab is the one operated by the San Diego Sheriff's Department. This crime lab serves the county of San Diego, providing forensic services to over 30 agencies. Except for the city of San Diego, the Sheriff's Crime Lab serves all cities and law enforcement agencies in San Diego County, including the District Attorney's office and the California Highway Patrol. The crime lab is located in a former hospital with over 100,000 square feet, two-thirds of which is devoted to the crime lab, and one-third serves as a centralized property and evidence area. The San Diego Sheriff's Lab employs over 56 personnel, including a lab manager, 32 criminalists, 8 latent print examiners, 2 document examiners, 2 lab assistants, and 5 forensic evidence technicians.[4]

At the other end of the country, Vermont is an example of a state with only one major forensic crime lab, operated by the state Department of Public Safety. The Vermont Forensic Laboratory was originally created in 1947 as part of the state police. Starting off with only photographic services, the lab grew to provide a full range of forensic services to all Vermont law enforcement agencies. In 1998, a civilian director was named to head the lab and, except for a state police officer assigned as an assistant director, all of the lab personnel were civilians. At present, the Vermont Forensic Lab employs a staff of 18, including 9 forensic chemists, 2 latent print examiners, 2 forensic photographers, a firearms and toolmark specialist, and an evidence technician.[5]

On the federal level, the FBI's new crime lab is one of the largest and most comprehensive forensic laboratories in the world, employing more than 700 employees in a state-of-the-art building covering 470,000 square feet. More than 1 million forensic examinations are conducted by this FBI Laboratory each year.[6]

Although the FBI has the most comprehensive crime lab, it is not the only federal agency with a forensic laboratory. Most federal investigative and law enforcement agencies have their own crime labs. For example, the Department of Homeland Security has a *Forensic Document Laboratory* under its Immigration and Customs Enforcement (ICE) division that is focused on travel and identity document fraud. The U.S. Fish and Wildlife Service maintains a wildlife forensics laboratory in Ashland, Oregon. The lab has a criminalistics section that includes firearms and fingerprint units. The lab "conducts visual, microscopic and instrumental examination on a wide range of evidence items, including wildlife parts and products, bullets, cartridge cases, shot pellets, fibers, paint, soil, and physical taggants."[7]

Crime Lab Accreditation

To ensure that their operations meet national standards, most modern crime labs seek accreditation through the Crime Laboratory Accreditation Program of the American Society of Crime Laboratory Directors/Laboratory Accreditation Board (ASCLD/LAB). This is a voluntary program in which a participating crime laboratory must demonstrate that its management, operations, personnel, procedures, equipment, physical plant, security, and personnel safety procedures meet established standards. The accreditation process is part of a laboratory's quality assurance program. The ASCLD/LAB inspects crime laboratories internationally, and its accreditation holds for a five-year period.

In 2002, the Bureau of Justice Statistics estimated that approximately 61 percent of the crime labs in the United States are accredited by the ASCLD/LAB. An additional 10 percent are accredited by some other organization.[8]

SERVICES PROVIDED BY CRIME LABORATORIES

As noted above, crime labs offer a variety of services to law enforcement agencies. Although this can be limited by the size of the law enforcement agencies and areas served, as well as level of funding, most crime labs provide certain support services. These include crime scene processing, analysis and testing of evidence, and expert witness testimony at trial. (See Exhibit 8.2.)

Crime Scene Processing

Specially trained crime lab personnel go to many crime scenes, especially those involving violent or serious property crimes, to assist investigators in the processing of the crime scene. Crime lab technicians and criminalists use sophisticated forensic equipment to help recognize, identify, collect, and preserve physical evidence for subsequent analysis.

Sketching and Documentation Services

Crime lab personnel may assist in the documentation of the crime scene. Many technicians are trained in the use of electronic distance measuring devices and Global Positioning Systems to diagram and sketch crime scenes.

Photography Services

Most crime labs have a crime scene photography unit and personnel trained in the professional use of a variety of photographic equipment and techniques. At the crime scene, photographers use several specialized cameras, including digital, video, infrared, and ultraviolet, to document the scene and identify and document evidence. At the crime lab, sophisticated photography equipment, including film and X-ray photographic processors, assist in developing and enlarging crime scene photos, as well as the preparation of photographic exhibits for use at trial.

Forensic Analysis and Testing

In addition to assisting with the processing of the crime scene, an essential service provided by crime labs is the subsequent forensic analysis and testing of this evidence. Most crime labs have sections or units with personnel who specialize in certain forensic testing procedures.

Latent Fingerprint and Impressions Analysis

latent
Not readily visible.

Technicians process crime scenes for **latent** fingerprints, collect them, identify prints in lab, and classify and compare them with suspects. This unit may also be responsible for the identification, collection, and comparison of other types of prints, including palmprints, lip prints, footprints, shoe prints, and tire prints.

dactylography
Study of fingerprint identification and classification.

The history of fingerprints can be traced back to 1892, when Francis Galton published a book on **dactylography**, the study of fingerprint identification and classification. In his study, Galton concluded that the chances of two fingerprints being identical were 64,000,000 to 1.

henry system
First fingerprint classification system, developed in 1901 at Scotland Yard, by Sir Edward Henry.

A few years later, in 1901, Sir Edward Henry established the first fingerprint classification system at Scotland Yard. This classification system, called the **Henry System**, is still used by crime labs.

Physical Sciences and Trace Evidence Analysis

This section uses scientific principles of physics and chemistry through forensic lab instrumentation and microscopic procedures to analyze physical evidence found at crime scenes. This can include analysis of glass, paint, drugs and controlled substances, fibers, hair, and explosives.

Biological and Serology Analysis

serology
Scientific study of blood and its properties.

Serology is the scientific study of blood and its properties. In 1901, Dr. Karl Landsteiner discovered that blood can be grouped into different categories, now recognized as A, B, AB, and O. In 1915, a professor in Italy, Leone Lattes, developed a technique for determining the blood group of a dried bloodstain.

Today, the serology section of a crime lab employs forensic chemists and biologists to identify, group, and compare bloodstains, seminal and body fluids, and tissue; and, conduct other biological analysis. DNA analysis has become a central part of this analysis, and many labs have separate units to conduct DNA testing.

CSI CHECKLIST 8.1

Blood Examination Request Letter

A blood examination request letter to the FBI Crime Lab must contain the following information:

- ❑ A brief statement of facts relating to the case.
- ❑ Claims made by the suspect(s) regarding the source of the blood.
- ❑ Whether animal blood is present.
- ❑ Whether the stains were laundered or diluted with other body fluids.
- ❑ Information regarding the victim(s)' and suspect(s)' health such as AIDS, hepatitis, or tuberculosis.

Source: FBI Crime Lab

Toxicology Analysis

toxicology
Detection and study of poisons.

The **Toxicology** section analyzes blood and urine samples, and body organs to determine the presence or absence of drugs and poisons. It is also used to determine the amount of alcohol consumption.

The study of toxicology as a forensic science dates back to 1814, when Mathieu Orfila, a professor of medicine in France, published a scientific article on the detection of poisons. He continued his work for many years and is considered the "father of forensic toxicology."

Ballistics Analysis and Toolmark Identification

ballistics
Analysis and identification of firearms and ammunition.

Ballistics is the scientific analysis and identification of firearms and ammunition. In a crime lab, this group is responsible for the examination, identification, and comparison of firearms, bullets, and cartridges. Specialists also test fire weapons, examining the objects and clothing fired at to detect discharge residues. In addition to firearms and ballistics analysis, this section is also usually responsible for the identification and comparison of tool marks and striations.

The history of ballistics goes back to 1913, when a scientific paper on firearms identification was published. In 1925, Philip Gravelle used a comparison microscope to compare bullets. The following year, Calvin Goddard, a U.S. Army physician, developed the standards for the newly termed science of ballistics.

Questioned Document Analysis

Questioned Document Examiners identify and compare handwriting, typewriting, and other questioned documents to resolve questions about age, source, or authenticity. This can include the analysis of paper and ink, document copying or production devices, document modification, and burned or charred documents.

questioned documents
Analysis and comparison of documents for identification purposes.

The use of these lab analysis techniques can be traced back to 1910, when Albert Osborn published the first text on **Questioned Documents**, the analysis and comparison of documents for identification purposes. Osborn also invented the comparison microscope for document analysis.

EXHIBIT 8.2   Census of 50 Largest Publicly Funded Crime Labs

A census of publicly funded forensic crime labs by the Bureau of Justice Statistics found that the 50 largest crime labs in the United States employed more than 4,300 full-time personnel and had total budgets exceeding $266 million. These labs received more than 994,000 new cases, including over 1.2 million requests for forensic services each year. These requests represented about half of all requests for forensic services handled by publicly funded labs nationally. The labs ended the year with over 93,000 backlogged cases.[9]

PRACTICE TIP 8.1

Research Crime Labs and Forensic Science

For more information about crime labs and the forensic sciences, check out the following Web sites:

American Society of Crime Laboratory Directors
http://www.ascld.org/forensicstudents.html
American Academy of Forensic Sciences
http://www.aafs.org/

CRIMINALISTICS

The word **criminalistics** was first used in a book, *System der Kriminalistik*, written in 1893 by Hans Gross, a public prosecutor and magistrate in Austria. In this classic treatise that would become the founding of the "science" of criminalistics, Gross emphasized the importance of physical evidence and the use of the scientific method in crime scene investigation. (See Exhibit 8.3.)

forensic science
Application of science and scientific method to crime scene investigation.

Criminalistics, often called **forensic science**, is the application of science to crime scene investigation. It involves the recognizing, collecting, identifying, analyzing, and comparing of physical evidence through the use of scientific methods, instrumentation, and analysis. This is accomplished through comparison and testing methods using a variety of forensic techniques and instrumentation. Once the evidence has been analyzed, the results are interpreted through the use of classification techniques.

EXHIBIT 8.3 History of Criminalistics

1814: Mathieu Orfila, in France, publishes on the detection and effect of poisons

1868: DNA discovered

1882: Alphonse Bertillon, a police clerk in France, develops *anthropometrical signalment*, a personal identification system that leads to mug shots and the *portrait parle*

1887: Sir Arthur Conan Doyle published his first Sherlock Holmes novel

1892: Francis Galton published a book on dactylography, a study of fingerprint identification and classification

1893: Hans Gross, a magistrate in Austria, wrote classic book on criminal investigation, *System der Kriminalistik*

1894: First criminal identification bureau in United States started in Chicago

1901: Sir Edward Henry established the first fingerprint classification system and identification bureau at Scotland Yard, called the Henry System

1901: Dr. Karl Landsteiner discovered blood grouping

1902: American courts begin to recognize firearms comparison as scientific evidence

1908: Bureau of Investigation, which became FBI, established in Washington, D.C.

1910: Edmond Locard established first police crime laboratory in Lyon, France

1910: Albert Osborn published the first book on *Questioned Documents*. (Osborn also later invented the comparison microscope.)

1911: American courts begin to recognize fingerprints as scientific evidence

1915: Leone Lattes, a professor in Italy, developed a technique for determining the blood group of a dried bloodstain

1924: FBI establishes an Identification Division for fingerprints

1925: Philip Gravelle uses comparison microscope for bullet comparisons

1926: Calvin Goddard, a U.S. Army physician, developed the standard for ballistics

1985: DNA identification and typing discovered by Alec Jeffreys

1987: Bristol Crown Court in England becomes the first court in the world to convict on DNA evidence when it sentenced a man to prison for rape

1990: U.S. District Court in Vermont rules that DNA profiling is sufficiently reliable to allow admissibility in criminal case to prove identity

Criminalist

criminalist
One who applies science and scientific method to crime scene investigation.

The practitioners of criminalistics are called **criminalists**, forensic scientists, crime lab technicians, fingerprint experts, document examiners, forensic chemists, and so on. To become a forensic criminalist usually requires at least a four-year or graduate degree in the natural sciences, with emphasis in chemistry, microbiology, or physics. However, some criminalists or forensic specialists are individuals with criminal justice or forensic science degrees, or law enforcement officers cross-trained in a specialty, such as fingerprint identification, ballistics comparison, or document examination.

What Criminalists Do

As noted in the previous section, criminalists apply scientific methods and testing to the investigation of crime. They are involved in recognizing, collecting, identifying, analyzing, and comparing physical evidence through the use of scientific methods, instrumentation, and analysis. This may include criminalists at the crime scene, using specialized forensic equipment, such as lasers or alternate light sources, to detect and identify evidence invisible to the naked eye. Criminalists may then use special techniques or scientific tools to collect the evidence, such as static lifters, casting compounds, or fluorescent powders.

At the crime lab, criminalists analyze the evidence collected through a variety of sophisticated scientific instruments, such as the scanning electron microscope. These tests may each involve numerous procedures, all of which must be properly documented and each test performed accurately. After testing evidence, criminalists analyze the findings and write a report for the case investigators. If a suspect is discovered, further testing may be involved as criminalists attempt to match evidence from the crime scene to the suspect. Once the suspect is charged with a crime, the criminalists involved in the case will have to testify in various court hearings and at trial. Finally, criminalists provide training and consultation in forensic science to law enforcement and other agencies.

PRACTICE TIP 8.2

For More Info on Criminalists

For more information on criminalists, check out one of the following Web sites:
ASCLD site with FAQ about careers in Forensic Science
http://www.ascld.org/forensicstudents.html
American Board of Criminalistics
http://criminalistics.com

WHY CRIMINALISTICS IS IMPORTANT

The sciences utilized under the broader term of "criminalistics" have always been important to crime scene investigation and the subsequent prosecution of crimes. At the crime scene, forensic identification and detection equipment help in the collection of evidence and have made it possible to discover physical evidence that was previously invisible to the naked eye. At the crime lab, trained criminalists, using sophisticated forensic instruments and testing equipment, are able to analyze this physical evidence and its value to the investigation. In court, criminalists can help to explain scientific evidence, complicated testing procedures, and the results of their comparisons and analysis.

CSI Effect

CSI Effect
Influence of popular *CSI* television shows on jurors' expectations of what criminalistics can and should do in a criminal investigation.

With the advent of new scientific discoveries and forensic technology, such as DNA identification and advanced computer systems, more criminal investigations are requesting forensic analysis of evidence found during an investigation. With the popularity of so many television shows focusing on crime scene investigation, more jurors are assuming that forensic analysis, especially DNA testing, will be conducted at all crime scenes, and that the testimony of a criminalist will be key in proving the case. This has been called the **CSI Effect** and many crime scene investigators and prosecutors believe that it has resulted in an unrealistic notion of what criminalistics can and should do in a criminal investigation, and how fast it can be accomplished.

BASIS OF CRIMINALISTICS

The basis of criminalistics is the analysis of physical evidence to determine the common origin or identity of the item, and the comparison of that item with some other evidence or object to determine if they come from the same source or share matchable characteristics. This is accomplished through various criminalistic methods, including microscopic, visual, and physical developmental techniques, DNA analysis, and instrumental analysis. However, interpreting the information from the analysis and testing is typically done through classification techniques. These techniques are based in a number of concepts and theories relative to identity.

Concept of Identity

concept of identity
A concept that although no two objects are identical, there are many factors that combine to establish identity to a certain mathematical probability.

In the scientific testing and analysis of physical evidence, we are always concerned with the **concept of identity**. We want to know answers to questions like: Did this chip of glass come from that broken window? Was this bullet fired from that gun? Whose fingerprint is this?

According to the strict concept of identity, no two objects are identical. There are always some characteristics by which they could be distinguished. However, there are many factors, which can combine to establish identity to a certain mathematical probability. Given these factors and the statistical probabilities that can result, expert witnesses can testify to the similarities or differences of a set of characteristics.

Set Theory

set theory
All objects can be divided and subdivided into various sets on the basis of their properties

Identification in criminalistics is aligned with the logic of **Set Theory**, that all objects can be divided and subdivided into various sets on the basis of their properties. In this use of set theory, we are concerned with narrowing the evidence from the *universal* set to a *unique* set from which we can determine origin or identity. To do this, we consider several factors, including *transfer theory*, *rarity*, and *probability theory*.

Transfer Theory: "Every Contact Leaves a Trace."

transfer or exchange theory
Whenever two surfaces are in contact with each other, there is a partial transfer of material from one to the other.

As described in a previous section, Edmond Locard, the French criminalist, believed that every time a criminal enters a crime scene, he leaves something behind in the way of trace evidence and takes something with him. According to this transfer theory, also called exchange theory, whenever two surfaces are in contact with each other, there is a partial transfer of material from one to the other.

Rarity

rarity
Evidence found at the crime scene that seems out of place.

Another factor that may be associated with identity is a rare or isolated circumstance that may be connected to a crime scene. An object that seems out of place at a crime scene may have increased value as a piece of evidence. The key is whether the evidence seems out of place.

To help with this, we consider the **rarity** of physical evidence found at the crime scene; that is, whether it seems unique, out of place, or does not appear to belong to the other objects or evidence found. When an object seems out of place at the crime scene, it may tend to increase the quality of its value as a piece of evidence. For example, a tie clasp found near the body of a woman may be of more evidentiary value than a hairpin.

Probability Theory

probability theory
Attempts to define the mathematical or statistical probability of a certain event occurring or an object having certain characteristics, usually in determining identity.

Probability Theory attempts to define the probability or odds of a certain event occurring or an object having certain characteristics, usually in determining identity. This is expressed as mathematical or statistical probability and described by using the ratio of the number of actual occurrences to the number of possible occurrences or odds. An example of mathematical probability is a simple coin toss. If you toss a coin, it will either land on heads or tails. There is no scientific validity to the coin landing on one side more than on the other.

Therefore, we would state that the *mathematical* or *statistical probability* of the coin landing on its head is: 1:1 or 50/50. This may not impress you for evidentiary purposes, but when you consider that this same statistical probability, when applied to the use of a fingerprint is 1:10 to the 60th power or 10 followed by 60 zeros. In other words, the probability of any two fingerprints being the same is:

1 in 10000000000000000000000000000000000000000 00000000000000000000.

For fingerprints, this means that no two prints in the entire world are alike. Some DNA testing is similar in its results, coming in somewhere around 1 in 300 million. When viewed in this statistical form of probability, scientists can offer opinions and conclusions as to whether there is a basis for similarities and if there is a match in establishing identity for physical evidence found at the crime scene.

Standards of Comparison

standard of comparison
A sample that is compared to evidence to determine whether both are identical or from the same source.

In crime scene investigation we are mainly dealing with probability in *comparison*. To be able to evaluate certain physical evidence, it must be compared to other samples. A **standard of comparison** is a similar item, source, or measure that is compared to the evidence to determine whether both are identical or from the same source.

For example, a bullet from a body is compared to a bullet fired from a suspect's gun; pry marks found at the point of entry is compared to pry marks made with suspect's screwdriver; or fingerprints found at scene are compared to the suspect.

For our purposes, an object has been identified when it can be shown that it has a sufficient number of characteristics that are like a *known* object or *standard of comparison*. The key concept is that an unknown object, found at the crime scene and marked *"Q"* for *Questioned* sample, is compared to a known object, usually that which has been taken from a suspect, and marked *"K"* for *Known*.

Matchable Characteristics

matchable characteristics
Identifying features that might prove the evidence is the same or from the same source as the sample.

Known samples and comparison samples are compared to find the number of **matchable** or different **characteristics**. If, in comparing these objects, we find that a sufficient number of characteristics are alike, then we could say that, based on our experience and the type of characteristics found, it would be extremely unlikely for the unknown object to be identified with any other object or that the mathematical probability of the questioned object to be identical to any other is "1:x." Thus, we conclude that the Questioned object is or is not the same as the Known compared sample. (See Exhibit 8.4.)

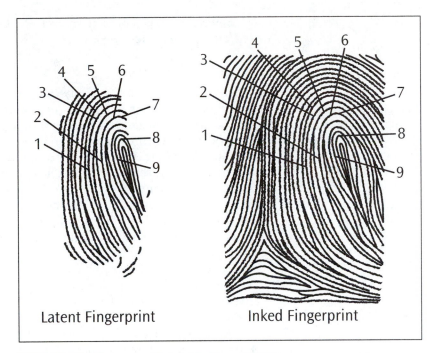

EXHIBIT 8.4 Comparing Matchable Characteristics

CSI CHECKLIST 8.2

Matchable Characteristics

Known samples and comparison samples are compared to find the number of matchable or different characteristics. When working on comparisons, follow these rules:

- ❏ Compare the same points from two separate samples.
- ❏ Draw and number a separate comparison line to each point on each sample.
- ❏ Lines should be drawn in a straight line and proceeding clockwise.
- ❏ Do not cross lines.

Class Versus Individual Characteristics

To recognize the potential value of physical evidence, we must first understand the difference between class characteristics and individual characteristics. In criminalistics, materials may be classified based upon characteristic properties exhibited by those materials.

There are two types of characteristics: *class characteristics* and *individual characteristics*.

Class Characteristics

class characteristics
When the characteristics of physical evidence are common to a group of objects or persons.

When the characteristics of physical evidence are common to a group of objects or persons, they may be termed **class characteristics**. Regardless of how thoroughly they are examined, such piece of evidence can only offer generalizations. Materials that exhibit class characteristics cannot be identified as coming from one individual or source to the exclusion of all other similar sources. An individual identification cannot be made as there is a possibility of more than one source for the material found. The evidentiary value of this type of evidence is based upon the probability factor. Evidence that generally exhibits only class characteristics includes fibers, paint, glass, and soil.

However, a preponderance of class characteristic evidence tying a defendant or the tools or weapons used in the crime to the scene strengthens the case. This is an example of *circumstantial evidence*.

In the famous Georgia case in which 30 young boys were reported murdered or missing, the suspect, Wayne Williams, was convicted on the basis of *fiber evidence*. During the trial, this fiber evidence was used to associate Williams with 12 of those victims.

Fibers from his bedspread were similar to those found on 12 of the victims. Fibers from his bedroom carpet similar to those found on 9 of the victims, fibers from his blanket similar to those found on 6 of the victims, fibers from his car carpet similar to those found on 4 of the victims; debris from his station wagon similar to that found on 8 of the victims; and animal hairs consistent with suspect's dog found on 11 of the victims.

Using figures and data from the carpet manufacturer, as well as the Atlanta Regional Commission for Housing, experts determined the mathematical probability of finding a house in Atlanta with a room having carpet like Williams to be 1 in 7,792. Taken alone, that would not constitute enough evidence to convict someone. However, when viewed along with the other evidence, it was sufficient to convince the jury beyond a reasonable doubt of William's guilt.

Individual Characteristics

individual or individualizing characteristics
When the characteristics of physical evidence can be identified as having originated with a particular person or source.

Unlike class characteristic evidence, evidence with **individual or individualizing characteristics** can be identified as having originated with a particular person or source. Objects and people have many characteristics that are common in other objects and people.

However, every person and many objects have individual characteristics that are unique and different from all others, such as fingerprints, footprints, DNA (from blood, semen, hair), impression evidence, and ballistics.

LEGAL CHALLENGES

Legal challenges to the crime lab and criminalistics generally fall in two areas: challenges to the crime lab or personnel, and challenges to the forensic equipment and procedures involved.

Legal Challenges to Crime Lab and Lab Personnel

Legal challenges may attack the credibility of the crime lab itself, or the lab personnel involved in the case. For example, an Illinois crime lab supervisor and chief of the lab's biochemistry section was accused of providing misleading testimony about scientific findings in examining blood evidence.[10] In a Washington state case, a crime lab scientist, who helped establish the lab's DNA section 10 years earlier, missed a marker in analyzing DNA and later tried to conceal this information. Other crime lab personnel were accused of sloppy analysis and drawing incorrect conclusions about their testing.[11] In eight criminal cases in Phoenix, lab personnel used the wrong statistical formula for calculating probability estimates in DNA tests.[12]

A crime laboratory can be challenged as to the credibility of the instruments, methods or testing performed from evidence gathered at the crime scene. To insure the integrity of the forensic testing and the accuracy of the results, labs first conduct **validation studies**. A validation study is a form of proficiency testing in which the crime lab or a particular technician working in the lab is given a sample to test that has already been tested by a validation lab. The results of the testing are then compared to the validation standard. These studies are performed to insure that the lab and its personnel are meeting certain professional standards. These validation studies can be obtained by the defense and subjected to attack in the courtroom through challenges to the procedures employed or the credibility of lab personnel or the lab itself.

Lab personnel typically maintain records and logs documenting every procedure and protocol utilized in the collection or receipt, testing, and analysis of forensic evidence. These documents and logs can also be examined by the defense, which may lead to legal challenges as to reliability or credibility of the records or the recordkeeper.

validation studies
A form of proficiency testing performed to insure that a crime laboratory and its personnel are meeting certain professional standards.

CSI CHECKLIST 8.3

Checklist for Challenging Crime Lab or Lab Personnel

❑ Were crime lab personnel improperly trained or supervised?
❑ Was the forensic evidence collected, preserved, and handled properly?
❑ Was there a failure to follow proper testing protocol or procedures?
❑ Were validation studies previously conducted, and if so, did the crime lab meet professional standards?

Legal Challenges to Forensic Equipment and Procedure

Legal challenges may also attack the way the forensic analysis was conducted or the equipment used. Examples of this include the use of forensic equipment to detect or analyze trace or impression evidence, or bodily fluids; and scientific testing instruments for determining DNA or blood alcohol content. These legal challenges may target whether the forensic equipment had been properly checked and tested, and whether it was operating accurately. For example, whether the chemicals used were of the correct kind and compounded in proper proportions. It may also challenge whether the proper procedures were used, such as whether the operator was properly trained and qualified to run equipment and the test was given in the proper manner. For example, a West Virginia court found that inaccuracies and irregularities in some forensic testing were "the result of systematic practice rather than an occasional inadvertent error" and recommended that "any testimonial or documentary evidence offered" by the criminalist involved "at any time in any criminal prosecution should be deemed invalid, unreliable, and inadmissible..."[13]

PRACTICE TIP 8.3

Legal Challenges to Crime Lab and Forensic Evidence

For an excellent Web site on legal challenges to crime labs and forensic evidence, see

A Beginner's Primer on the Investigation of Forensic Evidence, by Attorney Kim Kruglick http://www.kruglaw.com

CSI CHECKLIST 8.4

Checklist for Challenging Forensic Equipment and Procedure

❏ Was the equipment checked, tested, and operating accurately?

❏ If chemicals were used, were they the correct kind and compounded in proper proportions?

❏ Was the operator of the equipment properly trained and qualified to run equipment?

❏ Was the test given in the proper manner?

SUMMARY

Physical evidence that is collected from the crime scene is transported to either a secure evidence area, usually at a law enforcement facility, for storage until trial, or taken to the crime lab for analysis and testing. Evidence that is maintained at a law enforcement facility is usually kept in a specially built or equipped evidence room or locker. Many law enforcement agencies have an *Evidence Control Unit* or section with specially trained personnel who manage the receipt, handling, packaging, transfer, and storage of evidence. When evidence needs to be analyzed or tested, it is sent to the crime lab. This might be done directly from the crime scene or later from the evidence storage and control areas at a law enforcement agency. The crime lab is the forensics analysis and testing laboratory serving law enforcement agencies in a particular area. Crime labs provide a variety of essential services to crime scene investigations, including the processing of the crime scene, collection and analysis of evidence, and the providing of expert witnesses and courtroom testimony. There are almost 400 crime labs throughout the United States employing over 10,000 personnel. There are forensic laboratories at every level from federal crime labs to state labs, county labs, and labs in many city police departments. There are also private and military labs. Crime labs offer a variety of services to law enforcement agencies, including crime scene processing, analysis and testing of evidence, and expert witness testimony at trial.

Criminalistics, often called forensic science, is the application of science to crime scene investigation. It involves recognizing, collecting, identifying, analyzing, and comparing physical evidence through the use of scientific methods, instrumentation, and analysis. This is accomplished through comparison and testing methods using a variety of forensic techniques and instrumentation. The practitioners of criminalistics are called criminalists, forensic scientists, crime lab technicians, fingerprint experts, document examiners, and forensic chemists. The sciences utilized under the broader term of "criminalistics" have always been important to crime scene investigation and the subsequent prosecution of crimes, not only in helping to detect and collect physical evidence at the crime scene, but to analyze this evidence in the crime lab, and to help explain this scientific testing and evidence in court. The basis of criminalistics is the analysis of physical evidence to determine the common origin or identity of the item, and comparing that item with some other evidence or object to determine if they come from the same source or share matchable characteristics.

Interpreting the information from the analysis and testing is typically done through classification techniques. These techniques are based in a number of concepts related to identity, including the *Concept of Identity*, a concept that whereas no two objects are identical, there are many factors that combine to establish identity to a certain mathematical probability; *Set Theory*, that all objects can be divided and subdivided into various sets on the basis of their properties; and, *Probability Theory*, which attempts to define the probability or odds of a certain event occurring or an object having certain characteristics, usually in determining identity. Crime scene investigation mainly deals with probability in *comparison*. To be able to evaluate certain physical evidence, it must be compared to other samples, called standards of comparison, in which the sample is compared to the evidence to determine whether both are identical or from the same source. When the characteristics of physical evidence are common to a group of objects or persons, they may be termed class characteristics. Evidence with individual or individualizing characteristics can be identified as having originated with a particular person or source.

Legal challenges often target the crime lab, lab personnel, and criminalists. This includes challenges that crime lab personnel were improperly trained or supervised; that forensic evidence was improperly collected, preserved, or handled; that there was a failure to follow proper testing protocol or procedures; or that validation studies showed that the crime lab failed to meet professional standards. Legal challenges can also target forensic equipment and testing procedure. For example, the way the testing was conducted or the equipment used may be at issue. These legal challenges usually go to the weight, not the admissibility, of the forensic evidence.

KEY TERMS

Ballistics

Class Characteristics

Concept of Identity

Crime Lab

Criminalist

Criminalistics

CSI Effect

Dactylography

DNA

Evidence Control Unit

Exchange Theory

Forensic Science

Henry System

Individual or Individualizing Characteristics

Laboratory Information Management System (LIMS)

Latent

Matchable Characteristics

Probability Theory

Questioned Documents

Rarity

Serology

Set Theory

Standard of Comparison

Toxicology

Transfer or Exchange Theory

Validation Studies

REVIEW QUESTIONS

1. Explain what a crime lab is and its importance to crime scene investigation.

2. Define crime lab accreditation and discuss how this is obtained.

3. Describe the services offered by crime labs.

4. What is criminalistics?

5. What do criminalists do?

6. Distinguish between *concept of identity* and *set theory*, and describe how these pertain to criminalistics.

7. What are matchable characteristics?

8. Distinguish between class and individual characteristics. Give an example of each.

9. Explain what the legal challenges are to crime lab and criminalistics. Give an example for each.

CRITICAL THINKING QUESTIONS 8.1

1. What is the importance of the crime lab in crime scene investigations?
2. What do you think is one of the most important services offered by a crime lab? Why?
3. How has the evolution of crime labs and services influenced the collection of evidence at a crime scene?
4. What is the importance of criminalistics to crime scene investigation?
5. How do criminalistics and the use of forensic equipment and techniques discussed in this chapter influence crime scene investigations?

FORENSIC RESEARCH USING THE INTERNET

1. Search the Internet for specific crime lab Web sites. Assess at least three of the crime labs found, describing what personnel and services they offer, and how they compare or contrast with each other.

PRACTICE SKILLS:

Practice what you have learned in the following crime scene problems:

Crime Scene Analysis 8.1

1. Compare the DNA sample (see Exhibit 8.5.) taken from the crime scene, marked "K-1," with the DNA taken from S-1, S-2, and S-3. Do any of them match?

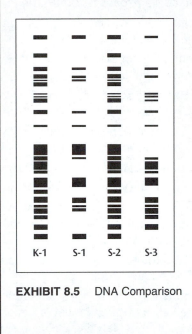

EXHIBIT 8.5   DNA Comparison

WEB SITES

American Academy of Forensic Sciences
   http://www.aafs.org/

American Board of Criminalistics
   http://criminalistics.com

American Society of Crime Laboratory Directors
   http://www.ascld.org/forensicstudents.html

FBI Lab
   http://www.fbi.gov/hq/lab/labhome.htm

Mesa, Arizona Police Crime Lab

http://www.ci.mesa.az.us/police/crimelab/

San Diego Sheriff's Crime Lab

http://www.sdsheriff.net/crimelab

Vermont Forensic Laboratory

http://www.dps.state.vt.us/cjs/forensic.html

ENDNOTES

[1] *The Evaluation of Physical Evidence in Criminalistics: Subjective or Objective Process?*, 60 J. Crim. L. & Criminology 97 (1969)

[2] Bureau of Justice Statistics, Census of Publicly Funded Forensic Crime Laboratories, 2002

[3] From the City of Mesa, Arizona Web site, http://www.ci.mesa.az.us/police/crimelab/

[4] See San Diego Sheriff's Crime Lab Web site, http://www.sdsheriff.net/crimelab

[5] Visit Vermont Forensic Laboratory's Web site, http://www.dps.state.vt.us/cjs/forensic.html

[6] See the FBI Lab Web site, http://www.fbi.gov/hq/lab/labhome.htm

[7] U.S. Fish and Wildlife Service Crime Laboratory, http://www.lab.fws.gov/

[8] Bureau of Justice Statistics, Census of Publicly Funded Forensic Crime Laboratories, 2002

[9] U.S. Department of Justice, Bureau of Justice Statistics, 50 Largest Crime Labs, 2002

[10] See article by Steve Mills & Maurice Possley, Report Alleges Crime Lab Fraud - Scientist is Accused of Providing False Testimony, Chi. Trib. (Jan. 14, 2001)

[11] See article by Ruth Teichroeb, Oversight of crime-lab staff has often been lax, *Seattle Post-Intelligencer Reporter*, July 23, 2004

[12] See article by Beth DeFalco, Police Say Lab Made Errors Analyzing DNA, AP Online, May 5, 2003.

[13] Investigation of the West Virginia State Police Crime Laboratory 190 W. Va. 321; 438 S.E.2d 501

FORENSIC VALUE OF PHYSICAL EVIDENCE

"Every human being carries with him from his cradle to his grave certain physical marks which do not change their character, and by which he can always be identified - and that without shade of doubt or question. These marks are his signature, his physiological autograph, so to speak, and this autograph can not be counterfeited, nor can he disguise it or hide it away, nor can it become illegible by the wear and mutations of time... This autograph consists of the delicate lines or corrugations with which Nature marks the insides of the hands and the soles of the feet."

—Mark Twain, *The Tragedy of Pudd'nhead Wilson*, 1894

"We used to think that our fate was in our stars. Now we know that, in large measure, our fate is in our genes."

—Francis Crick, Co-discoverer, structure of DNA

Chapter Outline

- Fingerprints
- Fingerprint Patterns
- Fingerprint Characteristics
- Fingerprint Comparison
- Footprints, Palmprints
- Lip, Ears, Voiceprints
- Bitemarks
- Shoe Impressions
- Tire Impressions
- Tools and Toolmarks
- Weapons and Ballistics
- Detecting Discharge of Weapons

- Explosives and Explosive Residue
- Soil
- Blood And Body Fluids
- Bloodstain Patterns
- Toxicology Examinations and Drugs
- Hair
- Fibers
- Glass
- DNA
- Questioned Documents and Handwriting Analysis
- Computers and Electronic Data
- Legal Challenges

INTRODUCTION

In Chapter 8, we examined the science of *criminalistics* that is used in the detection of crime and analysis of evidence. In analyzing evidence, we learned the difference between **individual characteristics**, which can identify evidence as having originated with a particular person or source, and **class characteristics**, which offers generalizations about evidence that is common to a group of objects or persons.

In this chapter, we will look at the forensic value of certain types of physical evidence, examining whether analysis of the evidence might provide individual characteristics leading to a positive identification or match, or class characteristics that can place it among a particular group or area.

FINGERPRINTS

At the end of each finger is a rounded area called the **bulb**. These areas contain a number of friction ridges that form a pattern and have characteristics that are different from any other human being. No two humans have the same fingerprint. Even identical twins have different fingerprints. The patterns and characteristics on each finger provide an identification unique to that individual. The palm side of the hands also contains these friction ridges. If a person grabs or touches something at a crime scene, an impression of these friction ridges may be left behind in the form of **latent prints**. The forensic value of fingerprints is the ability to positively identify a person through these patterns and characteristics. Unless altered by injury or surgery, fingerprints never change during a person's lifetime.

Fingerprint Patterns

All fingerprints fall into one of three general patterns or groupings: *arch*, *loop*, and *whorl*.

Arch

In an arch, the friction ridges enter on one side and tend to flow out the other side with a rise or wave in the center (See Exhibit 9.1).

---

individual characteristics
When the characteristics of physical evidence can be identified as having originated with a particular person or source.

class characteristics
When the characteristics of physical evidence are common to a group of objects or persons.

bulb
Rounded area at end of each finger.

latent prints
Fingerprints left at a crime scene, often not readily visible.

arch
Fingerprint pattern in which the friction ridges enter on one side and tend to flow out the other side with a rise or wave in the center.

loop

Fingerprint pattern in which the ridges flow inward and recurve back toward the point of origin.

Loop

In loops, the ridges flow inward and recurve back toward the point of origin (See Exhibit 9.2). Loops are subdivded into two basic types:

1. **Ulnar Loops**: Ridges flow from and recurve toward the little finger (ulnar bone side of hand)
2. **Radial Loops**: Ridges flow from and recurve toward the thumb (radius bone side of hand).

whorl

Fingerprint pattern with recurving ridges that flow in a circle or spiral.

Whorl

Whorl ridges have two delta-shaped divergences with recurving ridges in front of each, like a circle or spiral (See Exhibit 9.3).

Fingerprint Characteristics

Within the patterns of fingerprints are different types of characteristics that can be identified and matched.

type lines

Ridges that determine the pattern area of loops and whorls.

1. Type Lines

Type lines are ridges that determine the pattern area of loops and whorls. Arches lack type lines. The type lines originate as parallel ridges that diverge and surround the pattern area. The divergence is when the two parallel ridges begin to branch out in different directions.

delta

Point on the ridge formation located within the pattern area nearest to the divergence of the type lines.

2. Delta

A delta is a point < or > on the ridge formation located within the pattern area nearest to the divergence of the type lines (See Exhibit 9.4). The delta must be located so that it OPENS toward the center of the pattern: < O.

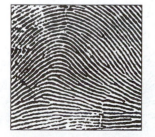

EXHIBIT 9.1   Arch Pattern
Source: FBI

EXHIBIT 9.2   Loop Pattern
Source: FBI

EXHIBIT 9.3   Whorl Pattern
Source: FBI

core
Center of the pattern area.

3. Core

The core is the center of the pattern area. It is within the innermost looping ridge. If the innermost loop has no ending ridge, then the core is placed on the end of the center rod. It is important to locate the core in loops for ridge counting (See Exhibit 9.4). This is not necessary with whorls.

ridge characteristics
Identifying characteristics on the friction ridges of fingerprints.

4. Ridge Characteristics

Ridges have certain basic characteristics that are used in identification (See Exhibit 9.5), including:

- **Ridge Endings** - and short ridges. **/**
- **Bifurcations**: the dividing of one ridge into two or more ridges. **Y**
- **Dots** .
- **Islands** or enclosures. **()**
- **Bridges**: a ridge connecting two parallel ridges.

Fingerprint Comparison

In comparing fingerprints, the latent print found at the crime scene must either be entered into a fingerprint identification system, like the FBI's national fingerprint database, **IAFIS** (Integrated Automated Fingerprint Identification System), or compared to a sample from a known subject or suspect. Comparisons are made based on pattern types, ridge features, and ridge counts. The object is to find corresponding points of comparison.

AFIS
Computerized fingerprint database, *Automated Fingerprint Identification System.*

IAFIS
FBI's national fingerprint database, *Integrated Automated Fingerprint Identification System.*

Many states or regions have their own computerized fingerprint database. These are generally known as **AFIS**, or automated fingerprint identification systems. The FBI's national fingerprint database, **IAFIS**, provides automated fingerprint and latent search capabilities to any law enforcement agency. If a fingerprint is submitted electronically, a search will be conducted and response sent

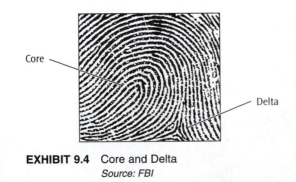

EXHIBIT 9.4 Core and Delta
Source: FBI

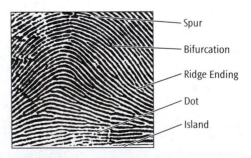

EXHIBIT 9.5 Ridge Characteristics

usually within an hour or two. According to the FBI, IAFIS maintains the largest biometric database in the world, containing the fingerprints and corresponding criminal history information for more than 47 million subjects in its Criminal Master File.[1]

In comparing with a known sample, examiners first look for general pattern similarities and eliminate patterns that are not similar (i.e., loop, arch, whorl) (See Exhibit 9.6). When a pattern is found, examiners look at the ridges for points of matchable characteristics. Generally, 10-12 points of matchable characteristics is required for positive identification. To put this into perspective, 12 points of matchable characteristics can be found in an area as small as a flat end of a pencil eraser!

Limitations of Latent Prints

Although fingerprints can be positively matched with enough point characteristics, it is impossible to determine the age of the print, or the age, race, or sex of the person leaving the print. In addition, investigators cannot identify the occupational groups for the person who left the print.

FOOTPRINTS AND PALMPRINTS

Footprints and palmprints are similar to fingerprints in their uniqueness. Both have individual characteristics that are capable of providing positive identification. Like fingerprints, no two people have the same palmprint or footprint. These prints or partial prints are found mostly at property crimes, usually at the point of entry and departure.

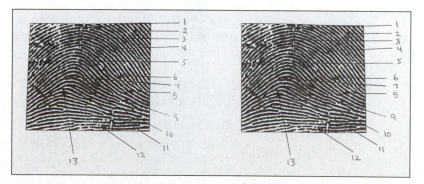

EXHIBIT 9.6   Comparing Matchable Characteristics

LIP, EARS, AND VOICEPRINTS

Lip and ear prints have not yet been accepted in many courts as positive identification, mainly because finding them is still rare and courts have been reluctant to admit them as reliable scientific evidence. Even so, they can yield both class and individual characteristics that can help build circumstantial evidence.

Lip prints and ear prints are usually found in property crimes; ears also in safe burglary; voice usually from telephone-related crimes, such as kidnapping, threats, and extortion. Lip and ear prints are latent and must be lifted, whereas voice must be taped. Voiceprints are compared through *sound spectrographs*, but are still regarded generally in many courts as class characteristics.

BITEMARKS

Bitemarks can be valuable in certain sexual assault cases, child abuse, and some homicides. They have the appearance of indentations and darkened bruising in semicircles on the skin.

Bitemarks can be found on the skin of the victim and also on objects that a suspect may have had in their mouth, like chewing items, apples, sandwiches, cigars, and cigarettes. Bitemarks yield both class and individual characteristics. To collect bitemarks, photograph the area first, then swab for trace evidence and cast with silicone rubber or dust. Bitemarks are compared with bitemarks made by the suspect.

SHOE IMPRESSIONS

Most impressions left by a shoe will have forensic value as evidence. Shoe prints and impressions can yield both class and individual characteristics. Class characteristics can include the size, type of shoe, and determination of the brand and manufacturer of the shoe. When a "known" shoe is obtained, it can be compared with the impression or print left at the crime scene to identify wear characteristics and random, identifying marks. If enough of these wear marks and random characteristics are present, a positive identification can be made (See Exhibit 9.7).

PRACTICE TIP 9.1

Do Not Step Into the Shoes...
Never attempt to step into a shoe print with your own shoe to determine the size of the shoe.

EXHIBIT 9.7   Shoe Print found at Crime Scene

TIRE IMPRESSIONS

Tire impressions yield both class and individual characteristics. Class characteristics can include the size, type of tire and tread, and determination of the brand and manufacturer of the tire. When a "known" tire is discovered, it can be compared with the impression left at the crime scene to identify tread marks and characteristics. If enough of these tread marks and characteristics are present, a positive identification can be made (See Exhibit 9.8).

EXHIBIT 9.8   Tire Impression found at Crime Scene

CSI CHECKLIST 9.1

Lab Report Results

On shoe or tire comparisons, generally lab report results will state one of the following:

❑ Insufficient detail or quality for comparison.
❑ The shoe or tire did not make the track.
❑ The shoe or tire could not be excluded as making the track.
❑ The shoe or tire could have made the track.
❑ The shoe or tire is highly probable as making the track.
❑ The shoe or tire did make the track.

TOOLS AND TOOLMARKS

Tools have microscopic characteristics and differences from their manufacturing that can leave unique toolmarks when used. These toolmarks are impressions left by a tool's shape, size, and the striations on the surface it comes in contact with. When the harder tool comes into contact with a softer object, like a door jamb, the softer area will yield to the harder one, resulting in an identifying mark or impression being produced upon the softer area's surface. These impressions are called toolmarks and are of two primary types: *striated* and *impressed*. Toolmarks yield both class and individual characteristics. Depending on the type of toolmark, we can tell the nature of a toolmark, type of tool used, the identification by manufacturer or group, any unusual and individualized characteristics, and how the tool was used. We can also make an individual comparison and match with a suspect tool. A toolmark is not compared to the suspect tool itself, but to a standard of comparison sample impression made with the suspect tool.

Striated Toolmark

striated toolmarks
Parallel striation markings produced when a tool is brought into contact with a softer surface and there is lateral movement between the surfaces at the moment of contact.

Striated toolmarks are markings produced when a tool is brought into contact with a softer surface and there is lateral movement between the surfaces at the moment of contact. The marks produced are a series of parallel striation markings, such as pry marks found on metal window or door frames, or the scrape marks caused by pliers. Striated toolmarks are generally of more forensic evidentiary value than the impressed toolmarks because striated toolmarks can be positively matched to a specific tool (See Exhibit 9.9).

EXHIBIT 9.9 *Comparison of Striation Marks*

Impressed Toolmarks

impressed toolmarks
Negative image or impression left by a tool that is brought into contact with a softer surface and there is no lateral movement between the objects at the moment of contact.

Impressed toolmarks are produced when a tool is brought into contact with a softer surface and there is no lateral movement between the objects at the moment of contact. The mark or marks produced are a negative image of the harder object. Examples of this include the impression of a pry tool (like a flathead screwdriver) in a wood frame, or the impression of a hammer head. Unless an impressed toolmark shows specific identifiable wear or damage markings, it is generally said to have class characteristics that would be consistent with a particular group of tools.

CSI CHECKLIST 9.2

Purpose of Tool and Toolmark Examination

❑ To determine the type of tool that made a toolmark or impression.
❑ To determine if a specific tool made a particular toolmark.
❑ The examination of toolmarks on different objects to determine if they were made by the same tool.
❑ The examination of fragments of tools to see if they can be physically matched with a particular tool.

WEAPONS AND BALLISTICS

ballistics
Science of projectiles in motion; used to examine firearms and the bullets fired from them.

Ballistics is the science of projectiles in motion and is used to examine firearms and the bullets fired from them. Because a bullet is larger than the diameter of the gun's bore, as it passes thru the barrel, "lands" grip it and cause it to rotate, causing individualized striations, or parallel scratch lines, of the bullet. In addition to the identifying striation marks on the bullet, there may also be identifying marks made on the fired cartridge case, which are caused by the firing pin, extractor, or ejector of the firearm (See Exhibit 9.10).

EXHIBIT 9.10   Comparison of Marks on Cartridge Cases

trajectory
Path of a bullet.

Ballistics allows us to determine both individual and class characteristics in the examination of firearms and bullets. With firearms, we can identify a bullet, shells, distance at which fired, position of shooter, and the ownership of the weapon. It is also possible to restore obliterated serial numbers. With a bullet, we can compare with other bullets to see if it was fired from the same gun, the distance fired, and the **trajectory**, or path of the bullet (See Exhibit 9.11).

According to the FBI lab, an analysis may yield one of three results: it may "positively conclude that the bullet or cartridge case was or was not fired by a particular firearm..., that there are not sufficient individual microscopic marks of value ... for identification purposes, or that the condition of the firearm precludes the possibility of making an identification."[2] From shot pellets and shotgun slugs, the type and size of shot and gauge of the slug can be determined. However, the shot cannot be matched to a specific shotgun barrel.

IBIS
Integrated Ballistic Identification System.

The FBI and Bureau of Alcohol, Tobacco, and Firearms (BATF) operate a national ballistics identification system, **IBIS**, which has automated database files and information on bullets and cartridge casings.

KNIVES AND KNIFE WOUNDS

Knives yield more class characteristics, but there are many questions that can be answered through the examination of knives and knife wounds. With knives, we can compare wounds, direction of force, position of assailant, probable sex, strength, and which hand held the weapon.

EXHIBIT 9.11   Ballistics Comparison
Source: FBI

Detecting Discharge of Weapons

There are tests associated with the field of weapons and ballistics that have forensic value in detecting whether a person has held or discharged a weapon. These are generally the *gunshot residue test* and the trace *metal detection technique*.

Gunshot Residue Test

gunshot residue (gsr) test
Detects the presence of gunshot residue from a fired weapon.

A weapon that is fired expels microscopic materials and vapor that contain elements of most cartridge primer mixtures, called *gunshot residue*. This residue can be detected through the use, within a limited time, of a **gunshot residue (GSR) test**. Although there are presumptive field tests available for use at crime scenes, more thorough testing and analysis is generally performed in the lab on a scanning electron microscope or using atomic absorption analysis. There is a limitation, however, to most GSR tests. Due to fragility of elements, the GSR must be collected within five hours of firearm discharge. Also, very few .22 rimfire cartridges contain the elements.

Trace Metal Detection Technique

trace metal detection technique (tmdt)
Field test that determines whether a person has held a metallic object such as a knife, pipe, or firearm.

The **trace metal detection technique (TMDT)** is a field test that helps to determine whether a person has held a metallic object such as a knife, pipe, or firearm. To conduct this test, a subject's hand is first sprayed with a test solution and the hand is examined under a short-wave ultraviolet lamp. Metallic traces on the hand will appear in colors varying with the metal compound detected. Pattern shapes also may appear, showing a pistol grip or a metal pipe. Any images discovered can then be recorded on color film, videotape, or digital media. The limitation of the TMDT is time. The TMDT should be conducted within four hours of the crime. If the GSR is also given, it should be conducted first.

EXPLOSIVES AND EXPLOSIVE RESIDUE

Evidence from explosive devices can provide valuable forensic information that yields both class and individual characteristics. Explosives can be examined to identify the components used to construct the device such as wiring, switches, batteries, detonators, and fuses. The main charge can be identified, as well as how the bomb or explosive device was constructed, and the specific assembly techniques employed by the builder(s) of the device. Explosive residue can be analyzed to determine the composition of the substances used, and the type of explosives.

SOIL

Soil can be an important investigative tool or piece of evidence in many types of crimes. It is especially important in homicide cases, or when the body has been moved. Soil yields class characteristics only, but analysis can narrow it down to a general location. Soil examinations can determine whether soils share a common origin by comparing color, texture, and composition.

density gradient tube technique
Used to compare soil specimens.

The **Density Gradient Tube Technique** is used to compare soil specimens where glass tubes are filled with different layers, mixing two particular liquids of different densities. When soil is added, its particles will sink to the portion of the tube that has a density of equal value and the particle will remain suspended at that point. Soil can also be examined through other methods to determine mineral content and subparticles within.

BLOOD AND BODY FLUIDS

Blood can have significant forensic value as evidence. Through DNA testing of blood, positive identification can be made. However, even without DNA testing, blood analysis can yield valuable forensic information. Most importantly, a stain can be analyzed to determine the presence or absence of blood. This analysis can determine whether the blood is human or animal.

Although blood analysis cannot, without DNA testing, adequately identify a person as the source, it can be useful in initially eliminating suspects because of different bloodgrouping. Blood is grouped according to four general types: 43% of the population has Type O; 42% have Type A; 12% Type B; and only 3% have Type AB blood.

Bloodstain Patterns

Another very important feature of blood evidence can be found in analyzing the patterns of blood splatters (also called blood splatter) and bloodstains discovered at the crime scene. Blood splatter and bloodstain pattern evidence have significant forensic value. These patterns can show direction of force, velocity, and the position of assailant. They can aid in the reconstruction of the events that happened to cause the blood splatter patterns (See Exhibit 9.12).

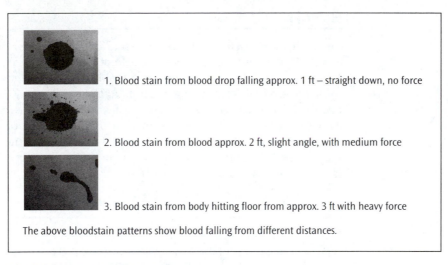

1. Blood stain from blood drop falling approx. 1 ft – straight down, no force

2. Blood stain from blood approx. 2 ft, slight angle, with medium force

3. Blood stain from body hitting floor from approx. 3 ft with heavy force

The above bloodstain patterns show blood falling from different distances.

EXHIBIT 9.12   Bloodstain Patterns

CSI CHECKLIST 9.3

Information Needed on Crime Scene Bloodstains

❑   Location of bloodstain.
❑   Size of bloodstain.
❑   Shape of bloodstain.
❑   Color of bloodstain.
❑   Kind of material that is bloodstained.

TOXICOLOGY AND DRUGS

Toxicology testing and analysis can determine the presence of drugs and poisons, and identify the type, mixture, and source of these chemicals. This can not only provide individualizing evidence in some cases (like possession of an illegal drug), but also determine the cause or circumstances in death investigations involving drugs or poisons. At the crime scene, certain drugs can be given a "field test" using a kit that will change to a blue color and give a "presumptive" reading to indicate illegal drugs. A full analysis can be made in the laboratory to determine the specific drug or combination of drugs.

HAIR

Through DNA testing, hair can be used for identifying characteristics and may serve as positive identification of its source. However, even without DNA testing, hair also yields important class characteristics and can offer strong circumstantial evidence. From hair, we can determine whether it is human or animal, the part of body it came from, whether it was bleached or dyed, freshly cut, pulled out or burned; and whether there was blood or semen on it. The animal species and family can be determined from hair analysis. In humans, the race can be determined.

FIBERS

Fibers have class characteristics that can be tested to determine type and origin of a fabric, such as whether it came from synthetic, wool, or cotton source. Fiber composition and construction can be examined and compared, and it can be tested to see whether it matches a comparison garment in type, pigment, manufacturer, and color. Fibers can be an excellent source of circumstantial evidence to help prove a case.

GLASS

Glass fragments are very valuable as forensic evidence. Glass can be examined and compared to determine whether the fragments originated from a broken source of glass. The direction and force of the breaking of glass can be determined by examining the glass fracture lines. For example, force causes glass to compress on the side that the force was applied and to stretch on the opposite side.

From the point that force was applied, circle cracks radiate out to form circles around the point of the force (called **concentric fractures**). Triangular lines radiate outward from point of impact and are called **radial fractures**. On the inside, there are parallel stress lines that curve downward toward the opposite side of the glass, indicating which side the force originated from. This can establish whether someone was breaking in to or out of a structure through a window or a door with glass (See Exhibit 9.13).

A side view can show the ridges that form from these fractures. The crime lab can examine these to determine direction of force. This examination can also enable a criminalist to determine the sequence or order of fractures occurring in a piece of glass, which can be particularly helpful in shooting investigations.

concentric fractures
Circle cracks in glass, radiating out to form circles around the point of impact.

radial fractures
Triangular lines in glass that radiate outward from point of impact.

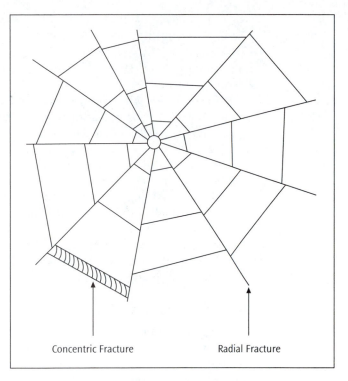

Concentric Fracture   Radial Fracture

EXHIBIT 9.13   Radial and Concentric Glass Fractures

DNA
Deoxyribonucleic acid,
found in the cells of every
person and containing a
unique genetic code that
can be profiled for posi-
tive identification of that
individual.

DNA

In 1865, Gregor Mendel conducted cross-breeding experiments
with peas, concluding that organisms carry and transmit heredi-
tary elements, or genes, to their offspring. His findings became the
basis of the theoretical principles of genetics, but it was not until the
next century that scientists recognized the existence of deoxyribonucleic acid, or DNA as we call it today, and its almost exclusive
location within the chromosome. Advances in recombinant DNA
techniques in the early 1970s provided the basis for analyzing the
DNA of individuals for identification purposes.

Scientists found that every human possesses a unique genetic
code, which carries the genetic "blueprint" for that individual. Chromosomes are used to hold this code and these are made of the
organic substance deoxyribonucleic acid, known as DNA. Geneti-
cally normal humans have 46 chromosomes in each body cell, 23
inherited from each parent. With the exception of identical twins, no
two people have the same DNA patterns.

The cells of each species contain the same number of chromosomes and within each organism, the DNA of each cell is identical. Any one cell of a person could provide a match with another cell from the same person. DNA found in hair would be identical to DNA found in blood.

In the 1980s, a British geneticist, Alec Jeffreys, developed a technique for DNA Fingerprinting. This technique was first used in a paternity case and later used in a rape-murder case in Leicester County, England, when a suspect who had confessed to two murders was exonerated when DNA tests demonstrated that his DNA did not match that found in traces of semen and blood on the victims. Police then took blood samples from more than 5,000 males before identifying the murderer and rapist of the teenagers. This murder case and the use of DNA was the subject for author Joseph Wambaugh's 1989 non-fiction book, *The Blooding*.[3] In 1987, the Bristol Crown Court in England became the first court in the world to convict on DNA evidence when it sentenced a man to prison for rape.

Forensic Value of DNA

Today, DNA has become a primary forensic tool in the identification of suspects from skin cells and bodily fluids or substances collected at the crime scene. Whether it is perspiration from inside a mask or cap, or saliva from a drinking glass, in chewing gum, or on a cigarette butt, DNA evidence can be retrieved and examined for identification of its genetic code. We can examine cells from different parts of the body, including bloodstains and hairs to "read" this genetic code and profile a DNA fingerprint to use it in eliminating suspects or helping to identify them.

The results of this DNA analysis of questioned samples are compared with the results of DNA analysis of known samples. This analysis can associate victims and suspects with each other or with a crime scene. There are two sources of DNA used in forensic analyses. Nuclear DNA (nDNA) is typically analyzed in evidence containing blood, semen, saliva, body tissues, and hairs that have tissue at their root ends. Mitochondrial DNA (mtDNA) is typically analyzed in evidence containing naturally shed hairs, hair fragments, bones, and teeth. Whereas mtDNA analyses do not provide the discrimination potential of some nuclear DNA tests, mtDNA data often are the only information that examiners can gather from degraded evidence, which is either old or has been exposed to the environment for a significant period of time.

CODIS

One of the ways that crime labs and law enforcement agencies can identify DNA profiles is through a national system of DNA identification called **CODIS**. CODIS is an FBI national database that allows federal, state, and local crime labs to exchange and compare DNA profiles.

CODIS
FBI national DNA database.

PRACTICE TIP 9.2

Want More Info On DNA?

Go to this online government source for more information on DNA.

http://www.dna.gov

QUESTIONED DOCUMENTS AND HANDWRITING ANALYSIS

Although still contested in many courts as to its reliability, questioned documents and handwriting analysis can yield both class and individual characteristics. Some handwriting may contain sufficient individualizing features to allow an analyst to conclude that it came from a specific source. Results may be inconclusive when there is a limited sample to analyze, when there has been a significant lapse of time between when the questioned and known writing was done, or when either writing was disguised. Even when this conclusion cannot be made, the examination of handwriting or document characteristics can sometimes determine its origin or authenticity, and can often serve to build a powerful case of circumstantial evidence through its class characteristics. Handwriting analysis cannot determine the age, sex, personality, or intent of its writer.

Questioned typewriting can be matched with the typewriter used to produce the writing, based on the individual characteristics that formed over continued use, as well as characteristics developed during the manufacturing process. Writing from computer word processing programs, printed on inkjet or laser printers will yield class characteristics. Photocopies can generally be matched with the photocopier machine that produced the copy.

COMPUTERS AND ELECTRONIC DATA

Evidence retrieved from computers and electronic data are generally admissible in court. The forensic value in this evidence is in associating or linking certain information retrieved from the computer to the owner or user of the computer, or as evidence of a particular crime involving computers. Generally, this would involve a form of class characteristics that would constitute circumstantial evidence. Information and evidence that can be retrieved from a computer includes:

- Specific files can be retrieved, including deleted data and converted files
- Type of files can be determined
- Time and sequence that files were created can be determined
- Passwords can be recovered and used to decrypt encoded files
- Source code can be analyzed

LEGAL CHALLENGES

In addition to the evidentiary challenges we will discuss in the following chapters dealing with expert testimony, or scientific evidence and testing, legal challenges to forensic evidence can range from how it was collected or preserved to whether a particular test was performed properly. As we learned earlier, the collection and preservation of forensic evidence is extremely important. Many cases have been weakened or lost due to improper collection techniques or a breakdown in the chain of custody or preservation of the evidence. According to many experts, forensic testing presents numerous opportunities for error and can be the subject of legal challenges.[4] One problem involves the integrity of the evidence samples found at the crime scene. Samples can be mixed with foreign debris or with DNA from other sources that may distort analysis. Samples, like other types of crime scene evidence, may be too small, too old, or damaged. Because some samples may be easily contaminated, a reliable chain of custody must be established.

In a New York case, the court excluded DNA test results in a murder trial because the laboratory improperly discounted as nonhuman contaminants two bands of DNA that did not match. In weighing the admissibility of the test results, the court looked at three factors:

(1) whether the theory of DNA testing is scientifically accepted;

(2) whether the techniques and experiments associated with DNA testing are scientifically accepted; and

(3) whether in the particular case at issue, the testing lab adequately performed the accepted scientific techniques.

The court acknowledged the first 2 points, but held that the testing procedures were not properly performed. [5]

SUMMARY

In this chapter, we looked at the forensic value of certain types of physical evidence, including whether analysis of the evidence might provide individual characteristics leading to a positive identification or match, or class characteristics that can place it among a particular group or area. At the top for individual characteristics were DNA and fingerprints. Palmprints and footprints also provided these individual characteristics, as did some shoe and tire prints, toolmarks, and firearms examination. Evidence having value only as class characteristics included fibers and soil. Legal challenges to forensic evidence can run from how it was collected or preserved to whether a particular test was performed properly.

KEY TERMS

AFIS	IBIS
Arch	Impressed Toolmarks
Ballistics	Individual Characteristics
Bulb	Latent Prints
Class Characteristics	Loop
CODIS	Radial Fractures
Concentric Fractures	Ridge Characteristics
Core	Striated Toolmarks
Delta	Trace Metal Detection Technique (TMDT)
DensityGradient Tube Technique	Trajectory
DNA	Type Lines
Gunshot Residue Test (GSR)	Whorl
IAFIS	

REVIEW QUESTIONS

1. Describe the forensic value of fingerprints.
2. Identify the fingerprint patterns and some of the identifiable characteristics of these patterns.

3. Explain how fingerprints are compared and identified.
4. Describe the forensic value for each of the following types of evidence:
   a. Footprints
   b. Palmprints
   c. Lip prints
   d. Bitemarks
   e. Shoe and Tire Impressions
   f. Tools and Toolmarks
   g. Glass
   h. Soil and Fibers
5. Identify the sources of DNA at a crime scene and assess its forensic value in crime scene investigation.
6. Discuss some of the legal challenges to forensic evidence.

CRITICAL THINKING QUESTIONS 9.1

1. What is the importance of understanding the forensic value of physical evidence found at a crime scene?
2. What is the importance of class characteristics if they cannot provide positive identification? Give examples.
3. How does the forensic value of evidence discussed in this chapter influence the collection of evidence at a crime scene?

FORENSIC RESEARCH USING THE INTERNET

Search the Internet for specific Web sites or articles dealing with the forensic value of physical evidence at a crime scene. Identify the physical evidence covered and describe whether the forensic value is class or individual.

PRACTICE SKILLS:

Practice what you have learned in the following crime scene problems:

Crime Scene Analysis 9.1

1. Compare the prints in Exhibit 9.14 to see how many points of comparison you can draw.

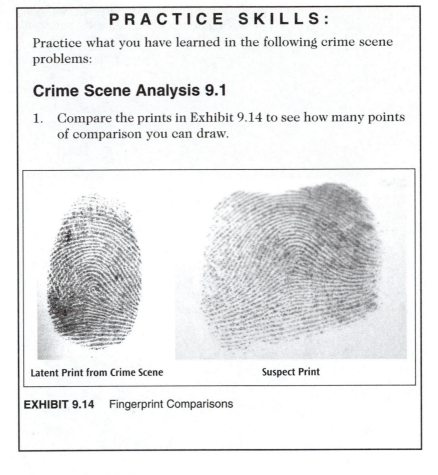

Latent Print from Crime Scene   Suspect Print

EXHIBIT 9.14   Fingerprint Comparisons

WEB SITES

Federal website on DNA
http://www.dna.gov

ENDNOTES

[1] Federal Bureau of Investigation. 2003. Handbook of Forensic Services. Quantico, VA: FBI Laboratory

[2] Federal Bureau of Investigation. 2003. Handbook of Forensic Services. Quantico, VA: FBI Laboratory

[3] Wambaugh, J. 1989. *The Blooding.* New York: Bantam.

[4] See, for example, Attorney Kim Kruglick's Web site on *A Beginner's Primer on the Investigation of Forensic Evidence* http://www.kruglaw.com

[5] *People v. Castro*, 545 NYS 2d 985 (1989)

CHAPTER **10**

FORENSIC EVIDENCE AND TESTING

"An expert, as the word imports, is one having had experience. No clearly defined rule is to be found in the books what constitutes an expert. Much depends upon the nature of the question in regard to which an opinion is asked."

—Oil Co. v. Gilson, 63 Pa. St. 146, 150 (1869)

"For every expert there is an equal and opposite expert."

—Arthur C. Clarke, 1998, who credits the quote to "Anonymous"

Chapter Outline

- Introduction: From Crime Lab to Courtroom
- What is Forensic Evidence and Testing?
- Importance of Forensic Evidence and Testing
- Admissibility Governed By Evidence Law
- Expert Witnesses
- Tests Used by Courts to Determine Admissibility
- *Daubert* Standard
- Effect of *Daubert* Decision
- Forensic Experts Who are Not Scientists
- Judge as Gatekeeper
- Abuse of Discretion
- Legal and Evidentiary Challenges

INTRODUCTION: FROM CRIME LAB TO COURTROOM

In previous chapters, we discovered the importance of physical evidence in crime scene investigation. We looked at how this evidence is found, identified, collected, and preserved.

We looked at the important role that the crime lab, its forensic personnel, and their sophisticated instrumentation play in the analysis and scientific testing of physical evidence. We examined how this analysis involved the concepts of *Set Theory*, *Concept of Identity, Probability Analysis*, and *Matchable Characteristics,* and how the application of these concepts helped to determine the forensic value of crime scene evidence.

In this chapter, we will look at the issues surrounding the admissibility of this forensic evidence and scientific testing, as testified to by crime scene and forensic experts. We will examine what the courts have determined as the legal *standard* and requirements for qualifying these experts and the results of their scientific testing. We will also look at where these legal standards came from, and how they are applied today in crime scene investigation.

CRIME SCENE REVIEW

Do you remember what these concepts mean and how they are used in crime scene investigation?

- ❏ Concept of Identity
- ❏ Set Theory
- ❏ Probability Analysis
- ❏ Matchable Characteristics

WHAT IS FORENSIC EVIDENCE AND TESTING?

forensic evidence and testing
scientific evidence and testing
Crime scene evidence and subsequent analysis of it that has a scientific or highly technical basis, requiring an expert witness with specialized knowledge to assist the trier of fact to understand it.

Forensic evidence and testing is the crime scene evidence and subsequent analysis of it that has a scientific or highly technical basis. It is also referred to as **scientific evidence and testing**. It requires an expert witness with specialized knowledge to assist the trier of fact to understand it. For example, forensic evidence includes (and tests analyze) weapons, blood, drugs, tire tracks, tool marks, fingerprints, and DNA. Tests scientifically determine the level of intoxication through a person's breath, blood, or urine. There are ballistics and various types of print comparisons, trace evidence detection, document examination, and voice identification. These are all examples of forensic evidence and testing that have undergone challenges to both the validity of the testing and the results. These challenges are generally directed toward the forensic expert witness who testifies in an attempt to establish a foundation and validity of the testing and results. They can also be directed toward the testing instrument or machine that is used by the forensic expert.

PRACTICE TIP 10.1

Reference Manual on Scientific Evidence

Check out this valuable reference manual on scientific evidence at the Federal Judicial Center:

Reference Manual on Scientific Evidence:
http://www.fjc.gov/

IMPORTANCE OF FORENSIC EVIDENCE AND TESTING

Whenever physical evidence has been collected from a crime scene, suspect, victim, or their environments, the analysis of that evidence becomes essential to the outcome of the case. Does it help to establish that a crime has been committed and to show the *corpus delicti* or *elements* of the crime? Does it help to identify a suspect, associate a suspect to the crime or crime scene, or exclude a suspect? Does it help to prove that a particular suspect committed a crime? Does it help to show the *who*, *what*, *when*, *where*, *how*, and *why* of crime scene investigation?

Consider the following case:

At 2 a.m., police respond to a report by neighbors of a gunshot heard at a private residence. When police arrive, they notice the front door open and the body of a female wearing pajamas inside on the hallway floor. The victim has contusions on her face and hands, and appears to have been shot in the stomach. A kitchen knife is found near the victim. The knife has bloodstains on it and several partial bloody fingerprints on the blade. Blood splatters are observed along the hallway floor leading from the kitchen. There are pools of blood splatters on the kitchen floor and blood on the wall. Small traces of dirt, several different fibers, and a hair not belonging to the victim are found on the kitchen floor and on the victim's hands. A window in the kitchen is open and the glass broken outward. Pry marks are observed on the outside of the window sill. A palmprint is also found on the sill. On the ground outside, shoe prints are discovered. Nothing else appears to have been disturbed inside the house or outside.

Forensic evidence and testing will play an essential role in the successful investigation and prosecution of this case. An autopsy of the victim will be conducted to determine time and cause of death, and to search for other evidence. The palmprint and fingerprints will be lifted and analyzed. The blood and hair will be analyzed and subjected to DNA testing. All of these could be used to identify a suspect. The bullet found in the victim will be examined and ballistics testing may determine what type of weapon was used. If the weapon is located, the bullet could be matched with it. The *trajectory* or path the bullet took through the victim's body will be analyzed to determine how close the suspect was standing when the shot was fired. Analysis might also reveal how tall the suspect is, and whether the suspect held the weapon in the right or left hand. The pry marks on the window could be matched with the tool used if the tool is recovered. Analysis of the blood splatters can reveal much about how and where the victim was standing, how the victim fell, whether the victim was crawling, walking, or running through the hallway, and whether there was a struggle. The fibers and dirt can be analyzed to determine their characteristics and general origin.

To be admissible in court, the results of the above analyses and testing will require testimony by each of the forensic experts who conducted or interpreted the tests. For the above case, this could involve several different expert witnesses, including a medical examiner, fingerprint technician, criminalist, ballistics examiner, and pry mark specialist. Prior to being allowed to testify, each of these forensic specialists will need to be qualified as an expert witness. The expert and his or her testimony regarding forensic evidence and testing will need to be admissible under the legal standards established by the rules of evidence and the courts.

ADMISSIBILITY GOVERNED BY EVIDENCE LAW

The admissibility of forensic witnesses, evidence, and testing is governed by rules and laws of evidence. **Evidence law** is a body of statutory rules and court decisions that help to govern conduct and determine what will be admissible in certain legal proceedings and trials. The federal courts use the **Federal Rules of Evidence**, enacted into law by Congress in 1975. States have their own set of evidence rules, although many states model their rules after the federal rules. **Case law**, through court decisions, helps to refine and interpret many of these evidence rules.

evidence law
Body of statutory rules and court decisions that help to govern conduct and determine what will be admissible in certain legal proceedings and trials.

Federal Rules of Evidence
Statutory evidentiary rules enacted by Congress in 1975 and used in all federal courts, and as a model for many states.

case law
Judge-made law through court decisions.

expert witness
A witness qualified by specialized skills or knowledge whose testimony or opinion can assist the trier of fact to better understand evidence in issue.

Expert Witnesses

Rules of evidence define and govern expert witnesses. According to the definitions of most evidence rules, an **expert witness** is one who is qualified by special knowledge, skills, experience, training, and/or education.[1] An expert witness can testify to and give opinions on matters that are outside of the knowledge of the average person, and that require special experience or knowledge of witnesses skilled in that particular science, art, or trade. These opinions can be based on first-hand observation, like a criminalist who examined and later performed tests on evidence from the crime scene, or it can be based on a hypothetical question posed to the expert, based on her training and expertise. (See Exhibit 10.1.)

TESTS USED BY COURTS TO DETERMINE ADMISSIBILITY

The three primary tests used by courts to determine the admissibility of expert testimony for forensic evidence and testing are the *General Acceptance Test* (also called the *Frye* Test), the *Reliability Test*, which in some states is a modification of or has been combined with the *Frye* text, and the *Daubert Standard*.

EXHIBIT 10.1   Examples of Rules for Admitting Expert Testimony on Forensic Evidence and Scientific Testing

New Jersey Rules of Evidence
Rule 702. Testimony by Experts
If scientific, technical, or other specialized knowledge will assist the trier of fact to understand the evidence or to determine a fact in issue, a witness qualified as an expert by knowledge, skill, experience, training, or education may testify thereto in the form of an opinion or otherwise.
California Evidence Code
Section 720 (a). A person is qualified to testify as an expert if he has special knowledge, skill, experience, training, or education sufficient to qualify him as an expert on the subject to which his testimony relates. Against the objection of a party, such special knowledge, skill, experience, training, or education must be shown before the witness may testify as an expert.
   (b) A witness' special knowledge, skill, experience, training, or education may be shown by any otherwise admissible evidence, including his own testimony.

General Acceptance Test

For more than 70 years, the accepted standard in this country for the admissibility of forensic evidence and testing was called the **Frye Test**, or **General Acceptance Test**. This test was based on the 1923 landmark case in which a federal court held that the results of a "scientific test" could be admitted if the test had "gained general acceptance in the particular field in which it belongs."[2]

Frye Test
General
Acceptance Test
Scientific evidence is admissible only if the principle upon which it is based is "sufficiently established to have general acceptance in the field to which it belongs."

CSI CHECKLIST 10.1

Guideline for Admitting Forensic Expert's Opinion under Frye General Acceptance Test

❑ Method of analysis that forensic expert's opinion is made from is sufficiently established to have gained general acceptance in the particular field in which it belongs

---

Frye Sets Precedent

precedent
A rule of law established by a court decision that sets a principle or is followed by other courts.

The 1923 Frye decision established a **precedent** that expert opinion based on a scientific technique was inadmissible unless the technique is "generally accepted" as reliable in the relevant scientific community. This required that "the thing from which the deduction is made must be sufficiently established to have gained general acceptance in the particular field in which it belongs."[3]

The *Frye* or general acceptance test was the standard for determining admissibility of novel scientific evidence at trial for more than 70 years. It is still followed by some states. For example, in Illinois, the "admission of expert testimony is governed by the Frye standard: whether the methodology or scientific principle upon which the opinion is based is sufficiently established to have gained general acceptance in the particular field in which it belongs."[4] Another Illinois court set forth what may be considered in determining the admissibility of evidence under Frye:

1. Scientific publications and law review articles
2. Prior court decisions in Illinois and other jurisdictions
3. Practical applications of the technique or method
4. Testimony or affidavits of experts regarding
   (a) the acceptance of the technique or method within the relevant scientific community (b) the attitudes of their fellow scientists[5]

Other states still use *Frye*, but in a modified form or in conjunction with the *Reliability Test*.

PRACTICE TIP 10.2

Does Your State Use the Frye Test?

Use one of the following Web sites to find out if your state's rules of evidence use the Frye general acceptance test:
Legal Information Institute (LII), Cornell Law School.
http://www.law.cornell.edu/states/listing.html
FindLaw. http://guide.lp.findlaw.com/casecode/

Reliability Test

Reliability Test
Determines admissibility of forensic evidence and testing by weighing probative value and reliability of scientific testing against the test's potential for prejudice

After the Federal Rules of Evidence were adopted, many courts began to refine the Frye general acceptance test to also ensure that the scientific testing was reliable and that the results were relevant. This newer federal standard was called the **Reliability Test**. Along with this newer test for determining scientific evidence, there was a growing controversy as to what effect Federal Rule 702 had on the Frye principle. At the time, this rule provided that a witness could testify and provide an opinion as an expert if qualified by "knowledge, skill, experience, training, or education," and "if scientific, technical, or other specialized knowledge will assist the trier of fact to understand the evidence."[6]

Reliability Test Increasingly Used

probative
Tends to prove something.

The Reliability test, which began being increasingly used by federal courts in the late 1980s to early 1990s, weighed the reliability and **probative** value of scientific testing against the test's potential for prejudice. In a 1985 Third Circuit case that laid the groundwork for this new test, the court stated that the admission of scientific evidence requires an examination of:

1. the soundness and reliability of the process or technique used
2. whether admitting the evidence would overwhelm, confuse, or mislead the jury
3. the proffered connection between the scientific research or test result to be presented and particular disputed factual issues in the case.[7]

In reaching this determination, the court looked to the rule requiring evidence to be relevant[8] and weighed it against the rule that even relevant evidence may be excluded if its probative value is substantially outweighed by the danger of unfair prejudice or confusion to the jury.[9]

Another example of the newer test being used in federal courts was a 1990 decision involving the introduction of DNA evidence. In this case, a court rejected a strict application of *Frye* in favor of the flexible approach afforded by the Reliability Test. The court concluded that the "appropriate considerations for the admission of novel scientific evidence were the same as those used to determine the admissibility of other evidence." The court went on to say that this test is "inherently a balancing one that weighs the probativeness, materiality, and reliability of the evidence against the tendency to mislead or confuse the jury, or unfairly prejudice the defendant." The court proceeded to outline factors to be considered when assessing whether a particular scientific technique is reliable:

1. The potential rate of error
2. The existence and maintenance of standards
3. The care with which the scientific technique has been employed and whether it is susceptible to abuse
4. Whether there are analogous relationships with other types of scientific techniques that are routinely admitted into evidence
5. The presence of failsafe characteristics

The court reasoned that one of the important characteristics of the reliability test was that it provided a "flexible standard that adapts to the exigencies of a particular scientific technique and case. Thus, when a scientific technique is more likely to mislead or confuse the jury, the test requires that a proportionally stronger showing of reliability must be made..."[10]

In 1990, another federal court looked even further for a proper foundation for any scientific testing to be admitted into evidence. The court adopted the following requirements:

1. Whether the evidence is generally accepted by the scientific community
2. Whether the testing procedures used are generally accepted if performed properly
3. Whether the testing was performed properly
4. Whether the evidence is more prejudicial than probative
5. Whether the statistics used to determine probability of someone having the same genetic characteristics is more probative than prejudicial[11]

CSI CHECKLIST 10.2

Checklist for Admitting Forensic Expert's Opinion under Reliability Test

❑ Scientific, technical, or other specialized knowledge will assist the trier of fact to understand the evidence or to determine a fact in issue

❑ Expert opinion is based on this scientific, technical, or other specialized knowledge

❑ Expert is qualified by knowledge, skill, experience, training, or education

❑ Basis for analysis and opinion rests on a reliable foundation

Reliability Test Used with Frye

Some states today use the *Reliability Test* in conjunction with or to modify *Frye*. For example, for new scientific methods and testing, Michigan as used the *Davis-Frye* Test, based on *Frye* and the Michigan case, *People v. Davis*.[12] The *Davis-Frye* test requires novel scientific methods be shown to have gained general acceptance in the scientific community to which it belongs before being admitted as evidence at trial. To be admissible, expert testimony must comply with a three-part test. First, the expert must be qualified. Second, the evidence must provide the trier of fact a better understanding of the evidence or assist in determining a fact in issue. Finally, the evidence must be from a recognized discipline. [13]

California uses the *Kelly* test.[14] Under the standard set forth in *Kelly,* "evidence based upon the application of a new scientific technique such as DNA profiling may be admitted only after the reliability of the method has been foundationally established, usually by the testimony of an expert witness who first has been properly qualified."[15] The *Kelly* test for new scientific methods requires the proponent of the evidence to:

1. Establish that the new technique or method is sufficiently established to have gained general acceptance in the particular field to which it belongs
2. Offer the testimony of a properly qualified expert regarding the technique and its application
3. Establish that correct scientific procedures were used in the case in question[16]

CASE

People v. Clevenger

Court of Appeal of California, Fifth Appellate District

2003 Cal. App. Unpub. LEXIS 11395 (2003)

Crime Scene Investigation

The victim, owner of a real estate investment office, was found bound and gagged with duct tape, stabbed, and strangled with his necktie. Based in part on fingerprint evidence collected at the crime scene, a woman who worked for the victim was tried and convicted of murder in the commission of a kidnapping.

Legal Issue

Defense attorneys attempted to exclude the fingerprint evidence as failing to meet guidelines for scientific evidence, pursuant to the *Kelly* test.

Holding of the Court

The California court found that "Fingerprint analysis is not a "new scientific technique." The California Supreme Court has repeatedly held, over a span of 57 years, that "fingerprints are the strongest evidence of identity of a person."[17]

Daubert Standard

An adaptation of the Reliability Test for determining the admissibility of scientific evidence by weighing probative value of scientific testing and its reliability against the test's potential for prejudice.

Daubert Standard

By the early 1990s, the federal courts and the states that followed the federal rules, had drawn battle lines over which test to use, the *Frye* precedent or the newer Reliability Test. Finally, in a landmark 1993 decision, the U.S. Supreme Court unanimously rejected the *Frye* test as a basis for determining the admissibility of scientific expert testimony. The Court established a new standard based on the Reliability Test, Relevancy, and Federal Rule 702. This became known as the **Daubert Standard**.[18]

CASE

Daubert v. Merrell Dow Pharmaceuticals, Inc.

United States Supreme Court

509 U.S. 579 (1993)

"...'general acceptance' is not a necessary precondition to the admissibility of scientific evidence under the Federal Rules of Evidence, but the Rules of Evidence, especially Rule 702, do assign to the trial judge the task of ensuring that an expert's testimony both rests on a reliable foundation and is relevant to the task at hand. Pertinent evidence based on scientifically valid principles will satisfy those demands..."

Effect Of Daubert Decision

The court in *Daubert* believed that the *Frye test* was outdated because of its exclusion of otherwise reliable and relevant expert scientific testimony. The court also believed that Frye might allow some questionable evidence as scientific—such as astrology—if it were based on general acceptance among astrologers. The Daubert court wanted to focus more on the reliability of the testing and data. Relying on reliability and relevance as baseline measures, the court went beyond the mere rejection of the *Frye* general acceptance test and set new standards for determining the admissibility of expert testimony in scientific evidence. The court held that the trial judge was to act as a "gatekeeper" with the responsibility of "ensuring that an expert's testimony both rests on a reliable foundation and is relevant to the task at hand." Whenever this expert testimony is proffered, the trial judge must determine if it is based on scientific or technical knowledge and whether it will assist the trier of fact to understand or determine a fact in issue.

To determine if it is based on scientific or technical knowledge, the trial judge needs to first conduct a "preliminary assessment of whether the reasoning or methodology underlying the testimony is scientifically valid" and then "whether that reasoning or methodology properly can be applied to the facts in issue." To help with this, the court listed five "considerations" that might be examined, including:

1. Whether it can be and has been tested
2. Whether the theory or technique has been subjected to peer review and publication
3. Known or potential rate of error
4. Existence and maintenance of standards controlling the technique's operation
5. Degree of general acceptance within relevant scientific community

Of these five factors, testing is essential. This is "what distinguishes science from other fields of human inquiry." The court indicated that the other factors, although "pertinent," were more "flexible" in their "consideration."

Although the Daubert court rejected the *Frye* "general acceptance" as the exclusive test for admitting scientific evidence, it can still be an important part of the process, especially in determining admissibility of new theories and technology that have not been generally accepted within the relevant scientific community. As the court stated in a 1985 case relied upon in *Daubert*:

"In many cases ... the acceptance factor may well be decisive, or nearly so. Thus, we expect that a technique that satisfies the Frye test usually will be found to be reliable as well. On the other hand, a known technique which has been able to attract only minimal support within the community is likely to be found unreliable."[19]

As "gatekeeper," it will be the responsibility of the trial judge to determine this reliability and to assess the validity of the proffered expert testimony.

The *Daubert* decision changed the law for determining scientific evidence in not only all of the federal courts, but most of the state courts as well. The effect of the Daubert decision is that once an "appropriate appellate court holds that the Daubert test of reliability is satisfied, lower courts can take judicial notice of reliability and validity of the scientific method, technique or theory at issue."[20] (See Exhibit 10.2.)

EXHIBIT 10.2 Examples of Post-Daubert Rules for Scientific Testing Testimony by Experts

Federal Rule of Evidence
Rule 702. Testimony by Experts
If scientific, technical, or other specialized knowledge will assist the trier of fact to understand the evidence or to determine a fact in issue, a witness qualified as an expert by knowledge, skill, experience, training, or education, may testify thereto in the form of an opinion or otherwise, if:

(1) The testimony is based upon sufficient facts or data

(2) The testimony is the product of reliable principles and methods

(3) The witness has applied the principles and methods reliably to the facts of the case

Ohio Rules of Evidence
702. Testimony By Experts
A witness may testify as an expert if all of the following apply:

(A) The witness's testimony either relates to matters beyond the knowledge or experience possessed by lay persons or dispels a misconception common among lay persons

(B) The witness is qualified as an expert by specialized knowledge, skill, experience, training, or education regarding the subject matter of the testimony

(C) The witness's testimony is based on reliable scientific, technical, or other specialized information. To the extent that the testimony reports the result of a procedure, test, or experiment, the testimony is reliable only if all of the following apply:

(1) The theory upon which the procedure, test, or experiment is based is objectively verifiable or is validly derived from widely accepted knowledge, facts, or principles

(2) The design of the procedure, test, or experiment reliably implements the theory

(3) The particular procedure, test, or experiment was conducted in a way that will yield an accurate result

CSI CHECKLIST 10.3

Scientific Testing Checklist

- ❑ Is it science?
- ❑ Can it be tested?
- ❑ Is it reliable?
- ❑ Is it relevant?

Forensic Experts Who Are Not Scientists

One of the unanswered questions left by the *Daubert* decision was how far the new standard extended. Clearly, it pertained to scientific evidence and testing by crime scene criminalists and forensic scientists at the crime laboratory. Did it also apply to other "experts" who were not scientists, but whose expertise or testing involved technical or specialized knowledge? For example, fingerprint technicians, handwriting analysts, or police officers with advanced training and experience in some aspect of crime scene investigation or analysis?

In 1999, the U.S. Supreme Court addressed this by looking at what "...technical, or other specialized knowledge" under Rule 702 as used in *Daubert* covered. In a case dealing with the testimony of an "expert in tire failure analysis,"[21] the Court held that the wording in Rule 702 made no distinction between "scientific" knowledge and "technical" or "other specialized" knowledge.[22]

The Court concluded that any such "specialized knowledge" might then become the subject of expert testimony. The Court held that it is the word "knowledge" in the rule that is key, not words like "scientific."[23] Therefore, as a matter of language, the *Daubert* decision applies its reliability standard to *all* scientific, technical, or "other specialized" matters within its scope. This would include any crime scene specialists, as long as their expert testimony and opinion is the product of reliable principles and methods, and the expert has applied the principles and methods reliably to the facts of the case.

Fingerprint Experts

The following case illustrates how a forensic witness, even though not a scientist, can be qualified as an expert when the witness's expertise or testing involves technical or specialized knowledge.

CASE

Louisiana v. Jones

Court of Appeal of Louisiana, First Circuit

593 So. 2d 1301 (1991)

Carl D. Jones (defendant) was charged by grand jury indictment with second degree murder. He pled not guilty and, after a jury trial, was found guilty of the responsive offense of manslaughter. He received a sentence of 21 years at hard labor, with credit for time served. Subsequently, the trial court granted defendant an out of time appeal

Crime Scene Investigation

The victim did not report to work on June 21. The next morning, Sunday, June 22, the victim's father... entered the victim's apartment and found her lifeless body on the bed. The victim's throat had been cut. Her upper body and the surrounding portion of the bed were covered with blood. A yellow note pad on the floor next to the victim's bed contained a bloody thumbprint and palm print. Several small fragments of hair were found on the victim's body and in her bed. The subsequent investigation focused on defendant.

One of the state's fingerprint experts, Kenneth Dunn, who was employed by the Federal Bureau of Investigation, testified the bloody right thumbprint on the yellow note pad matched defendant's right thumbprint. Dunn also testified the bloody palm print on the yellow note pad was defendant's...Dunn testified that when he received State-8, the yellow note pad containing a bloody right thumbprint and palm print, he had two photographs prepared, one of each print. After the photographs were returned to him, he checked them to make sure they were accurate. He then compared these photographs of the bloody prints to defendant's known fingerprint and palm print and discovered that the bloody right thumbprint matched defendant's right thumbprint. However, Dunn was not able to make a comparison of the bloody palm print. He then treated the bloody palm print with a chemical solution referred to as TMB. This solution enhanced the ridge detail of the palm print but destroyed the ridge detail of the right thumbprint. After treating the prints, he again ordered photographs to be made. He then compared defendant's known palm print to the photograph of the treated palm print and was able to identify it as defendant's.

....

Legal Issue

Defendant contends that the trial court erred in allowing Kenneth Dunn to be qualified as an expert in fingerprint identification and comparison... Noting that Dunn had only a high school education with no college or university training in the area of any science, defendant contends that Dunn should not have been qualified as an expert. Defendant also notes that Dunn was not board certified as a fingerprint specialist by any association, academy, or school, nor was he a member of any organization of forensic scientists.

Holding of the Court

"The acceptance of a witness as an expert is a matter entrusted to the discretion of the trial court. Its ruling will not be overturned on appeal absent an abuse of discretion ... Dunn testified that he had been employed by the FBI for 14-1/2 years. During that time, he received on-the-job training in fingerprint comparison and identification. Dunn testified that in 1986 alone he made approximately 450,000 fingerprint comparisons. He also testified he previously had qualified as an expert in federal and state courts. Considering the above, we find no abuse of the trial court's discretion in accepting Dunn as an expert witness in fingerprint identification and comparison.

...

For these reasons, we affirm the conviction and the sentence."

CSI CHECKLIST 10.4

Checklist for Admitting Forensic Expert's Opinion under Daubert Test and Federal Rule of Evidence 702

❑ Scientific, technical, or other specialized knowledge will assist the trier of fact to understand the evidence or to determine a fact in issue

❑ Expert opinion is based on this scientific, technical, or other specialized knowledge

❑ Expert is qualified by knowledge, skill, experience, training, or education

❑ Testimony of the expert is based upon sufficient facts or data

❑ Testimony is the product of reliable principles and methods

❑ Expert has applied the principles and methods reliably to the facts of the case

CSI CHECKLIST 10.5

Factors for Determining "Scientific Knowledge" under the Daubert Test

❑ Whether it can be (and has been) tested

❑ Whether the theory or technique has been subjected to peer review and publication

❑ What is its known or potential rate of error

❑ Whether there is existence and maintenance of standards controlling the technique's operation

❑ What is its degree of general acceptance within relevant scientific community

JUDGE AS GATEKEEPER

gatekeeper
Role of the trial judge in ensuring relevance and reliability of scientific evidence.

In *Daubert*, the Court stated that the role of the trial judge in determining the admissibility of scientific evidence was to act as a **gatekeeper**. In this role, the judge was responsible for "ensuring that an expert's testimony both rests on a reliable foundation and is relevant to the task at hand." In other words, is it science and is it relevant to assisting the trier of fact to understand or determine a fact in issue?

abuse of discretion
The standard of review that an appellate court should apply in reviewing a trial court's decision to admit or exclude expert testimony under Daubert.

Abuse of Discretion

After the Daubert decision, some federal courts wondered what standard of review would be applied by appellate courts in reviewing a trial court's decision to admit or exclude expert testimony. Prior to Daubert, **abuse of discretion** was the review standard. In 1997, this issue was resolved when the Supreme Court determined that *abuse of discretion* would remain the standard, holding that a "question of admissibility of expert testimony is not such an issue of fact, and is reviewable under the abuse of discretion standard."[24]

LEGAL AND EVIDENTIARY CHALLENGES

As we have seen in this chapter, certain evidentiary rules and major case decisions have set the standards for the admission of forensic evidence, testing, and expert testimony. The type of legal challenges to these depends on which standard is used in your state or jurisdiction.

One of the earliest standards to be used was the *Frye General Acceptance Test.* If you live in a state that still employs this test, you would raise a challenge or be facing a challenge that the method of analysis from which the expert testimony is made must be sufficiently established to have gained general acceptance in the particular field in which it belongs.

Many states have modified this test to include requiring that the basis for analysis and opinion rests on a *reliable* foundation. States also rely on modern evidence rules that require a forensic expert to be qualified by knowledge, skill, experience, training, or education, and that the expert's opinion is based on scientific, technical, or other specialized knowledge. The *Kelly* rule in California is an example of the modification of Frye with the reliability standard in dealing with new forensic and scientific techniques. It provides that evidence derived from a new scientific technique "'must satisfy *three* prongs, by showing, first, that the reliability of the new technique has gained general acceptance in the relevant scientific community, second, that the expert testifying to that effect is qualified to do so, and, third, that "correct scientific procedures were used in the particular case."[25] When demonstrating that there is general scientific recognition of novel scientific techniques or principles, it is necessary to present the testimony of disinterested and impartial experts whose livelihood is not intimately connected with the technique at issue.[26]

The *Daubert* standard took the above and added requirements that the testimony be based upon sufficient facts or data, the testimony be the product of reliable principles and methods, and the forensic expert has applied the principles and methods reliably to the facts of the case. Under *Daubert*, the legal challenges could include whether the forensic evidence can be and has been tested, whether the theory or technique has been subjected to peer review and publication, what is its known or potential rate of error, whether there is existence and maintenance of standards controlling the technique's operation, and what is its degree of general acceptance within the relevant scientific community.

CSI CHECKLIST 10.6

Factors for Determining Legal Challenges

Under the *Frye* "General Acceptance" Test

❑ Whether the method of analysis from which the expert testimony is made has been sufficiently established to have gained general acceptance in the particular field in which it belongs

Under the "Reliability Test"

❑ Whether the scientific, technical, or other specialized knowledge will assist the trier of fact to understand the evidence or to determine a fact in issue
❑ Whether the expert opinion is based on this scientific, technical, or other specialized knowledge
❑ Whether the expert is qualified by knowledge, skill, experience, training, or education
❑ Whether the basis for analysis and opinion rests on a reliable foundation

Under Federal Rule of Evidence 702

❑ Whether the scientific, technical, or other specialized knowledge will assist the trier of fact to understand the evidence or to determine a fact in issue
❑ Whether the expert opinion is based on this scientific, technical, or other specialized knowledge
❑ Whether the expert is qualified by knowledge, skill, experience, training, or education
❑ Whether the testimony of the expert is based upon sufficient facts or data
❑ Whether the testimony is the product of reliable principles and methods
❑ Whether the expert has applied the principles and methods reliably to the facts of the case.

continued

Under Daubert Standards

❑   Whether forensic evidence can be (and has been) tested
❑   Whether the forensic theory or technique has been sub-
      jected to peer review and publication
❑   What is its known or potential rate of error
❑   Whether there is existence and maintenance of standards
      controlling the technique's operation
❑   What is its degree of general acceptance within the rel-
      evant scientific community

PRACTICE TIP 10.3

Researching Evidence Laws on the Internet

Want some help in finding and researching your state or federal evidence laws? Try visiting one of the following Web sites:

Finding State Evidence Codes

*Legal Information Institute (LII), Cornell Law School:
      http://www.law.cornell.edu/states/listing.html*

Finding Federal Rules of Evidence

*LII searchable copy of the Federal Rules of Evidence:
      http://www.law.cornell.edu/rules/fre/overview.html*

SUMMARY

When forensic evidence or scientific testing is presented at trial, it often involves specialized knowledge or is so complicated and beyond the common knowledge of the jury, that a forensic expert is required to help the jury understand the evidence or a matter in issue. An expert forensic witness can testify if it can be shown that he or she has special skills, knowledge or experience, and that his or her testimony can help the jury understand certain evidence or matters in issue. If the testimony pertains to scientific evidence or testing, the *General Acceptance* test established by *Frye* was dominant in the courts for many years. This test required that the method of analysis from which the opinion about scientific evidence is made must be sufficiently established to have gained general acceptance in the particular field in which it belongs.

In 1993, a major decision by the U.S. Supreme Court in *Daubert* recognized a new test in the federal courts. The test requires that the scientific evidence or testimony be able to assist the trier of fact to understand the evidence or to determine a fact in issue. In addition, the expert testimony must consist of scientific or technical knowledge or experience supported by appropriate validation. This "knowledge" can be determined by considering five factors, including whether it can be (and has been) tested; whether the theory or technique has been subjected to peer review and publication; its known or potential rate of error; the existence and maintenance of standards controlling the technique's operation; and, the *Frye* standard for degree of general acceptance within the relevant scientific community. Under the *Daubert* test, the judge serves as the gatekeeper with abuse of discretion as the standard of review. The Daubert test is now used in all of the federal courts, as well as in many state courts. However, many state courts have yet to adopt the Daubert standard. The *Frye* test, or a modified version using *Reliability* of the forensic evidence or testing, is still used in some state courts, and is one of the five factors in determining admissibility under the *Daubert* standards. As such, the *Frye* test remains an important element in assessing the reliability of scientific evidence.

KEY TERMS

Abuse of Discretion	*Frye* Test
Case Law	Gatekeeper
Evidence Law	General Acceptance Test
Expert Witness	Precedent
Daubert Standard	Probative
Federal Rules of Evidence	Reliability Test
Forensic Evidence and Testing	Scientific Evidence and Testing

REVIEW QUESTIONS

1. What is forensic evidence and testing and why is it important?
2. What is an expert forensic witness?
3. What laws govern the admissibility of forensic evidence and testing?
4. Distinguish the *General Acceptance* test from the *Reliability* test.
5. What is the *Daubert* Standard and how is it used?

6. What is the effect of the *Daubert* Standard on the admissibility of forensic evidence and testing?

7. What are some of the legal and evidentiary challenges to forensic evidence and testing?

CRITICAL THINKING QUESTIONS 10.1

1. Why do we have rules that govern the admissibility of expert witnesses, forensic evidence and scientific testing?
2. Do you believe that the current rules or court tests discussed in this chapter provide adequate safeguards for this process?
3. What public policy issues or considerations do you think might be behind these rules or tests?
4. How do these rules and court tests influence the gathering of crime scene evidence or investigation of a crime scene?

FORENSIC RESEARCH USING THE INTERNET

1. Find your state's rules of evidence and look for rules that pertain to the admissibility of forensic evidence, testing, or expert witnesses. Compare and contrast with some of the rules and court tests listed in this chapter.

2. Find out if your state appellate court posts their case decisions on the Internet. If so, find a case that illustrates an issue discussed in this chapter dealing with the admissibility of forensic evidence or testing. If your state decisions are not on the Internet, go instead to the Web site for the U.S. Circuit Court of Appeals in your circuit, or search the U.S. Supreme Court decisions.

PRACTICE SKILLS:

Practice what you have learned in the following crime scene problems:

Crime Scene Analysis 10.1

For the crime scene described on page 209 regarding the gunshot heard at a private residence and police finding the body

continued

of a female wearing pajamas inside on the hallway floor, answer the following questions:

1. How should the crime scene be investigated? Searched? Processed?

2. Based on evidence found at the above crime scene, what is your *theory of the case*?

3. What else could be tested for?

Crime Scene Analysis 10.2

Based on evidence found at the crime scenes of several murders, a "psychological profile" is created by a forensic profiler, which is used in the investigation that leads to the arrest and prosecution of a suspect. At the subsequent trial of the alleged killer, the profiler testifies as an expert witness.

1. Does this testimony constitute "scientific knowledge"?

2. Should it be admitted under the *Frye* test?

3. Should it be admitted under the *Daubert* test?

Explain your reasons.

WEB SITES

FindLaw Case Codes

http://guide.lp.findlaw.com/casecode/

FindLaw U.S. Supreme Court Decisions

http://www.findlaw.com/casecode/supreme.html

Legal Information Institute (LII), Cornell Law School

http://www.law.cornell.edu/states/listing.html

LII (Legal Information Institute) searchable copy of the Federal Rules of Evidence

http://www.law.cornell.edu/rules/fre/overview.html

Reference Manual on Scientific Evidence

http://www.fjc.gov/

Supreme Court Collection of Cornell Law School

http://supct.law.cornell.edu/supct/

U.S. Supreme Court

http://www.supremecourtus.gov

ENDNOTES

1. See, for example, *Federal Rule of Evidence* 702

2. *Frye v. United States*, 293 F. 1013 (D.C. Cir. 1923)

3. *Frye v. United States*, 293 F. 1013 (D.C. Cir. 1923)

4. *Donaldson v. Central Illinois Public Service Co.*, 199 Ill. 2d 63, 767 N.E.2d 314 (2002) (see also footnote 1 (199 Ill. 2d at 80 n.1, 767 N.E.2d at 325-26 n.1), Illinois court has not yet considered adoption of a new standard consistent with *Daubert v. Merrell Dow Pharmaceuticals*

5. See *People v. Kirk*, 289 Ill. App. 3d 326, 681 N.E.2d 1073, 224 Ill. Dec. 452 (1997)

6. *Federal Rule of Evidence 702*

7. *United States v. Downing*, 753 F.2d 1224 (3d Cir. 1985)

8. *Federal Rule of Evidence 401*

9. *Federal Rule of Evidence 403*

10. *U.S. v. Jakobetz*, 747 F. Supp. 250, (Vt 1990) quoting *United States v. Williams*, 583 F. 2d 1194 (1990)

11. *U.S. v. Two Bulls*, 918 F.2d 56 (1990)

12. *People v. Davis*, 343 Mich. 348; 72 N.W.2d 269 (1955)

13. *People v. Wentworth*, 251 Mich. App. 560, 563; 651 N.W.2d 773 (2002)

14. *People v. Kelly*, 17 Cal. 3d 24 (1976)

15. *People v. Soto*, 21 Cal.4th 512 (1999)

16. *People v. Allen*, 72 Cal.App.4th 1093(1999)

17. *People v. Susan Diane Clevenger*, 2003 Cal. App. Unpub. LEXIS 11395 (2003)

18. *Daubert v. Merrell Dow Pharmaceuticals, Inc*, .509 U.S. 579 (1993)

19. *United States v. Downing*, 753 F.2d 1224 (3d Cir. 1985)

20. *United States v. Martinez*, 3 F.3d 1191 (3rd Cir. 1993)

21. *Kumho Tire Co. v. Carmichael*, 526 U.S. 137 (1999)

22. *Federal Rule of Evidence 702*

23. *Kumho Tire Co. v. Carmichael*, 526 U.S. 137 (1999)

24. *General Electric Company v. Joiner*, 522 U.S. 136 (1997)

25. *People v. Roybal*, 19 Cal.4th 481(1998)

26. *People v. Haywood*, 209 Mich. App. 217, 530 N.W.2d 497 (1995)

ADMISSIBILITY OF FORENSIC EVIDENCE AND TESTING

"We balance probabilities and choose the most likely. It is the scientific use of the imagination."

—Sherlock Holmes, *The Hound of the Baskervilles*

"When the question involved does not lie within the range of common experience or common knowledge, but requires special experience or special knowledge, then the opinions of witnesses skilled in that particular science, art, or trade to which the question relates are admissible in evidence."

—*Frye v. United States*, 293 F. 1013 (D.C. Cir. 1923)

Chapter Outline

INTRODUCTION

In Chapter 10, we looked at forensic evidence and testing, with a focus on what the courts have determined as the legal *standards* and requirements for admitting expert witnesses and their testimony about the results of their scientific testing. In this chapter, we will look at the admissibility of specific types of forensic evidence and the legal challenges and evidentiary issues involved.

CRIME SCENE REVIEW

Do you remember what these concepts mean and how they are used in crime scene investigation?
- ❏ Frye Test
- ❏ Daubert Standard

ADMISSIBILITY OF FORENSIC EVIDENCE AND TESTING

The Daubert Standard and the modification of the Frye Test has brought some changes in the admissibility of forensic evidence and testing. It has had more of an impact, however, on newer techniques and testing than some of the traditional forms of forensic evidence.

Fingerprints

There was a flurry of challenges after *Daubert* to fingerprint evidence considered to be one of the more reliable forms of physical evidence. In one of these cases, a federal judge in Pennsylvania initially held in a 2002 decision that while "fingerprint identifications have been used for over 100 years..." and "fingerprint examinations conducted under the general ACE-V rubric are generally accepted as reliable by fingerprint examiners, this by itself cannot sustain the government's burden in making the case for the admissibility of fingerprint testimony under Federal Rule of Evidence 702."

The court went on to state, "There are no mandatory qualification standards for individuals to become fingerprint examiners, nor is there a uniform certification process." The court found that "fingerprint evidence "does not adequately satisfy the "scientific" criterion of testing (the first Daubert factor) or the "scientific" criterion of peer review (the second Daubert factor). Further, the court found that the information of record is unpersuasive, one way or another, as to ACE-V's "scientific" rate of error (the first aspect of Daubert's third factor), and that, at the critical evaluation stage, ACE-V does not operate under uniformly accepted "scientific" standards (the second aspect of Daubert's third factor).

The court held that it would "take judicial notice of the uniqueness and permanence of fingerprints" and that the parties "will be able to present expert fingerprint testimony (1) describing how any latent and rolled prints at issue in this case were obtained, (2) identifying, and placing before the jury, such fingerprints and any necessary magnifications, and (3) pointing out any observed similarities and differences between a particular latent print and a particular rolled print alleged by the government to be attributable to the same persons."

However, the court held that "the parties will not be permitted to present testimony expressing an opinion of an expert witness that a particular latent print matches, or does not match, the rolled print of a particular person and hence is, or is not, the fingerprint of that person."[1]

Then, a few months later, the court was asked for a reconsideration of its decision. After hearing other expert witnesses, the court changed its mind and held:

> "On reviewing these issues on the basis of the expanded record I reach the following conclusions:
> (a) Whatever may be the case for other law enforcement agencies, the standards prescribed for qualification as an FBI fingerprint examiner are clear: To be hired by the FBI as a fingerprint trainee, one must be a college graduate, preferably with some training in one of the physical sciences; to become a certified fingerprint examiner, the trainee must complete the FBI's two-year in-house training program which winds up with a three-day certifying examination. The uniformity and rigor of these FBI requirements provide substantial assurance that, with respect to certified FBI fingerprint examiners, properly controlling qualification standards are in place and are in force.
>
> ... [C]ontrary to the view expressed in my January 7 opinion, I am now persuaded that the standards which control the opining of a competent fingerprint examiner are sufficiently widely agreed upon to satisfy *Daubert*'s requirements.
> ....
>
> I have found, on the record before me, that there is no evidence that certified FBI fingerprint examiners present erroneous identification testimony, and, as a corollary, that there is

no evidence that the rate of error of certified FBI fingerprint examiners is unacceptably high.

....

English and American trial courts have accepted fingerprint identification testimony for almost a century. The first English appellate endorsement of fingerprint identification testimony was the 1906 opinion in *Rex v. Castleton, 3 Cr. App. R. 74.* In 1906 and 1908, Sergeant Joseph Faurot, a New York City detective who had in 1904 been posted to Scotland Yard to learn about fingerprinting, used his new training to break open two celebrated cases: in each instance fingerprint identification led the suspect to confess—important early indices of the reliability of fingerprint identification techniques when responsibly practiced. The first American court of last resort to consider the admissibility of such evidence was the Illinois Supreme Court: in *People v. Jennings, 252 Ill. 534, 96 N.E. 1077 (1911),* the court concluded that such evidence was admissible and affirmed appellant's murder conviction.

....

By agreeing to reconsider my prior ruling, I had the opportunity to acquire information not previously presented, or that I had not fully digested, on the record made in another courtroom more than two years ago.

....

Based on the foregoing considerations, I have concluded that arrangements which, subject to careful trial court oversight, are felt to be sufficiently reliable in England, ought likewise to be found sufficiently reliable in the federal courts of the United States, subject to similar measures of trial court oversight. In short, I have changed my mind. "Wisdom too often never comes, and so"—as Justice Frankfurter admonished himself and every judge—"one ought not to reject it merely because it comes late."[2]

PRACTICE TIP 11.1

Find Out More about Legal Challenges to Fingerprints

To find out more about the cases presenting legal challenges to fingerprints, check out the following Web site for fingerprint professionals:

http://onin.com/fp/daubert_links.html

Other Forensic Evidence and Testing

The challenges continue today, but almost all courts have upheld the reliability of fingerprint evidence. This is also true of other traditional forms of forensic evidence and testing, like footprints and palm-prints, ballistics, blood, fiber, and hair testing. The reason for this may be that some forensic tests and theories have gained such widespread acceptance over the years as to be **judicially noticed** by the courts. (See Exhibit 11.1.) In discussing this, one federal court stated that "in future cases with a similar evidentiary issue, a court could properly take judicial notice of the general acceptability of the general theory and the use of these specific techniques. Beyond such judicial notice, the threshold for admissibility should require only a preliminary showing of reliability of the particular data to be offered, i.e., some indication of how the laboratory work was done and what analysis and assumptions underlie the probability calculations.... Affidavits should normally suffice to provide a sufficient basis for admissibility."[3]

judicial notice
When a judge recognizes and accepts a certain fact that is commonly known in the community or capable of accurate and ready determination.

EXHIBIT 11.1 Examples of Cases Dealing with Admissibility of Forensic Evidence

Type of Forensic Evidence	Admitted or Excluded	Case	Summary
Lip print	Admitted	*Smallwood v. Gibson*, 191 F.3d 1257 (1999)	"Lip print was not used for ID of either the victim or accused, but as evidence that contradicted the defendant's statements. ... Cups located in the living room and bedroom showed bloody lip prints, suggesting the victim had been conscious enough to drink from containers at least twice before being beaten and/or bludgeoned"
Lip print	Admitted	*People v. Davis*, 304 Ill. App. 3d 427 1999	"The appellate court affirmed defendant's first-degree murder while attempting to commit an armed robbery... Lip print identification expert testimony was properly admitted ..."
Glass fragments	Admitted	*Brown v. Easter*, 1995 U.S. App. LEXIS 31448 (1995)	"The FBI obtained a warrant to search Brown's house, garage and vehicle for glass, blood and a brown vest. Glass found in Brown's vehicle at that time matched the glass found at the crime scene and on Harris' body...."

EXHIBIT 11.1 Examples of Cases Dealing with Admissibility of Forensic Evidence *Continued*

Type of Forensic Evidence	Admitted or Excluded	Case	Summary
Voice identification	Excluded	*People v. Persaud*, 226 A.D.2d 402 (1996)	"Defendant sought to establish that a spectrographic analysis of the 911 tape recording, when compared with a spectrographic analysis of a tape recording of his voice, revealed that he was not the anonymous caller. However, defendant failed to proffer evidence sufficient to establish that the use of spectrographic voice analysis to negate a voice print match was a technique or procedure generally accepted within the scientific community as capable of being performed reliably."
Computer-generated Images	Admitted	*State v. Tollardo* Court of Appeals of New Mexico, *2003 NMCA 122* (2003)	"Trial court did not abuse its discretion in determining that the methods used to generate the images were valid uses of computer technology."
Shoe impressions	Admitted	*United States v. Allen*, 208 F. Supp. 2d 984 (2002)	Expert opinion is admissible "as to whether two shoe impressions are a "match." Certainly, defense counsel is free to challenge [the] conclusions based upon the use of this methodology... "Daubert instructs that 'vigorous cross-examination, presentation of contrary evidence, and careful instruction on the burden of proof are the traditional and appropriate means of attacking shaky but admissible evidence...'"
Footprints	Admitted	*State of North Carolina v. Fleming*, 350 N.C. 109 (1999) Graham v. State, 239 Md. 521	"It is now well established that the correspondence of footprints found in connection with a crime with the print made by the shoe of the accused, is admissible in evidence to identify the accused as the guilty person."
Footwear impression	Admitted	*United States v. Allen*, 208 F. Supp. 2d 984 (2002)	A forensic expert offered opinion testimony that a footwear impression taken from the scene of the bank burglary could have been the same shoe as the shoe worn by defendant. Forensic expert had 11 years of experience in the general field of impression evidence which included fingerprints, palm prints, footwear, tire track and other physical comparisons. He had undergone over 200 hours of training specific to footwear, tire track, and physical match comparisons. The court found that the expert employed a reliable methodology in reaching his conclusion and would be permitted to provide his expert opinion as to whether the two shoe impressions are a "match."

EXHIBIT 11.1 Examples of Cases Dealing with Admissibility of Forensic Evidence   *Continued*

Type of Forensic Evidence	Admitted or Excluded	Case	Summary
Shoe impression	Excluded	*People v. Ferguson,* 172 Ill. App. 3d 1, (1988).	Testimony of a "shoe-print identification" expert who claimed that each person made a unique impression in the wear patterns of the sole of the shoe, which led her to conclude the defendant was responsible for the shoe print left at the crime scene "beyond a reasonable doubt" failed the Frye Test in that the expert's theory lacked "general acceptance."
Hair	Admitted	*Johnson v. Commonwealth,* 12 S.W.3d 258 (1999).	Microscopic examination of hair has sufficiently met the scientific reliability standard and a Daubert hearing was no longer required.
Blood spatters	Admitted	*State v. Moore,* 458 N.W.2d 90, 97 (Minn. 1990)	Recognized blood spatter analysis as a scientific technique.
Blood splatters	Admitted	*State v. Scudder,* 643 N.E. 2d 524 (Ohio 1994)	Expert forensic testimony that victim was alive while being raped. Analysis based on "blood splatter" (or blood spatter) evidence on victim's eyelid showing that victim had blinked while still alive.
PCR method of DNA testing	Admitted	*State v. Begley,* 956 S.W.2d 471, 477 (Tenn. 1997)	The Tennessee Supreme Court has held "the PCR method of DNA analysis an inherently trustworthy and reliable method of identification."

Ballistics and Firearms Identification

As described in a previous chapter, there are a variety of tests and comparisons that can be made on firearms and bullets, from shot pattern and trajectory to the markings made by a gun's barrel rifling, and ejection and extraction mechanisms. Courts have long accepted these forms of forensic evidence and expert testimony. At the November 2003 murder trial of sniper John Allen Muhammad, a ballistics expert for the federal Bureau of Alcohol, Tobacco, Firearms and Explosives, testified that the assault-style rifle found in the back of Muhammad's vehicle had fired the bullets that killed nine people and wounded three "to the exclusion of all other firearms."[4]

Bite Marks

The following Michigan case is representative of the majority of states in admitting bite mark evidence.

CASE

People v. Wright

1999 Mich. App. LEXIS 1677 (1999)

Crime Scene Investigation

The victim's body was discovered at approximately 9:00 a.m. on August 4, 1992. The next day, Dr. Warnick examined the victim and collected various pieces of evidence with respect to the bite marks on the victim's body. After defendant became a suspect, Dr. Warnick examined defendant in April, 1993, and collected various pieces of evidence with respect to defendant's teeth at this time.... Dr. Warnick testified that during his examination of defendant he photographed defendant, registered defendant's dentition... took impressions of defendant's teeth... and made molds of defendant's upper and lower teeth.... (He also) testified that each person's dentition is unique and that in this case defendant's teeth exhibited several unusual characteristics.... Dr. Warnick testified that he had compared defendant's teeth to the bite marks found on the victim by actually placing the mold of defendant's upper teeth onto the molds of the bite marks on the victim... (and he) demonstrated this technique for the jury.... Dr. Warnick testified that based on these techniques he had concluded in his ... police report that the "comparison of the wound pattern injuries found on the [victim] was highly consistent with the dentition found on [defendant]."

Legal Issue

Defendant argues that the trial court erred in admitting Dr. Warnick's testimony concerning bite marks, including his testimony with respect to the statistical probability that defendant made the bite marks found on the victim. Defendant contended that the statistical evidence "is a fairly new field" and "is not . . . widely accepted."

Holding of the Court

.... Bite mark analysis is one of the four main areas of the field of forensic odontology....The fundamental underlying theory of bite mark analysis is that every person's dentition is unique and can, therefore, leave a recognizable mark.... Once the evidence is collected, the forensic odontologist then uses a variety of comparison techniques to determine to what extent the suspected biter's dentition matches the bite mark.... Bite mark comparison evidence is currently admissible in at least thirty-five states...

(T)he bite mark comparison techniques employed by Dr. Warnick do not involve near total reliance on scientific interpretation to establish a question of fact. Rather...the jury is able to see the bite mark comparisons for itself by comparing the photographs, molds and other physical evidence. We conclude, therefore, that the observational bite mark comparison techniques employed by Dr. Warnick were sound and created a trustworthy foundation for his conclusion that defendant was the person who made the bite marks on the victim...."

Tool Marks

As described in Chapter 10, toolmarks are the marks or impressions made by certain tools used at a crime scene. For example, a burglary may have been committed through the forcing open of a door or window using a pry tool or screwdriver. The marks left behind on the door or window by the tool may later be compared with a suspect tool to determine whether they match. Tool Mark identification and analysis has generally been accepted in courts.

The following Mississippi case deals with whether a forensic expert may offer an expert opinion at trial about a particular tool being consistent with particular injuries to a victim.

CASE

McGowen. v. Mississippi

Supreme Court of Mississippi

859 So. 2d 320 (2003)

Crime Scene Investigation

[This case dealt with the crime scene investigation of a murder of a four-year old girl, Shelby Lynn Tucker.] The State's ... witness was Dr. Paul McGarry, a forensic pathologist from the coroner's office of Orleans Parish, Louisiana... Dr. McGarry, who performed the autopsy on Shelby's body... testified that his observations revealed a violent struggle had taken place. He found her vaginal opening stretched and torn, abrasions on her inner thighs, eleven dark brown hairs around her genital region, bruises on her face, knees, shins, hips, and shoulders, bleeding in the tissues of her neck indicating strangulation, bleeding and tearing in the tissues of her mouth indicating smothering, and five deep round disk-shaped bruises on the left side of her head where her skull had been fractured and crushed. Despite defense objections, photographs were introduced comparing Shelby's head injuries to the mallet found in Charles McGowen's truck. Dr. McGarry was permitted to testify that the diameter of the mallet and the diameter of the wound patterns were the same...

Legal Issue

The ... question this Court must answer is whether a forensic pathologist may render an expert opinion at trial as to whether a particular instrument or weapon in evidence was consistent with particular injuries to a victim...

Holding of the Court

... Dr. McGarry did not testify that the mallet found in the back of McGowen's brother's truck in fact caused Shelby's head wounds. Rather, Dr. McGarry simply stated the shape of the mallet was consistent with the shape of the wounds...Dr. McGarry's testimony ... is distinct from the kind of tool-mark testimony disallowed in *Fowler v. State, 566 So. 2d 1194 (Miss. 1990)*. In *Fowler*, the prosecution's objection was sustained by the trial judge when the defense expert witness testified that certain blood stains pictured in a photograph presented at trial were arterial blood squirts from the right side of the victim's head. The prosecution objected that the expert could not know whether the squirts were from the victim's head or his finger. In McGowen's trial, Dr. McGarry did not testify with the specificity and certitude asserted by the expert in *Fowler*. Dr. McGarry merely stated the shape of the mallet in evidence was consistent with the shape of Shelby's head injuries. He did not assert that the mallet in evidence was *the* weapon in fact used to inflict Shelby's injuries in the same way the expert in *Fowler* testified the photographed blood stains were caused by blood squirts specifically from the victim's head.

.... a forensic pathology expert may offer an expert opinion at trial about whether a particular instrument in evidence was consistent with particular injuries to a victim.

Blood Spatter (or Splatter) Analysis

Most courts recognize blood spatter (or splatter) analysis as forensic evidence.[5] In the following case, this Illinois court must decide on whether to accept a defense witness as an expert in the fields of luminol interpretation and blood splatter analysis.

CASE

Illinois v. Kaczmarek

Appellate Court of Illinois, First District, Third Division

318 Ill. App. 3d 340 (2000)

Crime Scene Investigation

A neighbor called police after discovering a broken window and open back door to the apartment of an 86-year old woman. Chicago police responded and noticed several pieces of glass that had been broken from a window. Officers entered the kitchen and observed spots of blood on the kitchen floor leading to a nearby bedroom. The officers further noticed blood spots on the bedroom door frame, and found a kitchen knife, which was bloodstained, on a small table immediately outside the bedroom. Inside the bedroom, officers found the victim lying in bed, face up in a pool of blood. The officers observed blood on the floor and walls near the bed. The bedroom, including the rest of the apartment, had been ransacked, and no signs of forced entry were readily apparent.

....

The detectives found defendant early the next morning asleep in his car and observed blood stains on the right and left sleeves of defendant's quilted jacket. The detectives placed defendant under arrest and, upon obtaining defendant's written consent, they searched the trunk of the vehicle. In the trunk, the detectives found jewelry boxes, which appeared to be stained with blood, jewelry, serving plates and platters. The detectives also discovered a pair of blood-stained jeans and several tools, including a glass cutter.

....

Pamela Fish, an expert in electrophoresis, serology and DNA testing with the microanalysis unit of the Chicago Police Department, detailed the results of her examination conducted of the physical evidence ... Fish examined blood samples obtained from defendant, the victim, the victim's kitchen floor, and the knife found in the apartment. Fish also inspected the substances resembling blood found on defendant's jacket and jeans, and the jewelry boxes recovered from the trunk of defendant's vehicle. Fish determined that the victim had Type A blood and that defendant had Type B blood. Fish further determined that the substances taken from defendant's jeans and quilted jacket were human blood possessing Type A characteristics. Fish additionally examined the blood samples to ascertain their particular genetic markers for purposes of making an identification. Fish testified that the blood found on the jeans and quilted jacket was consistent with the victim's blood and could not have come from defendant. In fact, according to Fish, all the enzymes from the blood taken from defendant's clothing was consistent with those found in the victim's blood.

....

Mitch Rea was called by the State as an expert in luminol testing and interpretation. During voir dire examination of his qualifications, Rea stated he ... had previously worked over 26 years as a police

continued

officer with the Phoenix Police Department in Arizona. Of his time at the department, Rea spent ten years working as a detective in the homicide unit where he processed over an estimated 350 murder crime scenes. Rea has received training in crime scene investigation and specialized training in chemical blood detection involving luminol. Rea has additionally attended and participated in numerous seminars dealing with luminol and luminol testing, has taught and trained other law enforcement officers in these fields, has conducted hundreds of experiments involving luminol, has participated in several workshops covering luminol testing, and has previously testified in court as a luminol expert. Rea detailed the application and use of the luminol chemical as a detecting agent, and described its glowing effect when it reacts with particular substances, including blood. Rea acknowledged that luminol is not specific to blood and that it reacts with other substances, such as metals and cleansers.

Upon questioning by defense counsel, Rea acknowledged never being educated or trained in the field of chemistry. Rea further admitted that he does not perform any additional testing, like DNA analysis, to ensure the accuracy of results indicating the presence of blood. Over defendant's objection, Rea was accepted by the court as an expert and testified that he performed luminol tests on defendant's quilted jacket ... Rea explained that an application of luminol to the right front panel of the jacket produced a bright luminance of several small spots. According to Rea, these luminances indicated the presence of blood. Rea further observed luminances about sections of the jacket which had been previously removed for Fish's examination, the right sleeve and cuff, and both the elbow region and back portion of the left sleeve. Rea stated that each of the foregoing luminances were consistent with the presence of blood. On cross-examination, Rea explained he did not perform any additional tests to confirm that the luminol reactions he observed were in fact reactions to blood.

Rod Englert, an expert in crime scene reconstruction and blood splatter, described three different categories of blood splatter: low velocity splatter which result from drops of blood falling straight down; medium velocity splatter which results from blunt force trauma; and high velocity splatter which results from gunfire. With respect to medium velocity splatter, Englert explained that blood does not splatter on the first blow of force, and that regardless of the severity of the beating, very little blood gets on the offender although the scene may be terribly bloody. Englert explained that a minimal amount of blood would be found on the offender in such cases because the force is always directed away at the victim. Englert additionally discussed blood transfer stains, and explained that they occur when blood is swiped against someone or something.

Englert examined the physical evidence and photographs in the case and concluded that the blood on the victim's kitchen floor appeared smeared, indicative of a struggle in which someone bled. Englert stated that the absence of bloody shoe prints was not unusual given how quickly blood dries. Englert noted the blood on the kitchen wall immediately outside the bedroom represented classic medium velocity splatter suggestive of blunt force being inflicted upon the victim. Given the low angle of projection, Englert opined that the victim received numerous blows while on the kitchen floor...

In examining photographs of the luminol testing performed on defendant's jacket by Rea, Englert stated the stains on the right and left sleeves and on the front of the jacket represented medium velocity splatter. Englert also observed transfer stains on the back of the sleeves and on the right front pocket.

In Englert's opinion, the victim was first attacked in the kitchen, near the entry of the bedroom, where she received numerous blows while on the floor...The victim, struggling to break free, was then taken to the bedroom and thrown on the bed where she was attacked again and ultimately killed. According to Englert, the bleeding represented by the amount of blood found in the bed would have occurred after the victim had died. Englert opined the physical evidence he examined was consistent with the person causing the death of the victim.

continued

....

To rebut the testimonies of Rea and Englert, the defense offered Dr. Kenneth Siegusmund as an expert in the fields of luminol processing and blood splatter analysis. .... Dr. Siegesmund has performed luminol testing well over a hundred times, and was "familiar" with the study of blood splatter. Dr. Siegesmund indicated that he had been qualified in court as an expert in forensic sciences about 250 times, and specifically as a blood splatter expert about 20 times. Dr. Siegesmund did not indicate whether he had ever been previously accepted as an expert in luminol application or testing.

On cross-examination, the State initially went to great lengths to undermine Dr. Siegesmund's credibility...Dr. Siegesmund described himself as an expert in, among other areas, crime scene reconstruction, blood splatter, blood identification and luminol testing. The doctor has never taken a course in crime scene reconstruction and has never been to a crime scene under investigation. Dr. Siegesmund has never had any formal training in crime scene processing or in techniques of physical evidence collection. His only exposure in this area has been through yearly, one-week seminars held by the American Academy of Forensic Scientists. Dr. Siegesmund believed he last attended such a conference in 1994, but was not sure. ....

Responding to the defense's tender of Dr. Siegesmund as an expert, the [trial] court remarked that the doctor "appears to be a jack of all trades and a master of none." Finding the doctor's qualifications lacking, the court refused to accept Dr. Siegesmund as an expert in blood splatter analysis and luminol interpretation...

....

Defendant ... asserts error in the rulings of the trial court regarding (1) the presentation of expert testimony by a witness offered by the State and (2) the nonacceptance of his tendered expert, Dr. Siegesmund.

Legal Issue

What factors are considered by a court in qualifying a witness as an "expert?" The defendant was convicted of murder and appealed, arguing that the trial court erred in allowing Mr. Rea as an expert in luminal interpretation, but not allowing Dr. Siegesmund as a defense expert.

Holding of the Court

"An individual will be allowed to testify as an expert if his experience and qualifications afford him knowledge beyond that of the average person, and where his testimony will aid, and not invade, the province of the trier of fact in reaching its conclusions...The courts do not employ any predetermined formula for how an expert acquires specialized skill or knowledge, and the indicia of expertise is not an assigned level of academic training. An expert may acquire his expertise from a variety of outlets, including practical experience, scientific study, education, training and/or research...

We find no error in the trial court's decision. Based on his extensive work experience, training and independent study, Rea possessed knowledge not commonly known to the average person that would have assisted the jury in making its determinations concerning defendant's guilt. Although Rea has never taken a college-level chemistry course as defendant correctly observes, the law is clear that an expert is not required to have any particular level of academic training, and that the witness may acquire his particular expertise and training through other means. Notably, defendant fails to explain the importance a general chemistry class would serve in understanding and performing testing with luminol.

continued

... A review of the record shows that Dr. Siegesmund simply possesses a general knowledge of forensic studies, and does not hold any specialized understanding of luminol interpretation and blood splatter analysis. Indeed, the doctor never stated he knew how to interpret particular luminol reactions, and merely explained that he has conducted numerous luminol testing without indicating whether he ever interpreted the results. Although not determinative, Dr. Siegesmund additionally has received no training in luminol application and interpretation and has never performed such work in any crime lab. With respect to blood splatter analysis, Dr. Siegesmund merely stated he was "familiar" with the subject. He has neither received training in the field nor performed such work in a crime lab setting...

We find no error in the trial court's determination that, based on the testimony presented, Dr. Siegesmund did not possess a sufficient level of knowledge and expertise to testify as an expert in the fields of luminol interpretation and blood splatter analysis.

....

We affirm defendant's conviction for murder ..."

Handwriting Analysis

Handwriting analysis is an area that is still subject to contest in the courts. Some courts admit it as reliable, and some do not. One California court stated that it is "apparent to the Court that handwriting opinion testimony on unique identification does not have the validity and reliability of fingerprints or DNA evidence."[6] On the other hand, a Kentucky trial court "determined that handwriting evidence had been admissible for a long period of time and therefore a Daubert hearing was not necessary." The appellate court upheld this, stating that "trial judges in Kentucky can take judicial notice that those methods or techniques have achieved the status of scientific reliability."[7]

The following Massachusetts case examines whether expert testimony can be admitted at trial on the subject of handwriting comparison.

CASE

Commonwealth v. Glyman.

Superior Court of Massachusetts, at Worcester

2003 Mass. Super. LEXIS 431 (2003)

Legal Issue

The Commonwealth has indicated an intention to offer expert testimony at trial on the subject of handwriting comparison. The defendants seek to exclude such testimony on the ground that its reliability is not sufficiently established...

continued

Holding of the Court

Massachusetts, like other jurisdictions, has long admitted handwriting comparison by a qualified expert... Massachusetts Courts have considered the reliability of such testimony to be so firmly established as to obviate any need for preliminary screening. Federal Courts, like Massachusetts, have long admitted expert testimony on handwriting comparison... [H]andwriting comparison, unlike some other areas of expert evidence, is accessible to jurors; they are familiar with the subject matter from everyday experience, and are capable of understanding and evaluating expert testimony on it through their own observation. For that reason, there is little risk of "undue prejudice from the mystique attached to experts."

....

Two ...federal district court decisions...admitted expert testimony as to handwriting comparison, but imposed certain limitations on the opinions to be expressed (holding handwriting analysis in general admissible ...but precluding expert from expressing ultimate conclusion on authorship...

Among the reasons recognized in both of these decisions for admitting the testimony... is the familiarity of handwriting comparison to jurors, enabling them to understand and evaluate expert testimony on the subject. Indeed, the Supreme Judicial Court has held that, although expert testimony is helpful, jurors are competent to perform handwriting comparison themselves, without expert testimony. Unlike other types of expert testimony, which jurors often must evaluate based largely on pure credibility determinations, jurors themselves can see the points of comparison on which a handwriting analyst relies. An expert may point out similarities and differences that untrained jurors would otherwise miss, and may explain their significance in light of the expert's training and experience, but the actual comparison falls ultimately to the jurors themselves. The overwhelming weight of authority, both before and since *Daubert*, as well as sound reason, thus favors admission of expert testimony on handwriting comparison.

...Defendants' Motion to Exclude Expert Testimony Concerning Handwriting Comparison ...is *denied*."

New and Novel Forensic Evidence and Testing

Newer areas of forensic evidence and testing are subject to more scrutiny and legal challenges under both the Daubert Standard and the modified Frye Test still used in many states. As stated by one federal appeals court, "the import of *Daubert* was not to compel 'wholesale exclusion of a long-accepted form of expert evidence.' Rather, *Daubert* provides a framework for courts 'to entertain new and less conventional forms of expertise,' admitting what is reliable, even if not yet generally accepted, among such new fields, but screening out the unreliable."[8]

DNA

One of the most heavily challenged newer areas of forensic evidence in the courts over the past 15 years has been the admissibility of DNA. As described in Chapter 9, every human possesses a unique genetic code, which carries the genetic "fingerprint" for that individual. Chromosomes are used to hold this code and these are made of the organic substance known as DNA, deoxyribonucleic acid. We can now examine cells from any part of the body, including bloodstains and hairs to "read" this genetic code and profile a DNA "fingerprint" to use in eliminating suspects or helping to identify them. A single cell can provide a match with another cell from the same person. With the exception of identical twins, no two people have been found to possess the same DNA patterns.

The Office of Technology Assessment's evaluation of DNA testing has concluded that "forensic uses of DNA tests are both reliable and valid when properly performed and analyzed by skilled personnel."[9] The National Research Council's report on DNA evidence stated, "The state of the profiling technology and the methods for estimating frequencies and related statistics have progressed to the point where the admissibility of properly collected and analyzed DNA data should not be in doubt."[10]

Although still the subject of intense legal challenges in the courts, the admissibility of DNA has been steadily gaining in most states. However, as testing methodology evolves and becomes even more sophisticated, it is expected that legal challenges will continue as to the reliability of these newer testing procedures. The following Texas case illustrates the legal challenges to the reliability of the testing procedures.

CASE

Reese v. State of Texas

Court of Appeals of Texas, Fourteenth District, Houston

2003 Tex. App. LEXIS 8656 (2003)

Crime Scene Investigation

Appellant Reese was convicted by a jury of two counts of aggravated sexual assault of a child, a first-degree felony. His DNA was found on A.H.'s vagina, thigh, and a mixture of appellant's and A.H's DNA was found on the crotch of A.H's pajamas... During the hearing to determine the admissibility of the State's DNA expert's testimony, Mr. Cockrell testified that he had worked for the Houston Police Department Crime Laboratory for seven years, and had been performing DNA analysis for five years. Mr. Cockrell holds a Bachelor's and Master's Degree in biology, received in-house training at the Houston Police Department Crime Laboratory, and attended several training seminars on DNA testing and analysis. With regard to the testing performed in this case, Mr. Cockrell explained that STR DNA testing was performed. He stated that STR, or short tandem repeats, is an upgraded version of PCR DNA testing, and that STR DNA testing is accepted world-wide and considered an accurate form of genetic testing. He explained the processes he used to perform the test: the first step is extraction, performed by "removing everything from [the] stain but the exception of DNA." After extraction, he quantified the DNA present and then amplified it to develop a DNA profile through a

continued

process of electrophoresis. Once a profile is developed, it is typed to determine whether it is consistent with a known sample. He further stated that he followed the proper procedures in performing the DNA testing and analysis in this case.

On cross-examination, appellant's counsel questioned Mr. Cockrell regarding the procedures employed by the lab to guarantee the DNA evidence was not contaminated. Mr. Cockrell explained that negative and positive controls are always used to ensure the evidence is not contaminated and the test is performed properly. He stated the positive controls ensure the test "ran exactly as it should have been," and the negative controls "determine whether or not you have any contamination in your evidence." Appellant's counsel asked for a document to verify whether these controls were in fact used in this case. Mr. Cockrell testified that two tests were actually performed with each DNA sample, called the profiler and co-filer kits. Mr. Cockrell, however, only produced a print-out of the positive and negative controls used in the co-filer kit. He consistently and repeatedly stated that the positive and negative controls were used for both the profiler and the co-filer kits and explained that the "exact same" positive and negative controls used on the co-filer kit were also used on the profiler kit.

Legal Issue

[A]ppellant contends the trial court erred in admitting the State's DNA expert's testimony: (1) Mr. Cockrell was not qualified to interpret the results of the DNA analysis, and (2) Mr. Cockrell's analysis was not reliable because he did not produce documentation showing that tests were performed to ensure the DNA evidence had not been contaminated.

Holding of the Court

... The trial court is guided by *Texas Rule of Evidence 702* in determining whether expert testimony should be admitted. *Rule 702* provides: "If scientific, technical, or other specialized knowledge will assist the trier of fact to understand the evidence or to determine a fact in issue, a witness qualified as an expert by knowledge, skill, experience, training, or education may testify thereto in the form of an opinion or otherwise." The trial court serves as "gatekeeper", admitting evidence only if it is sufficiently reliable and relevant to assist the jury.

Appellant complained to the trial court, and now complains on appeal, that the DNA testing, and thus Mr. Cockrell's testimony, is unreliable because Mr. Cockrell did not produce documentation showing positive and negative controls were used on the profiler kit. The trial court concluded the State had shown by clear and convincing evidence that the STR DNA testing was sufficiently reliable and relevant to help the jury in reaching accurate results. We agree.

(1) Mr. Cockrell testified, and it was not disputed, that STR DNA testing is accepted world-wide; (2) he has a Bachelor's and Master's degree in Biology, as well as, five years' experience in DNA testing; (3) Mr. Cockrell testified that STR DNA testing is an accurate form of genetic testing; (4) based on the world-wide acceptance of STR DNA testing, there would be a number of other experts available to test and evaluate the technique; (5) Mr. Cockrell was able to explain the underlying scientific theory and technique with clarity; and (6) a vast amount of scientific literature exists discussing STR DNA testing. The trial court has great discretion in deciding whether to admit or exclude evidence. We find nothing in the record demonstrating the trial court abused its discretion by admitting Mr. Cockrell's testimony in the absence of *written* documentation showing positive and negative controls were used on the profiler kit.

Accordingly, we hold the trial court did not abuse its discretion in concluding the State demonstrated by clear and convincing evidence that Mr. Cockrell's testimony concerning STR DNA testing, as well as its interpretation, was reliable and relevant to aid the jury in determining appellant's guilt or innocence on the charged offense."

CSI CHECKLIST 11.1

FBI Checklist for Determining Legal Challenges to DNA

❑ If DNA evidence is not properly documented, collected, packaged, and preserved, it will not meet the legal and scientific requirements for admissibility in a court of law.

❑ If DNA evidence is not properly documented, its origin can be questioned.

❑ If DNA is not properly collected, biological activity can be lost.

❑ If DNA is not properly packaged, contamination can occur.

❑ If DNA is not properly preserved, decomposition and deterioration can occur.

Source: FBI Crime Laboratory Guidelines for Admissibility of DNA

PRACTICE TIP 11.2

Research DNA Testing and Standards for Crime Labs

Find out more about DNA testing and the standards for crime laboratories testing DNA:

Bureau of Justice Statistics, Survey of DNA Laboratories
http://www.ojp.usdoj.gov/bjs/pub/pdf/sdnacl01.pdf
The Future of Forensic DNA Testing: Predictions of the Research and Development Working Group—National Institute of Justice
http://www.ojp.usdoj.gov/nij/pubs-sum/183697.htm

Global Positioning System (GPS) Technology

GPS
Global positioning system used in criminal investigation for tracking and determining locational positioning.

In the 2004 Scott Peterson double-murder trial in California, prosecutors wanted to present evidence of **GPS** (global positioning system) technology that police used to track the defendant prior to his arrest for the murder of his wife and unborn son. The defense tried to prevent this GPS tracking evidence from being admitted at trial, saying that GPS technology had not been generally accepted by the scientific community. The defense went on to cite several tracking errors noted in the systems that police used, including one tracking system that didn't work for several weeks. The judge, however, admitted this new forensic evidence, saying that global positioning technology was "generally accepted and fundamentally valid."[11]

Voiceprints and Voice Identification

voiceprints
Voice identification based on analysis and comparisons of voice recording samples.

The admissibility of **voiceprints** is still being contested and varies from state to state. Some states have allowed forensic evidence on voice identification. Some states still do not regard it as reliable. In the following Louisiana case, the issue is whether the testimony of a forensic voice identification expert can be admitted.

CASE

State of Louisiana v. Gary Morrison

Court of Appeal of Louisiana, First Circuit

2003 La. App. LEXIS 2479 (2003)

Legal Issue

This case dealt with the admissibility of a voice identification expert.

Holding of the Court

"At a hearing to determine the admissibility of expert evidence on [voice identification], defense counsel offered the testimony of Dr. Al Yonovitz, a voice identification expert. Upon the conclusion of Dr. Yonovitz's testimony, the trial court held that the defendant failed to satisfy the requirements of *Daubert* and ordered the expert testimony of Dr. Yonovitz inadmissible at trial. The defendant seeks review of that ruling. For the following reasons, we deny the writ.

....

Voice identification analysis consists of both "critical listening," which requires an expert to carefully listen to the qualities of two voices, and spectrographic analysis. In the latter phase, a computer-based instrument compares the frequencies and amplitudes of a voice on a questioned recording with those of a known sample. According to Dr. Yonovitz's testimony, the State could test or retest the information, and if an examiner had the same raw data that he used, the examiner could fully replicate his findings....When questioned concerning his error rate, Dr. Yonovitz answered that the error rate in his measurement of formats was very low, but he stated he did not know specific error rates...

Although Dr. Yonovitz testified in favor of the voice identification analysis technique, he did not introduce supporting documentation to verify the error rates and studies conducted within the field or to support his claims concerning the development of this field. The inconsistency in error rates clearly illustrates the uncertainty of this method, and a proper foundation has not been established pursuant to the factors listed within *Daubert*. Moreover, other courts considering the uncertainty of the law regarding the reliability and admissibility of expert voice identification evidence have also concluded that there are problems concerning the reliability and scientific validity of the method.

Accordingly, the defendant's writ application seeking review of the district court's denial of the admissibility of Dr. Yonovitz's expert testimony is hereby denied."

LEGAL CHALLENGES BASED ON COURT STANDARDS

As we have seen in this chapter and Chapter 10, the standards for the admission of forensic evidence and testing is set by evidentiary rules and case decisions. The type of legal challenges to these depends on which standard is used in your state or jurisdiction. The *Frye*[12] *General Acceptance* challenge would require that the method of analysis from which the expert testimony is sufficiently established to have gained general acceptance in the particular field in which it belongs.

Many states have modified this test to include requiring that the basis for analysis and opinion rests on a *reliable* foundation.[13] States also rely on modern evidence rules that require a forensic expert to be qualified by knowledge, skill, experience, training, or education, and that the expert's opinion is based on scientific, technical, or other specialized knowledge.

The *Daubert* standard[14] took the above and added requirements that the testimony be based on sufficient facts or data, that the testimony be the product of reliable principles and methods, and that the forensic expert has applied the principles and methods reliably to the facts of the case.

CSI CHECKLIST 11.2

Factors to Consider in Admitting Forensic Evidence

❑ Does the matter at issue require scientific, technical, or other specialized knowledge?

❑ Will the forensic evidence or expert assist the trier of fact to better understand the evidence?

❑ Is the witness providing testimony about the forensic evidence or testing qualified as an expert by knowledge, skill, experience, training, or education?

❑ Is the testimony based on sufficient facts or data?

❑ Is the testimony the product of reliable principles and methods?

❑ Did the forensic expert apply these principles and methods reliably to the facts of the case?

LEGAL CHALLENGES OF FORENSIC TESTING AND EQUIPMENT

In addition to the overall forensic or scientific validity of the evidence, legal challenges may include the way the testing was conducted or the equipment used. As discussed in an earlier chapter, legal challenges may target the equipment used; whether the equipment had been checked, tested, and was operating accurately; or, how the testing was done—whether the analyst was properly trained and qualified to run equipment, or whether the test was given in the proper manner.

Legal challenges may also focus on the crime lab or its personnel. The focus here would be to attack the credibility of the crime lab itself, or the lab personnel involved in the testing and analysis of the evidence. For example, in one Baltimore case, a police chemist admitted on the stand that she did not follow certain steps in her testing procedure and did not understand the "science" behind some of the tests that she performed.[15]

PRACTICE TIP 11.3

Legal Challenges to Forensic Evidence

For an excellent Web site on legal challenges to forensic evidence and testing, see

A Beginner's Primer on the Investigation of Forensic Evidence, by Attorney Kim Kruglick
http://www.kruglaw.com

Legal Challenges to Reliability

The admissibility of forensic evidence and testing can be challenged through evidentiary rules and standards established through court decisions. A party can also challenge the reliability of a particular person, test, or of the crime lab itself by a "showing of sloppy handling of samples, failure to train the personnel performing the testing, failure to follow protocol, and the like. Such a challenge, however, will go to the weight, not the admissibility, of... evidence."[16]

SUMMARY

The Daubert Standard and the modification of the Frye Test has brought some changes in the admissibility of forensic evidence, testing, and expert testimony. It has had more of an impact, however, on new techniques and testing than some of the traditional forms of forensic evidence. For example, after *Daubert* there was a flurry of challenges to fingerprint evidence which is considered to be one of the more reliable forms of physical evidence. The challenges still go on today, but almost all courts have upheld the reliability of fingerprint evidence. This is also true of other traditional forms of forensic evidence and testing, like footprints and palmprints, ballistics, blood, fiber, and hair testing. The reason for this may be that some forensic tests and theories have gained such widespread acceptance over the years as to be judicially noticed by the courts. Newer areas of forensic evidence and testing are subject to more scrutiny and legal challenges under both the Daubert Standard and the modified Frye Test still used in many states.

One of the most heavily challenged newer areas of forensic evidence in the courts over the past 15 years has been the admissibility of DNA. Although still the subject of intense legal challenges in the courts, the admissibility of DNA has been steadily gaining in most states.

The standards for the admission of forensic evidence and testing is set by evidentiary rules and case decisions. The type of legal challenges to these depends on which standard is used in your state or jurisdiction. In addition, however, there are other legal challenges that can be utilized in addition to the rules and case standards. These include challenging forensic equipment, testing, or personnel. For example, the way the testing was conducted or the equipment used may be at issue. The personnel involved in the testing may be challenged as to the procedure used or the credibility of the analyst. These challenges go to the weight, not the admissibility, of the forensic evidence.

KEY TERMS

GPS   Voiceprints
Judicial Notice

REVIEW QUESTIONS

1. Describe how the Daubert Standard has affected the admissibility of some forensic evidence and testing. Give an example.

2. Using examples, discuss the admissibility of some of the traditional forms of forensic evidence and testing.

3. Using examples, discuss the admissibility of some of the newer forms of forensic evidence and testing.

4. Identify some of the legal challenges to forensic evidence and testing and describe how they might be used.

CRITICAL THINKING QUESTIONS 11.1

1. Why do we have standards as discussed in this chapter that govern the admissibility of forensic evidence and scientific testing?
2. If it were up to you, would you keep these standards and rules as they are, or would you delete, narrow, or expand them? Explain your reasoning.
3. How do these standards and court rules influence the gathering of crime scene evidence or investigation of a crime scene?

FORENSIC RESEARCH USING THE INTERNET

1. Find your state's rules of evidence and look for rules that pertain to the admissibility of forensic evidence, testing, or expert witnesses. Compare and contrast with some of the rules and court tests listed in this chapter.

2. Find out if your state appellate court posts its case decisions on the Internet. If so, find a case that illustrates an issue discussed in this chapter dealing with the admissibility of forensic evidence or testing. If your state decisions are not on the Internet, go instead to the Web site for the U.S. Circuit Court of Appeals in your circuit, or search the U.S. Supreme Court decisions.

PRACTICE SKILLS

Practice what you have learned in the following crime scene problems:

Crime Scene Analysis 11.1

Handwriting Analysis

At trial, a detective testified as to his training as a handwriting analysis expert, and that his opinion in the case was based on the handwriting samples provided. Specifically, the detective testified that he completed a questioned document course offered by the United States Secret Service and he also participated in a two-year internship in the field. As a questioned document examiner, he is a member of the association of questioned document examiners and members of this

continued

organization exchange notes and compare experiences. The detective also testified that he has trained other questioned document examiners who have completed the course. He stated that he performs examinations for the police and privately and has performed about 120 examinations.

The detective also testified about the science of handwriting analysis. He stated that "handwriting is even more precise than DNA for identification purposes." To perform an examination, the detective testified that an examiner must have known samples and compare them with the questioned documents.

1. Should the detective be allowed to testify as a forensic expert in handwriting analysis? Why or why not?

2. Besides a challenge to his qualifications as a forensic expert, what other challenge would you raise to his testimony?

WEB SITES

Attorney Kim Kruglick's Web site on *A Beginner's Primer on the Investigation of Forensic Evidence*

> http://www.kruglaw.com

Bureau of Justice Statistics, Survey of DNA Laboratories

> http://www.ojp.usdoj.gov/bjs/pub/pdf/sdnacl01.pdf

FindLaw Case Codes

> http://guide.lp.findlaw.com/casecode/

FindLaw U.S. Supreme Court Decisions

> *http://www.findlaw.com/casecode/supreme.html*

Future of Forensic DNA Testing: Predictions of the Research and Development Working Group—National Institute of Justice

> http://www.ojp.usdoj.gov/nij/pubs-sum/183697.htm

Legal Cases Challenging Fingerprints and Other Forensic Evidence

> http://onin.com/fp/daubert_links.html

Supreme Court Collection of Cornell Law School

> http://supct.law.cornell.edu/supct/

U.S. Supreme Court

> http://www.supremecourtus.gov

ENDNOTES

1 *United States v. Plaza,* 179 F. Supp. 2d 492 (January, 2002)

2 *United States v. Plaza,* 188 F. Supp. 2d 549 (March, 2002)

3 *United States v. Jakobetz,* 955 F.2d 786 (2d. Cir., 1993)

4 November 2003 murder trial of sniper John Allen Muhammad

5 *State v. Moore,* 458 N.W.2d 90 (Minn. 1990)

6 *United States v. Santillan,* 1999 WL 1201765 (N.D.Cal. Dec. 3, 1999)

7 *Florence v. Commonwealth Of Kentucky,* 120 S.W.3d 699 2003

8 *United States v. Crisp,* 324 F.3d at 268

9 U.S. Congress, Office of Technology Assessment, *Genetic Witness: Forensic Uses of DNA Tests, OTA-BA-438* (Washington, D.C.: U.S. Government Printing Office, July 1990)

10 Committee on DNA Forensic Science. 1996. *The Evaluation of Forensic DNA Evidence.* Committee on DNA Forensic Science: An Update, National Research Council, National Academy of Sciences, Washington, D.C.: National Academies Press

11 Order of Judge Alfred A. Delucchi in *State v. Peterson* murder trial, February 2004

12 *Frye v. United States,* 293 F. 1013 (D.C. Cir. 1923)

13 See, for example, *People v. Kelly,* 17 Cal. 3d 24 (1976)

14 *Daubert v. Merrell Dow Pharmaceuticals, Inc,* .509 U.S. 579 (1993)

15 See *Baltimore Sun* article by Stephanie Hanes, *Chemist quit crime lab job after hearing...* (March 2003)

16 *State v. Begley,* 956 S.W.2d 471, 477 (Tenn. 1997)

PRESENTING CRIME SCENE EVIDENCE IN COURT

"The first thing we do, let's kill all the lawyers."

—William Shakespeare, *Henry VI*

"Take nothing on its looks; take everything on evidence. There's no better rule."

—Charles Dickens, *Great Expectations*

Chapter Outline

- Criminal Prosecution
- Preliminary Hearing
- Pre-Trial Motion Hearings
- Criminal Trial
- CSI Effect
- Order of Trial
- Role of Witnesses at Trial
- Expert Witnesses
- Lay Witnesses
- Impeachment of Witnesses

- Preparing to Testify
- Accuracy in Documentation
- Demeanor
- Preparing Evidence and Exhibits for Trial
- Presenting Evidence at Trial
- Laying a Foundation
- Identification and Authentication
- Effect of Identification and Authentication Requirement
- Chain of Custody

INTRODUCTION

As this book has shown, a crime scene investigation involves a methodical process, attention to detail, the ability to organize and analyze information and evidence, and effective communication skills, both verbal and written. Success in this requires focus and a high degree of professionalism. However, this focus and professionalism must not end with the investigation. If evidence from the crime scene and the subsequent investigation has identified a suspect and will prove the elements of the crime, a prosecution will be initiated, and the focus will turn to the courtroom. In this chapter, we will look at the courtroom, how a criminal trial proceeds, and how both testimony and evidence are presented in court.

CRIMINAL PROSECUTION

grand jury indictment
A process of charging someone with a crime, where a grand jury is convened to determine if probable cause exists.

information
A process of charging someone with a crime, where a prosecutor files a paper with the court.

A criminal prosecution is formally initiated when a prosecutor either obtains a **grand jury indictment** or files a charging document, called an **information**, with the court. After a suspect has been formally charged with a crime, that person becomes the defendant and is either summoned to appear or arrested and brought before a court in an initial appearance, often known as an arraignment. At this court appearance, the defendant is formally informed of the criminal charges against him, is given an opportunity to enter an initial plea to the charges, has bail set, and a subsequent court date set. The court will also ensure that the defendant is represented by counsel.

Because this initial court appearance only involves the formal charging of the defendant and scheduling of court dates, there is no need for any crime scene investigators or personnel to be present or testify.

Preliminary Hearing

preliminary hearing
probable cause hearing
A court hearing, before a judge only, where prosecution must present, and defense is allowed to challenge, evidence to show probable cause that a crime has been committed and that the defendant committed the crime.

After the initial arraignment of a defendant, there is generally a follow-up court hearing scheduled, called a **preliminary** or **probable cause hearing**, where the prosecutor must present enough evidence to show probable cause that a crime has been committed and that the defendant committed the crime. At this stage, there will be a need for crime scene investigators and personnel to testify. If the court finds that probable cause did exist for the arrest and charging of the defendant, the court will bind the defendant over for trial.

burden of proof
The duty to meet a certain standard or establish the requisite degree of belief in the mind of the trier of fact regarding the evidence submitted.

beyond a reasonable doubt
Requires the trier of fact to believe something to be "almost certainly true" and leaving no reasonable doubt.

motion to suppress
A request made by the defense asking the judge to prevent certain evidence from being admitted at trial because it violates a law or rule of evidence.

Burden of Proof

Burden of proof is the legal duty to meet a certain standard or establish the requisite degree of belief in the mind of the jury regarding the evidence submitted. In a criminal case, the burden of proof is **beyond a reasonable doubt**. This burden requires the jury to believe something to be "almost certainly true" and leaving no reasonable doubt. This applies to every element of a particular crime. Every element must be proven beyond a reasonable doubt. For example, if a burglary is defined as an "unlawful entry into a building with the intent to commit a theft or felony therein," then every one of the elements making up this definition must be proven beyond a reasonable doubt: that there was an *entry*, that the entry was *unlawful*, that the entry was into a *building*, and that the entry was made *with the intent to commit a theft or felony therein*.

Pre-Trial Motion Hearings

Prior to trial, there may be court hearings to decide motions filed in the criminal case. A typical hearing in which a crime scene investigator or criminalist might have to testify is a **motion to suppress** evidence. A motion to suppress is a request made by the defense asking the judge to prevent certain evidence from being admitted at trial because it violates a law or rule of evidence. For example, evidence collected from a crime scene may be challenged because no search warrant was obtained beforehand. Some crime scene photos may be challenged because of their inflammatory or prejudicial nature. Scientific evidence may be challenged because of the way it was collected, tested, or analyzed. Motions are initially filed as written documents to the court, and must then be argued before the judge in a hearing.

In each of these examples, crime scene investigators or crime lab personnel may be called to testify in support of the prosecution's argument to admit the evidence. An investigator may testify as to why no search warrant was needed at the crime scene (consent had been given, for example, or the evidence was viewed in plain view upon the initial entry). A crime lab technician may testify as to the authenticity of a crime scene photo in accurately representing the scene as found. A criminalist may testify about the scientific standards and procedures used in the collection or analysis of evidence.

Criminal Trial

Criminal trials, if they are jury trials and not before a judge only, begin with the selection of a jury. Prospective jurors are seated in the courtroom and questioned by the defense and prosecution. This

voir dire
Meaning *to speak the truth*, the process of questioning by defense and prosecution of prospective jurors.

questioning process is called **voir dire**, meaning *to speak the truth*, and is considered an essential part of trial strategy for both the defense and prosecution. Both sides have a limited number of *challenges* that they may use to exclude a prospective juror. Either side may challenge a juror found to be biased, and the judge may be requested to exclude the juror *for cause*.

CSI Effect

The questioning of jurors is especially important in criminal cases that involve evidence found at the crime scene and subsequently tested and analyzed at the crime lab. In recent years, with the popularity of so many television shows focusing on the crime scene (e.g., CSI, Forensic Files), many people have developed their own perception of what can and should be done by crime scene investigators and technicians. These perceptions have resulted in expectations on the part of many jurors as to the capabilities of crime scene personnel and evidence. This has been referred to as the **CSI Effect**. Often, these perceptions and expectations are unrealistic, as when jurors expect that DNA can be found at any crime scene, or that all evidence can be properly analyzed for definitive results about the crime. Proper questioning of prospective jurors will help identify and address these issues before they cause later problems at trial or in jury deliberations. Often, however, attorneys must adjust some of their trial strategy and handling of forensic experts if they suspect the CSI effect from the questioning of jurors.

CSI effect
Perceptions, often unrealistic, of jurors who have watched television shows about crime scene investigations and expect similar techniques and results from real-life crime labs and personnel.

Order of Trial

After a jury has been selected, the prosecution, who is usually seated closer to the jury box, begins their opening argument, presenting an overview of what they hope to prove. The defense may then present their opening argument. When opening arguments are completed, the prosecution opens their case by presenting witnesses and evidence to establish that a crime has been committed and that the defendant committed that crime.

After the prosecution presents their witnesses and evidence, the defense may present their own witnesses to counter the prosecution's case. At the conclusion of evidence, both sides present a closing argument to the jury, the judge instructs the jury as to the law in this particular case, and the jury retires to deliberate and reach a verdict. (See Exhibit 12.1.)

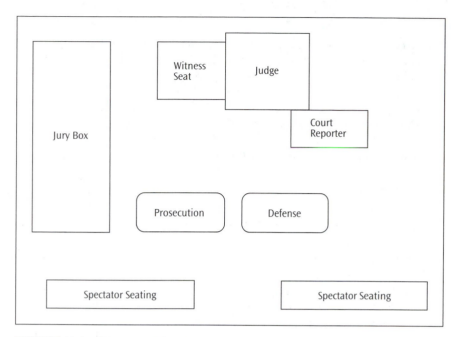

EXHIBIT 12.1   Example of Courtroom Layout

Role of Witnesses at Trial

Witnesses are central to the introduction of evidence and the proving of a case at trial. We look to witnesses to provide evidence in the form of testimony to help the triers of fact better ascertain the truth. Unless the witness qualifies as an expert, testimony must be from firsthand, personal knowledge. Crime scene investigators and personnel may also be called to lay a foundation for crime scene evidence being offered, to identify and authenticate this evidence, even to offer their opinions as to how this evidence was obtained or what it means. (See Exhibit 12.2.)

Expert Witnesses

expert witness
A witness qualified by specialized skills or knowledge whose testimony or opinion can assist the trier of fact to better understand evidence in issue.

An **expert witness** is one qualified by special knowledge, skills, experience, training, and/or education.[1] An expert witness can testify to and give opinions on matters outside of the knowledge of the average person, and that require special experience or knowledge of witnesses skilled in that particular science, art, or trade. These opinions can be based on first-hand observation, like a criminalist who examined and later performed tests on evidence from the crime scene, or it can be based on a hypothetical question put to the expert, based on her training and expertise.

lay witness
A person who testifies at trial, generally from first-hand knowledge about a fact at issue.

Lay Witness

A **lay witness** is a person who can give a firsthand account of something from personal knowledge. The witness does this by being called to the stand, taking an oath, and testifying to firsthand perception (i.e., what she saw, heard, felt, smelled, or tasted). Unless they are testifying about matters that require special knowledge or skills, most law enforcement officers initially testify as lay witnesses. Lay witnesses may also include victims and other individuals who saw or heard something that pertained to the crime scene.

Personal Knowledge

personal knowledge
A lay witness must be able to testify from a firsthand perception of having seen, heard, felt, touched, or smelled something.

To help ensure reliability in the fact-finding process, a lay witness must have **personal knowledge** about the matter being testified to, as opposed to a mere opinion. A Mississippi Rule of Evidence, for example, states that a "witness may not testify to a matter unless evidence is introduced sufficient to support a finding that the witness has personal knowledge of the matter."[2] Personal knowledge involves *perception* and *recollection*. A witness must be testifying about an event that the witness perceived through one of her senses (sight, hearing, etc.). It must be firsthand knowledge, and not what she has heard from others. She must also be able to recollect it. Evidence to prove personal knowledge usually comes from the witness's own testimony. (See Exhibit 12.3.)

EXHIBIT 12.2 Examples of Evidence Rules Governing Testimony by Witnesses

New Jersey Rules of Evidence
Rule 602. Lack of Personal Knowledge
Except as otherwise provided by Rule 703 (bases of opinion testimony by experts), a witness may not testify to a matter unless evidence is introduced sufficient to support a finding that the witness has personal knowledge of the matter. Evidence to prove personal knowledge may, but need not, consist of the testimony of the witness himself.
Rule 702. Testimony by Experts
If scientific, technical, or other specialized knowledge will assist the trier of fact to understand the evidence or to determine a fact in issue, a witness qualified as an expert by knowledge, skill, experience, training, or education may testify thereto in the form of an opinion or otherwise.

EXHIBIT 12.3 Example of Testimony Lacking Personal Knowledge

Defense:	You don't know whether the defendant had access to this storage room at the crime scene in question?
Witness:	No, I was told that she did not have access.
Defense:	You don't have personal knowledge of whether she did?
Witness:	No, only what I was told by my supervisor.
Defense:	I move to strike the last answer. It's based on what witness was told by others, not based on her personal knowledge or based on anything within this witness' ability to speak from her personal knowledge.

Impeachment of Witnesses

impeachment
Attacking the credibility of a witness in order to convince the jury that the testimony given is not truthful or that the witness is unreliable.

Impeachment is a form of attacking the credibility of a witness in order to convince the jury that the testimony given is not truthful or that the witness is unreliable. There are a variety of methods for impeaching a witness and different state rules will emphasize these various methods. Georgia rules of evidence, for example, include methods where a witness may be impeached by disproving the facts testified to by him, contradictory statements, or by evidence as to his general bad character.[3] In Florida, the credibility of a witness may be impeached by introducing statements of the witness that are inconsistent with the witness's present testimony; showing that the witness is biased; attacking the character of the witness; showing a defect of capacity, ability, or opportunity in the witness to observe, remember, or recount the matters about which the witness testified; or, by proof by other witnesses that material facts are not as testified to by the witness being impeached.[4]

The various rules have a common framework. They provide for impeachment by attacking competence and credibility. Competence may be impeached by showing that the witness has a problem in testifying from personal knowledge, or lacks the ability to perceive an event, remember, or communicate what was perceived. Credibility may be impeached by showing bias, prejudice, or an interest in the outcome of the case that might have influenced the testimony of the witness. Credibility may also be impeached by attacking the untruthful character, bad reputation, or contradictory or inconsistent statements of the witness.

PREPARING TO TESTIFY

The time for preparing to testify at trial begins with the initial crime scene investigation. Following a thorough and methodical plan of investigating and processing the crime scene and collecting evidence will help later at trial, when the defense will attempt to look for and exploit discrepancies and inconsistencies.

Accuracy in Documentation

It is essential that not only the crime scene investigation is carried out in a methodical procedure, but that the entire process is accurately documented. Defense attorneys will try to discredit crime scene witnesses and shed doubt on the investigation by attacking any inaccuracies, either in the way the investigation was carried out or in how it was documented. Even minor points, such as different times or measurements on reports can be seized on by the defense to persuade jurors that they should not believe the witness or that the investigation was flawed. *If they make mistakes on these facts or did not spot them later, what else did they miss?* To avoid this potential danger, all reports and documentation should be verified, checked, and re-checked for any errors. If any are found, they should be brought to the attention of the prosecutor.

Demeanor

Juries have evolved over the past 20 years. Today's jurors are more diverse, better educated, and have watched more television, especially shows featuring dramatized crime scene investigations and court trials. As a result, jurors have their own notions, right or wrong, of how witnesses should testify in the courtroom. They look closely at not only *what* a witness says, but *how* it is said, and how the witness looks and acts while saying it. The demeanor of a witness is extremely important and carefully watched by jurors. Surveys of juries have consistently shown that when witnesses fail to connect with or win the trust or respect of a jury, the jury tends to discount that testimony and evidence. This can lead to serious outcomes in the trial, possibly resulting in a deadlocked jury or acquittal.[5]

To avoid this, crime scene investigators and personnel must ensure that their courtroom presence and demeanor is as focused and professional as their investigation. This begins with how they *dress* for court. Conservative attire (no loud colors or flashy dress) should be the rule. Dark blue or gray business suits (for men or women) and white shirts still project authority, competence, and veracity.

Surveys show that some law enforcement personnel fail to connect with juries because they do not show the jurors the proper attention or respect, like standing when the jurors enter the courtroom or making eye contact with jurors when testifying.[6] Subtle gestures such as a respectful nod and eye contact with a juror in the hallway can make the difference later.

The effective witness is one who appears professional, confident (without appearing arrogant), comfortable, open, and honest. Body language, facial expressions, and movement of the eyes are especially important. Investigators and crime lab personnel should sit up straight in the witness chair and speak clearly. Pausing briefly before answering shows that the answer is being thoughtfully considered. (However, taking too long to answer may also convey deception.) Eye contact should be maintained with the questioner and the jury. There should be no distracting, reactive, or hostile facial expressions or hand movements. Keeping the hands open, palms up projects a sense of openness. To emphasize a point, a witness should lean slightly forward, toward the jury, making eye contact. After testifying, this professional demeanor must be maintained. The witness should maintain good posture, acknowledge the jury (e.g., with a nod), and portray confidence in leaving the courtroom.

PRACTICE TIP 12.1

Testifying in Court

Dress right
Sit up straight, don't slouch
Speak clearly, firmly
Be polite; avoid cynicism or hostile remarks
Maintain eye contact with lawyers and jury
Answer questions directly, do not volunteer info
Pause briefly before answering
Avoid police jargon or highly technical scientific terms
Be honest, never try to bluff or fake an answer
Always act professional

PREPARING EVIDENCE AND EXHIBITS FOR TRIAL

As described earlier, there are four forms of evidence: testimonial, physical, documentary, and demonstrative. Of these, witness testimony will be the primary source of evidence at trial. Evidence is usually presented in the order that the legal action took place. Sometimes, in order for one witness to testify, another person must first testify to establish the qualification of the witness to testify about a particular matter. For example, a police officer may testify that she administered a breath test to a suspect at a crime scene. To show that the police officer was properly trained and certified in how to administer the breath test, the officer will need to either establish this on the stand or another witness, the training instructor as example, may need to testify. Similarly, when a witness testifies to properly administering the test, another witness, the criminalist, may have to be called to explain what the test results mean. This all underscores the need for the prosecution to properly plan and organize the list of witnesses in a manner to present the most effective case.

exhibit
An item offered in evidence that is properly marked for later identification.

The same principle applies to exhibits. An **exhibit** is an item offered in evidence that is properly marked for later identification. Aside from testimonial evidence, the other forms of evidence will generally require that they be presented in the form of an exhibit. For example, physical evidence in the form of a fingerprint, the weapon of a crime, or tool will all need to be marked and identified as evidentiary exhibits. *State's Exhibit A*, for example.

Again, the need for proper planning of these exhibits is most important. Exhibits need to be organized so that they support witness testimony and are introduced at the right point in the trial. The key throughout this planning is to employ the Scout motto to "be prepared." Plan, gather, verify, plan more, organize and manage all witnesses and evidence.

CSI CHECKLIST 12.1

Organizing and Managing Crime Scene Evidence Exhibits

❑ What is the evidence?
❑ Who found or collected it?
❑ Who can identify it in court?
❑ How can it be identified?
❑ Where was it found or collected?
❑ Why would it be in this location?
❑ What were the circumstances around finding it?

continued

❑ Was there anything unusual or out of place?
❑ Was it photographed or documented at this scene?
❑ If so, by whom and in what capacity?
❑ Did it require any examination or analysis by a lab?
❑ If so, what lab, what results, and who did analysis?
❑ What does this evidence tend to prove or disprove?
❑ What legal citations or authorities can be used to support this evidence?
❑ Where in the trial should this evidence be presented?
❑ What challenges are anticipated to its introduction?
❑ What evidence and legal citations can be used to overcome these challenges?
❑ What offer of proof can be presented?
❑ What exhibit number will be assigned to the evidence?

PRESENTING EVIDENCE AT TRIAL

Evidence at trial is introduced through the testimony of a witness. The witnesses and evidence are usually presented in chronological order, taking the jury through each step of the original report of the crime, the initial response, and the investigation. Witness testimony is also required in order to identify and authenticate other forms of evidence presented, whether physical, documentary, or demonstrative.

Testimonial Evidence

direct examination
Initial questioning of a witness by the party that called the witness to the stand.

object
To challenge evidence or testimony introduced at trial.

cross-examine
Questioning of a witness by the opposing party on matters within the scope of the direct examination, usually to discredit the testimony of the witness or to develop facts that may help the cross-examiner's case.

Testimonial evidence is introduced by calling a specific witness to the stand, swearing them in, and asking questions of them, called **direct examination**. An example of this process might be:

Prosecutor: "Your honor, we call Detective John Jones to the stand."

Court: "Detective Jones, do you swear or affirm to tell the truth, the whole truth and nothing but the truth?"

Witness: "I do."

Court: "State may begin."

Prosecutor: "Thank you, your honor. Detective Jones, were you on duty during the evening of March 5th of this year?"

While direct examination is going on, the other side has an opportunity to **object** to the questions asked or to the witness's answers, and, afterward, will have the opportunity to **cross-examine** the witness in order to clarify answers given or attempt to discredit the witness.

Unless an opinion is allowed, testimony is limited to the witness's personal knowledge of the matter before the court. This is generally accomplished by having the witness testify to what she saw or heard.

Laying a Foundation

laying a foundation
Presenting evidence that sets the groundwork for other evidence, authenticating and identifying the evidence.

In order to be admitted, crime scene evidence must be properly offered to the trier of fact. Often, this will first require an explanation of how the witness came to be in the place where some event was witnessed, or how an item of evidence was obtained, maintained, or tested. This process is called **laying a foundation**. For example, to have a witness testify to what she saw at a crime scene, you must first show that the witness was in a position to see this event at that time and location, that is, what the witness was doing at the crime scene. If an item collected from the crime scene is introduced as evidence at trial, the person who collected or documented that item of evidence at the scene must first be called to the witness stand to identify the evidence and describe the details surrounding its collection.

Physical, Documentary, and Demonstrative Evidence

All physical, documentary, demonstrative, and scientific evidence must have a proper foundation in order to be admissible as evidence at trial. These forms of evidence must be properly identified and authenticated. It must also be shown that the custody and integrity of the evidence was maintained. (See Exhibit 12.4.)

EXHIBIT 12.4   Steps for Laying a Foundation

There are certain steps for laying a foundation to introduce physical, documentary, or certain demonstrative evidence into court. Here is an example of one procedure:

Step 1   Have the proposed piece of evidence marked as exhibit for identification (e.g., *State's Exhibit #1 in Identification*).

Step 2   Identify and authenticate the exhibit by having a witness testify that it is what it purports to be, that it is relevant to the disputed issues, and that its condition has not substantially changed.

continued

EXHIBIT 12.4   Steps for Laying a Foundation   *Continued*

Step 3	Offer the proposed evidence to opposing counsel for inspection. At this point, opposing counsel may state any objections to the admissibility of the proposed evidence.	
Step 4	The court will rule on the admissibility.	
Step 5	Once admitted as evidence, the exhibit will be named *State's Exhibit #1 in Evidence* and it may be viewed and examined by the jury.	

Identification and Authentication

identification
Part of laying a foundation, where a witness testifies that she can recognize a piece of evidence and identify it.

authentication
Part of laying a foundation, where a witness testifies that evidence is what it purports to be.

There are two requirements to laying a proper foundation for the introduction of this evidence: **identification** and **authentication**. According to Wyoming Evidence Rule 901, which reflects the majority trend in evidence law, these requirements are satisfied "by evidence sufficient to support a finding that the matter in question is what its proponent claims."[7] Identification is satisfied by having a witness testify that she recognizes the object in question and can identify it. Authentication can be done through the witness testifying to the object's authenticity, that it is what it purports to be, or, in the case of demonstrative evidence like photographs or diagrams, that it is a true and accurate representation of the scene where it was obtained. (See Exhibit 12.5.)

EXHIBIT 12.5   Requirement of Identification or Authentication

Tennessee Rules of Evidence
Rule 901 (a). General provision. The requirement of authentication or identification as a condition precedent to admissibility is satisfied by evidence sufficient to support a finding that the matter in question is what its proponent claims.

C S I   C H E C K L I S T   1 2 . 2

Elements Required for Identification

- ❑ Witness must be able to recognize the evidence in question
- ❑ Witness must be able to identify the evidence in question

---

CSI CHECKLIST 12.3

Elements Required for Authentication

❑ Evidence must be sufficient to support a finding that the matter in question is what it purports to be or what its proponent claims it is

or, in the case of *Demonstrative Evidence*:

❑ The demonstrative evidence must be a true and accurate representation of the scene it depicts or where it was obtained

---

Effect of Identification and Authentication Requirement

The effect of an authentication and identification requirement is to provide a standard to ensure that evidence presented at trial is genuine; that it is what the party presenting it says it is. Simply because evidence has been authenticated does not mean that it will be found credible or reliable by the trier of fact. Authentication only establishes that the evidence has been shown to be what it purports to be. The opposing side may still offer evidence to counter the authentication.

Problems arise when the authentication involves more complex issues, such as in how certain scientific evidence is collected or tested, or whether some items can be authenticated, like computer-generated documents and images, tape recordings, and videotapes. Another problem with authentication deals with how the legal integrity of evidence has been maintained until trial—called the *chain of custody*.

Chain of Custody

chain of custody
Means for verifying the authenticity and integrity of evidence by establishing where the evidence has been and who handled it prior to trial.

legal integrity of evidence
The principle that evidence must not be tampered with, altered, substituted, or falsified.

The **chain of custody** is the means for verifying the authenticity and **legal integrity of evidence** by establishing where the evidence has been and who handled it prior to trial. Also called the *chain of evidence*, this area of evidence law establishes the criteria for maintaining this integrity and the procedure for establishing and verifying its identity at trial. An investigator, for example, may testify that a weapon in question is the same weapon that was taken from a crime scene. She may identify and authenticate the evidence from initials that she had marked on the weapon or from the serial number that she had noted. After establishing this identity and authentication, the investigator will be asked to verify that the evidence has been kept safe, without tampering, prior to bringing it to trial. Any person who had contact with the evidence must also be accounted for.

Chain Only as Strong as Weakest Link

There should be as few persons as possible that have custody of evidence and those who do must be identifiable or explained in the chain of custody. Because a chain is only as strong as its weakest link, the chain of custody may be broken or vulnerable to attack if the evidence has been damaged, tampered with, or found to be unaccounted for during any period of time. For example, one court established the rule still followed in most jurisdictions that where "evidence has passed out of the possession of the original receiver and into the possession of others, a chain of possession must be established to avoid any claim of substitution, tampering, or mistake, and failure to submit such proof may result in the exclusion of the evidence or testimony as to its characteristics."[8]

Another court stated the rule as, "Where the substance analyzed has passed through several hands the evidence must not leave it to conjecture as to who had it and what was done with it between the taking and the analysis."[9] Still another court stated, "Proof of a chain of custody is necessary to establish that the evidence recovered by the police is the same as that tested by the laboratory."[10]

In the following Alabama case, the court described the "links" in the chain of custody and how these links need to be identified and documented.

CASE

Knight v. State of Alabama

Court of Criminal Appeals of Alabama

659 So. 2d 931 (1993)

Opinion: McMillan, Judge

The appellant was convicted of receiving stolen property in the first degree. He was sentenced to 15 years' imprisonment.

The appellant contends that the State failed to prove a proper chain of custody for pieces of broken glass taken from the crime scene for purposes of fingerprint examination. Specifically, he contends that the State failed to present any evidence as to "how the glass got to the police station." The evidence presented by the State tended to show the following: Officer Derek Wilson testified that he was the evidence technician who "lifted" the fingerprints off of the glass. He testified that he went to the "supply house" where the evidence was stored to pick up the glass and the supply form. He testified that the evidence was listed on the supply form as having been discovered during a burglary investigation. He further testified that the supply form indicated that the evidence had been delivered to the supply house by Officer P. L. Flemming, who had investigated the crime. He testified that, after lifting the fingerprints, he returned the glass to the supply house.

continued

In *Ex parte Holton, 590 So. 2d 918, 920 (Ala. 1991),* the Alabama Supreme Court stated:

"The chain of custody is composed of 'links.' A 'link' is anyone who handled the item. The State must identify each link from the time the item was seized. In order to show a proper chain of custody, the record must show each link and also the following with regard to each link's possession of the item: '(1) [the] receipt of the item; (2) [the] ultimate disposition of the item, i.e., transfer, destruction, or retention; and (3) [the] safeguarding and handling of the item between receipt and disposition.' Imwinklereid, The Identification of Original, Real Evidence, *61 Mil.L.Rev . 145, 159 (1973).*

"If the State, or any other proponent of demonstrative evidence, fails to identify a link or fails to show for the record any one of the three criteria as to each link, the result is a 'missing' link, and the item is inadmissible. If, however, the State has shown each link and has shown all three criteria as to each link, but has done so with circumstantial evidence, as opposed to the direct testimony of the 'link,' as to one or more criteria or as to one or more links, the result is a 'weak' link. When the link is 'weak,' a question of credibility and weight is presented, not one of admissibility."

Applying the Holton principles to the instant case, we conclude that the State failed to prove a proper chain of custody for the pieces of broken glass. Although Officer Wilson testified that Officer Flemming had initially seized the glass and delivered it to the supply house, the record is devoid of any evidence, either direct or circumstantial, concerning Officer Flemming's "safeguarding and handling of the item between receipt and disposition." Hence, there was a "missing link" in the chain of custody of the evidence, and the glass should not have been admitted into evidence.

Will a "Missing Link" Break the Chain?

Some courts have held that a missing link in a chain of custody will not affect the admissibility of evidence as long as it has been properly authenticated and shown that it has not been altered or contaminated. One federal court stated:

The "chain of custody" rule is but a variation of the principle that real evidence must be authenticated prior to its admission into evidence. The purpose of this threshold requirement is to establish that the item to be introduced, is what it purports to be. Therefore, the ultimate question is whether the authentication testimony was sufficiently complete so as to convince the court that it is improbable that the original item had been exchanged with another or otherwise tampered with. ... [P]recision in developing the "chain of custody" is not an ironclad requirement, and the fact of a "missing link does not prevent the admission of real evidence, so long as there is sufficient proof that the evidence is what it purports to be and has not been altered in any material aspect."[11]

A state court summed up the rule that in a criminal case, the prosecution "is not required to eliminate all possibility of tampering, but it must show with reasonable certainty that the item [has] not been altered, substituted, or contaminated prior to analysis . . . ."[12]

Does Failure to Preserve Useful Evidence Constitute Denial of Due Process?

due process clause
Constitutional protection under the Fourteenth Amendment that provides a person with the right to reasonable notice of charges and the right to confront witnesses and evidence against him.

When the state has failed to adequately preserve or test an evidence sample, another legal challenge by defense has been that it constituted a violation of the **Due Process Clause** of the Fourteenth Amendment. This constitutional protection provides a person with the right to reasonable notice of charges and the right to confront witnesses and evidence against him.

The United States Supreme Court addressed this in a case decision, holding that the police do not have any constitutional duty to perform a particular test on any evidence. In the Arizona case before the Court, the victim, a 10-year-old boy, was molested and sodomized. After the assault, the boy was taken to a hospital where a physician used a swab from a "sexual assault kit" to collect semen samples from the boy's rectum. The police also collected the boy's clothing, which they failed to refrigerate. A police criminologist later performed some tests on the rectal swab and the boy's clothing, but was unable to obtain information about the identity of the boy's assailant. At trial, expert forensic witnesses for the defense testified that defendant might have been completely exonerated by timely performance of tests on properly preserved semen samples. Instead, the defendant was convicted of child molestation, sexual assault, and kidnapping in an Arizona state court. The Arizona Court of Appeals reversed the conviction on the ground that the State had breached a constitutional duty to preserve the semen samples from the victim's body and clothing.

On appeal, the United States Supreme Court held that the Due Process Clause of the Fourteenth Amendment did not require the state to preserve the semen samples even though the samples might have been useful to respondent. The Court stated that unless a criminal defendant can show *bad faith* on the part of the police, failure to preserve potentially useful evidence does not constitute a denial of due process of law. The Court said that here, the police's failure to refrigerate the victim's clothing and to perform tests on the semen samples could at worst be described as negligent. However, none of this information was concealed from defense at trial, and the evidence—such as it was—was made available to the defense expert, who declined to perform any tests on the samples. There was no suggestion of bad faith on the part of the police. Moreover, the Court held that the Due Process Clause was not violated because the State failed to perform a newer test on the semen samples. "The police do not have a constitutional duty to perform any particular tests."[13]

Although this decision is still the standard in federal courts, many state courts have rejected the "bad faith" part of it, holding that their state constitutions have set a different standard. Most of these states have employed some type of balancing test, "weighing the reasons for the unavailability of the evidence against the degree of prejudice to the accused." Some state courts have held that more specifically, "the trial court must balance the totality of circumstances surrounding the missing evidence, including the following factors: the materiality of the missing evidence, the likelihood of mistaken interpretation of it by witnesses or the jury, the reason for its nonavailability to the defense, and the prejudice to the defendant caused by the unavailability of the evidence."[14]

PRACTICE TIP 12.2

United States Supreme Court Decisions

Do you want to read the above Supreme Court case in full or other U.S. Supreme Court cases? Go to one of the following court resources:

> *Findlaw—United States Supreme Court Decisions*
> *http://www.findlaw.com/casecode/supreme.html*
> *United States Supreme Court*
> *http://www.supremecourtus.gov/*

SUMMARY

The focus and professionalism involved in a crime scene investigation must not end with the investigation. If evidence from the crime scene and the subsequent investigation has identified a suspect and will prove the elements of the crime, a prosecution will be initiated, and the focus will turn to the courtroom. Crime scene investigators and crime lab personnel may have to testify in several different court proceedings, including preliminary hearings, pretrial motion hearings, and the criminal trial. The time for preparing to testify at trial begins with the initial crime scene investigation. Following a thorough and methodical plan of investigating and processing the crime scene and collecting evidence will help later at trial, when the defense will attempt to look for and exploit discrepancies and inconsistencies.

Evidence at trial is introduced through the testimony of a witness. The witnesses and evidence are usually presented in chronological order, taking the jury through each step of the original report of the crime, the initial response, and the investigation. Witness testimony is also required in order to identify and authenticate other forms of evidence presented, whether physical, documentary, or demonstrative.

To be effective witnesses, crime scene investigators and lab personnel must ensure that their courtroom presence and demeanor is as focused and professional as their investigation. The effective witness is one who appears professional, confident (without appearing arrogant), comfortable, open, and honest.

Evidence exhibits also need to be organized so that they support witness testimony and are introduced at the right point in the trial. To be admitted, evidence must be properly offered. Often, this will first require an explanation of how the witness came to be in the place where some event was witnessed, or how an item of evidence was obtained, maintained, or tested. This process is called *laying a foundation*. There are two requirements to laying a proper foundation for the introduction of this evidence: *identification* and *authentication*. Identification is satisfied by having a witness testify that she recognizes the object in question and can identify it. Authentication can be done through the witness testifying to the object's authenticity, that it is what it purports to be, or, in the case of demonstrative evidence like photographs or diagrams, that it is a true and accurate representation of the scene where it was obtained. *Chain of custody* is the means for verifying the authenticity and legal integrity of evidence by establishing where the evidence has been and who handled it prior to trial. Because a chain is only as strong as its weakest link, the chain of custody may be broken or vulnerable to attack if the evidence has been damaged, tampered with, or is unaccounted for during any period of time.

KEY TERMS

Authentication

Beyond a Reasonable Doubt

Burden of Proof

Chain of Custody

Cross-Examine

CSI Effect

Direct Examination

Due Process Clause

Exhibit

Expert Witness

Grand Jury Indictment

Identification

Impeachment

Information

Lay Witness

Laying a Foundation

Legal Integrity of Evidence

Motion to Suppress

Object

Personal Knowledge

Preliminary Hearing

Probable Cause Hearing

Voir Dire

REVIEW QUESTIONS

1. Identify some of the court proceedings in which a crime scene investigator or lab personnel may have to testify.

2. Distinguish between lay and expert witnesses. Give an example of what each might testify to.

3. Describe how crime scene personnel might prepare for testifying in court.

4. Explain what is meant by *laying a foundation.*

5. Distinguish the terms *identification* and *authentication,* and describe how they are used in the presentation of evidence?

6. Distinguish *chain of custody* from the *legal integrity of evidence.*

7. Explain how *chain of custody* can be established and why it is important in presenting evidence.

CRITICAL THINKING QUESTIONS 12.1

1. What is the importance of understanding how to present evidence and testify effectively in court?

2. What public policy considerations do you think might be behind some of the legal procedures for presenting evidence in court or ensuring the chain of custody for evidence as discussed in this chapter?

3. How do you think the CSI effect discussed in this chapter might influence the testimony of crime scene investigators or personnel at trial? The gathering of crime scene evidence or investigation of a crime scene?

FORENSIC RESEARCH USING THE INTERNET

Find the specific court Web sites covering your state or federal circuit. Search these sites for case decisions that deal with the presentation of crime scene evidence or testimony at trial. Summarize the cases that you find and describe how they pertain to the topics studied in this chapter.

PRACTICE TIP 12.3

Finding State Court Sites

A good source for finding your state court case decisions is to go to the official Web site for your state. If you do not know how to access this site, go the Google search engine (www. google.com) and type in the name of your state and "court opinions" in www.google.com or go to one of these valuable court resources:

> *Legal Information Institute listing of state courts and laws*
> *http://www.law.cornell.edu/states/listing.html*
> *National Center for State Courts*
> *http://www.ncsconline.org/d_kis/info_court_web_sites.html*

PRACTICE SKILLS:

Practice what you have learned in the following problem.

Crime Scene Analysis 12.1

Conduct a portion of a court proceeding in which an item of physical evidence collected from a crime scene is to be admitted into evidence at trial. Call at least two different crime scene personnel to testify regarding the evidence: one of the investigators and one of the criminalists or crime scene specialists. In addition to these witnesses, role players should include a judge, prosecution, defense attorney, and a jury. In the introduction of the evidence and testimony of the witnesses, cover the following topics:

- Expert versus Lay Witness
- Preparation and Demeanor of Witnesses on Stand
- Direct Examination
- Laying a Foundation
- Identification
- Authentication
- Chain of Custody
- Cross-Examination

After testimony has concluded, conduct an assessment and critique of the witnesses, whether a proper foundation was provided, whether the evidence was properly identified and authenticated, and whether a chain of custody was established.

WEB SITES

Findlaw—United States Supreme Court Decisions
    http://www.findlaw.com/casecode/supreme.html
Google Search Engine
    http://www.google.com
Legal Information Institute listing of state courts and laws
    http://www.law.cornell.edu/states/listing.html
National Center for State Courts
    http://www.ncsconline.org/d_kis/info_court_web_sites.html
United States Supreme Court
    http://www.supremecourtus.gov/

ENDNOTES

1   See, for example, *Federal Rule of Evidence* 702

2   *Mississippi Rules of Evidence,* Rule 602. Lack of Personal Knowledge

3   *Georgia Evidence Codes,* Sections 24-9-82, 24-9-83, and 24-9-84

4   *Florida rules of Evidence 90.608* Who may impeach.

5   Joe Navarro, "Testifying in the Theater of the Courtroom," *FBI Bulletin*, Sept. 2004

6   Amy Singer, "How to Connect with Jurors," *Trial* 35, no. 4 (1999): 22.

7   *Wyoming Rules of Evidence*, Rule 901

8   *Graham v. State of Indiana*, 253 Ind. 525 (1970)

9   *Rodgers v. Commonwealth,* 197 Va. 527, 90 S.E. 2d 257, 260 (1955)

10   *Robertson v. Commonwealth,* 12 Va. App. 854, 406 S.E. 2d 417 (1991)

11   *United States v. HowardArias, 679 F.2d 363 (4th Cir. 1982)*

12   Washington v. Commonwealth, 323 S.E. 2d 577 (1984)

13   *Arizona v. Youngblood*, 488 U.S. 51 (1988)

14   *State v. Morales*, 232 Conn. 707, 657 A.2d 585 (1995)

FUTURE OF CRIME SCENE INVESTIGATION, CRIMINALISTICS, AND THE LAW

"The future is now."
—Nam June Paik

"The future ain't what it used to be."
—Yogi Berra

Chapter Outline

- Future is Now: Recent Innovations in Crime Scene Investigation
- Future of Crime Scene Investigation and Criminalistics
- Improving Existing Forensic Tools and Technologies
- Miniaturization (Lab-on-a-Chip)
- Automation
- Tele-Forensics
- Standardization
- Future of Laws Governing Crime Scene Investigations
- Technology and Law
- Scientific Evidence
- Trends in Crime Scene Search Laws
- CSI Effect

INTRODUCTION

We will conclude this book by looking at recent innovations in crime scene investigations and criminalistics, and at some expected future changes and innovations, and the factors that are expected to drive these changes.

FUTURE IS NOW: RECENT INNOVATIONS IN CRIME SCENE INVESTIGATION

The quote above by Nam Paik is especially pertinent for crime scene investigation, which has been undergoing significant changes over the past several years. "The future is now." For crime scene investigation, this future really started with the adaptation of the laser, DNA, the computer and its related technology for law enforcement and crime scene investigative purposes. Through innovations in science and technology, we have seen dramatic advances in our forensic identification, analysis, and testing capabilities.

Alternate Light Source

alternate light sources
Specialized forensic lighting that allows detection of evidence that cannot be seen by naked eye.

For example, we have highly specialized forensic lighting, called **alternate light sources**, which allow the detection of fingerprints, body fluids, and trace evidence at a crime scene that previously could not be seen by the naked eye.

New research in these alternate light sources are developing reflective ultraviolet imaging systems (RUVIS), which can work in ambient light, like full daylight or darkness, to detect latent prints.[1]

Lasers

laser trajectory projection
Use of laser to determine trajectory and path of a bullet.

laser profilometry system
Three-dimensional laser scanning equipment able to compare, analyze, transmit, and store images of evidence.

We also have portable lasers that can help reveal evidence invisible to the naked eye, like fingerprints and other impression evidence, including the outline of a shoeprint in a carpet. Lasers are being adapted to other uses in crime scene investigation. Bullet trajectories can now be determined through **laser trajectory projection**, pinpointing not only the path of the bullet, but where it might be found.

In the future, a laser system, called the **laser profilometry system** is expected to replace or supplement the crime lab microscope. This system has a computerized three-dimensional laser scanning equipment that will be able to compare, analyze, transmit, and store images of evidence, all in a more accurate and faster manner than conventional methods.

electrostatic lifting
Electrostatic dust-lifting film that collects dust from a surface to the film, allowing an impression to be lifted without damage to the impression.

GPS
Global positioning system used to sketch and diagram a crime scene.

image processing software
Specialized software that enhances digital images at crime scenes or on victims that need more detail shown, such as fingerprints or bite marks.

Electrostatic Lifting

We have new ways to "lift" latent prints, or prints that were previously difficult to attempt to lift without damage. For example, **electrostatic lifting** allows a footprint impression to be lifted from dust, without damaging the impression.

GPS

To sketch and document crime scenes, technicians are starting to use electronic distance measuring devices and **GPS**, Global Positioning Systems. To help record a crime scene, we have digital cameras and camcorders that also allow the images to be instantly transmitted to outside or remote locations for others to view.

To receive this transmitted digital information, we have computerized databases and evidence control systems that can help analyze and track digitized impressions of evidence from a crime scene. We have **Image Processing Software** that can enhance these digital images from crime scenes that need more detail shown, such as fingerprints or bite marks.

FUTURE OF CRIME SCENE INVESTIGATION AND CRIMINALISTICS

The technological advances and innovations in crime scene investigation and criminalistics are expected to continue at a rapid pace in the future. Driving some of this change is the need for better technology to combat terrorism and ensure domestic security in our post-9/11 world. As governments encourage development of new and improved security devices, biometrics, and identification systems, forensic science will benefit as these new products are adapted for related law enforcement and crime scene investigative purposes.

Most importantly, new advances in crime scene investigation and criminalistics will be driven by four key factors: improving existing forensic tools and technologies, miniaturization, automation, and standardization.

Improving Existing Forensic Tools and Technologies

There are many forensic tools and technologies in use at crime scenes and crime labs. As described above, there are also many new products developed over recent years. The future need will be to further test and improve these existing tools and technologies, making them better, smaller, and easier to use in the field.

Better Visualization of Latent Prints

For example, traditional methods to lift latent prints have been utilized for years. However, as noted above, there have been many recent innovations to improve the visualization of latent prints at a crime scene. To help in this visualization problem and to speed up the detection process, fingerprint-retrieving devices using cyanoacrylate fuming techniques combined with ultraviolet dyes have been developed for nonporous areas. Small areas of a crime scene or the entire building can be more quickly fumed and processed. This also helps to eliminate the problem of print degradation due to the time spent looking for prints. For porous areas, new ninhydrin analogs have been developed that can work with non-chlorofluorocarbon solvents to more effectively detect latent prints, and are environmentally sensitive.[2]

In the future, these existing innovations will be greatly improved upon and new methods will be found to improve the discovery, visualization, and collection of impression evidence at a crime scene. The focus will be on standardizing and automating the methods used. At the top of this list will be the use of new, more powerful digital cameras and mobile retrieval devices specifically designed to collect and transmit prints and impression evidence. These devices would then instantly transmit an image of the impression to a database where an identification and further information could be automatically retrieved and analyzed.

Photogrammetry

photogrammetry
Computerized method used to map and precisely measure a crime scene and the objects in it from digital photographs.

Photogrammetry is a computerized method used to map, sketch, and precisely measure a crime scene and the objects in it from digital photographs. Measurements are taken and the crime scene is photographed from several directions and views. From this, the sizes of any objects or evidence in the photos can then be determined and displayed.

Pictometry

To help with the sketching and mapping of a crime scene using photogrammetry, a new form of aerial photography, called **pictometry**, can map and depict images in 3D.[3]

pictometry
Aerial photography that can map and depict images in 3D.

Digital photos taken at the crime scene can also be "sewn" together, creating a panoramic, 360-degree, photo of a crime scene, allowing views of all objects in relation to each other. Sound can be embedded so that a viewer could select a piece of evidence viewed in the photo, put a cursor over it, and hear crime scene personnel describe the evidence, how it was found and how it will be collected.

Distance Measuring Devices

In the future, technicians will be able to create precise mapping and sketches of a crime scene in both regular and 3D using the above digital photographic techniques, along with laser and electronic distance measuring devices (like the GPS system discussed above). These systems will replace the sketching techniques now done by hand.

Miniaturization

miniaturization
lab-on-a-chip
Use of microchips to develop smaller, more efficient forensic identification and testing instruments.

New innovation in forensic tools and technology is being driven in large part by the need for **miniaturization**; to make things smaller and easier to use in the field.

Lab-on-a-Chip

Referred to as **lab-on-a-chip**, this technology uses microchips and nanotechnology to develop smaller, more efficient forensic instrumentation, which is now only found in full size at the crime lab. These miniaturized instruments could then be used at crime scenes to more quickly discover, identify, and analyze evidence. It would be like bringing an entire crime lab to a crime scene in a shoebox.

Gas Chromatography

gas chromatograph
A crime lab testing instrument that analyzes by separating substances into their components.

For example, a **gas chromatograph** is an important crime lab testing instrument that is used for analysis of certain crime scene evidence, such as drugs or explosive residue. For the past several years, research has been in progress to develop a miniaturized gas chromatograph that could easily be transported to and used at a crime scene. The goal of the research is to have one that was as small as a wrist watch and that would take no more than a few seconds to complete its analysis (compared to almost 40 minutes in the lab).[4]

Microchip Blood Analysis

Researchers are developing a miniature, disposable microchip device capable of collecting blood and other biological samples at a crime scene, processing and analyzing the sample, and sealing it for transport and preservation of evidence.

DNA on a Chip

DNA profiling and identification has revolutionized crime scene investigation in recent years. The problems with current methods, however, have been in the complexity of the testing procedures and the length of time from collection to analysis. The future for DNA profiling is an exciting one. Research has been undertaken to simplify, speed up, and miniaturize the process. One project, funded by the National Institute of Justice, will develop a unit that can be used at a crime scene to analyze DNA using electric fields on a silicon microchip. This technology would provide greater than 99 percent probability of identity, and allow simultaneous analysis and comparison of two individuals on one chip. The system would be easier to operate than current methods, with the operator simply adding crude tissue or sample for analysis and genetic information in less than a minute.

Another project underway is researching the use of *Laser desorption mass spectrometry* (LDMS) to analyze DNA. This method would reduce analysis time to a few minutes per sample.[5]

Smaller, Better, Faster

Miniaturization will not only result in forensic identification and analysis instruments that are more portable and easier to use, but they will be cheaper, need less sample, and be much faster in producing results. A test that can take hours when sent to a lab can be completed in seconds at the crime scene.

Automation

automation
Connectivity technology allowing faster and more open sharing, retrieval, and analysis of information, directly from the crime scene.

Automation refers to computerized and electronic connectivity technology that will allow faster and more open sharing, retrieval, and analysis of information, directly from the crime scene. An example of this is database connectivity, such as the FBI's automated fingerprint identification system. Better technology will soon be developed to allow crime scene technicians to digitally photograph and "collect" impression evidence found at the crime scene. Automated features embedded in this technology will immediately transmit the print to the appropriate electronic database for analysis and identification. These automated features will also link with other data-mining databases and investigative links to compare with other cases and related crimes or MOs.

Data-Mining and Linkage

This automation technology will be utilized throughout each step of the crime scene investigation. Procedures, information, and evidence at the scene will be documented, identified, "collected," and analyzed. Relevant case and investigative information will be documented and linked to relevant analytic, investigative, and pattern recognition databases. Data-mining and computer-assisted analysis tools will automatically track and help to manage the crime scene investigation, providing linkage with partnering agencies and signaling investigators with related information or suggestions. Investigators at the crime scene will be informed of any investigative leads and connections discovered through any of these links.

Teleforensics

teleforensics
Remote viewing of a crime scene through electronically transmitted images.

The future of miniaturization and automation will significantly impact another important area in crime scene investigation, currently being used. **Teleforensics** is the remote viewing of a crime scene through electronically transmitted images. These images can be transmitted by a digital camera or camcorder. At present, some agencies are experimenting with this method by having an officer go into the crime scene carrying a handheld or helmet camcorder, outfitted with a wireless transmitter. The images are then transmitted in real time to a remote location, where other investigators and crime lab personnel can view the scene and determine what is needed.

Teleforensics in Use

Teleforensics can be a valuable tool, and has tremendous potential for future applications in crime scene investigation. Currently, using teleforensics can protect the crime scene and evidence from contamination, can document the scene before it is disturbed by processing personnel, can identify important evidence, and allow more investigators and crime lab personnel to view the original scene so that proper plans can be made for the investigation and processing. Teleforensics can reduce the need for a walk-through and speed up the actual investigation. The crime scene images can be transmitted to outside investigators or consultants so that they can provide important analysis and recommendations. For example, digitized images of blood splatter evidence could be transmitted to an expert in another state, who could then evaluate the pictures and offer recommendations.

Future Use of Teleforensics

thermal imaging
Imaging technology that detects and converts infrared radiation into heat images based on relative warmth.

In the future, teleforensics will be the primary means for approaching many crime scenes, especially those where the crime is unknown or those involving violent crimes. The procedure will include the use of **thermal imaging**, a technology that can detect heat images, which can be identified based on their relative warmth. This imaging will let officers know whether there are humans inside the crime scene, where they are, and whether they are alive and seriously injured. This will allow for officer safety in the initial response to the crime scene.

robotics
Technology associated with the design and use of robots.

Robotics

Another major innovation that will assist teleforensics is the development of **robotics**, technology associated with the design and use of robots. Already in use to find bombs, and by military special operations and law enforcement S.W.A.T. teams to find barricaded suspects, robots will change the way crime scenes are investigated. Using miniaturization and air-cushion or hover technology, small robots with digital transmission and imaging technology will be able to enter and move through crime scenes without disturbing any evidence. Infrared lighting can be attached to allow maneuvering in darkness.

As miniaturization is developed in forensic applications, robots can be equipped with detection and analysis instrumentation. These robots can document the crime scene, identify evidence, and perform examinations on the evidence. For example, a blood stain could be detected with the robot's embedded evidence identification technology. The robot could then analyze the blood stain using its attached DNA microchip analysis. This analysis would be immediately transmitted via the robot's wireless communication system to the DNA identification database, and linked through the robot's automation technology to any other relevant site or database.

Teleforensic robots could be equipped with a variety of testing and analysis devices to be able to safely and effectively find, scan, and analyze a variety of evidence at a crime scene.

Standardization

In recent years, law enforcement crime labs have been the subject of criticism over lab backlogs (especially DNA testing backlogs), qualifications of lab personnel, and standardization of testing criteria and methodologies. With the future of crime scene investigation moving toward the lab-on-a-chip, field-based testing concepts, it is expected that more standardization will occur to address these issues.

Although there are plans in effect now to deal with the problem of backlogs in DNA testing at crime labs, it is not expected to be as bad of a problem in the future. With miniaturization, lower costs, and field-based testing, especially in DNA analysis instrumentation used directly from the crime scene, the backlogs of DNA testing from crime scenes will be eliminated. This will relieve pressure on the crime labs, which often are backlogged by drug and alcohol testing. The problem then will be who will provide these lab-on-a-chip services at different crime scenes and how will the testing and analysis be conducted.

To deal with providing crime lab services, it is expected that there will be more consolidation, standardization, and regionalization. At present, crime labs can be found at city, county, and state levels. Often, budgetary restrictions dictate how much funding or equipment a particular crime lab may have, which affects the level and quality of services that lab may provide to law enforcement. In the future, there will be more consolidation of smaller crime labs with more focus on mobile units capable of field-based testing and analysis directly at the crime scene. Smaller crime labs lacking adequate budgets will be consolidated into larger, regional labs that will oversee the mobile units and conduct regular lab testing and analysis (e.g., drugs and alcohol).

Current State of Regulation

Currently, crime labs are not regulated and lack standardized testing and quality control criteria. As described in an earlier chapter, to ensure that their operations meet national standards, most modern crime labs seek accreditation through the Crime Laboratory Accreditation Program of the non-profit American Society of Crime Laboratory Directors/Laboratory Accreditation Board (ASCLD/LAB). This is a voluntary program in which a participating crime laboratory must demonstrate that its management, operations, personnel, procedures, equipment, physical plant, security, and personnel safety procedures meet established standards.

Unfortunately, almost half of the crime labs in the United States are not accredited by this voluntary program. As a result, there is a lack of standardized testing, quality control, or analyst qualification criteria at many labs. In an assessment of California crime labs by the California State Auditor, the report concluded that "because many of the laboratories have neither designated quality managers nor implemented other essential elements of a quality control system, they cannot achieve or maintain ASCLD/LAB accreditation."[6]

The Rand Corporation, a research think tank followed up by reporting that the California State Auditor's statement was "indicative of the condition of labs across the country." The Rand report concluded that "there are substantial needs for improved facilities, modern equipment, continuing training, and quality control."[7]

Future Standards and Regulation

In the future, these concerns will be addressed through government regulation. States and the federal government will enact laws regulating crime labs and personnel. Standardized testing, quality control, and analyst qualification criteria will be required and regulated by government agencies, or through mandated accreditation and review by the ASCLD. (See Exhibit 13.1.)

EXHIBIT 13.1   Recommendations for Crime Labs

To ensure that they meet and maintain ASCLD/LAB standards for accreditation, a California Auditor report recommended local laboratories should do the following:

❑ Appoint quality managers and support staff at sufficient levels to implement and maintain quality control and safety programs, including documentation and periodic auditing.

❑ Implement a proficiency testing program.

❑ Implement a court testimony monitoring program.

❑ Work with their respective parent organization to budget the funds necessary for accreditation inspections and self-evaluations to demonstrate continued compliance with ASCLD/LAB standards.

❑ Develop, implement, and document a formal training program.

❑ Consider consolidating or regionalizing services, including DNA testing.

❑ Continue to consider consolidating laboratories within a specific region.[8]

FUTURE OF LAWS GOVERNING CRIME SCENE INVESTIGATIONS

As with innovations in forensics, law and legal procedure in the future will be impacted by technology. There will be some changes in how scientific evidence is viewed by the courts, and the laws pertaining to crime scene search will be relaxed.

Technology and Law

With the advent of miniaturization and wireless connectivity, the courtroom of the future will allow the judge and each of the parties to have a computer in front of them. Witnesses may no longer always have to appear "live" in the courtroom to testify. Video conferencing may allow a witness to testify "live" from any location throughout the world, including a crime lab.

Evidence will be viewed through the individual monitors and on a big screen computer projection screen. Gone will be the time-consuming routine of handing exhibits of evidence around for viewing, or passing out photos one by one, or of a witness trying to set up and write on a board to illustrate something, or point something out of a sketch from an accident or crime scene. The forensic witness or investigator will simply click a button and the item of evidence pops up on the big screen computer projection screen, simultaneously shown on the small monitor in front of each juror. Using an **Evidence Presentation Software** program for exhibiting evidence, or one of the presentation software applications, the forensic witness will utilize computer animation and graphics to illustrate and explain the crime scene evidence or forensic testing.

evidence presentation software
A computer program specially designed for the organizing of evidence exhibits and the animated presentation of evidence.

computer animation evidence
A newer form of demonstrative evidence that utilizes sophisticated computer-generated graphics and animation to illustrate and reconstruct evidence or crime scenes.

Computer Animation in Presenting Crime Scene Evidence

Computer animation evidence is already being used in many courtrooms. In the following California case, the court wrestled with what may be the portentous concern of the future—the role of computer animation as evidence.

CASE

People v. Hood

53 Cal. App. 4th 965 (1997)

[Hood was convicted of first degree murder in the shooting death of an employee. Hood fired seven bullets into the victim, killing him. The prosecutor contended that the killing was deliberate and premeditated; the defense contended that the victim had threatened Hood beforehand and was in the process of pulling out a gun when Hood shot him in self-defense.

....

Before the first trial, the prosecution moved to be permitted to introduce a computer animation of the shooting, based upon information supplied by Hood's secretary and the detective who did measurements at the scene and on the reports and opinions of the pathologist who performed the autopsy on the victim and prosecution ballistics and gunshot residue experts. Hood opposed admission of the animation, claiming that ... computer animation had not gained the scientific acceptance necessary for admissibility. The trial court ruled that the animation was illustrative, similar to an expert who draws on a board, and was not being introduced as evidence in and of itself, but only to illustrate the testimony of various prosecution experts.

....

Before the prosecution's computer animation was played for the jury, the trial court gave the jury the following instruction: ". . . [Y]ou're reminded that . . . this is an animation based on a compilation of a lot of different experts' opinions. And there are what we call crime scene reconstruction experts who could, without using a computer, get on the stand and testify that based on this piece of evidence and this piece of evidence and this piece of evidence that they've concluded that the crime occurred in a certain manner. And then they can describe to you the manner in which it occurred. And they can sometimes use charts or diagrams or re-create photographs to demonstrate that. And the computer animation that we have here is nothing more than that kind of an expert opinion being demonstrated or illustrated by the computer animation, as opposed to charts and diagrams."

....

Hood contends that the trial court abused its discretion in determining that the probative value of the prosecution's computer animation outweighed its prejudicial impact. Aside from reiterating the points made and rejected below, Hood asserts that the animation was emotionally charged and preyed on the emotions of the jury. We disagree. The animation was clinical and emotionless. This, combined with the instruction given the jurors about how they were to utilize both animations, persuades us that the trial court did not abuse its discretion in this regard.

The judgment is affirmed.

Scientific Evidence

Another area of current change and the subject of significant future uncertainty is how scientific evidence is viewed by different courts. As we have seen in our readings, for over 70 years in this country, the accepted test for scientific evidence and testing was called the *Frye* standard, or *General Acceptance Test*. This standard was based on a 1923 case where a federal circuit court held that the results of a "scientific test" could be admitted if the test had "gained general acceptance in the particular field in which it belongs."

In 1993, a major decision by the U.S. Supreme Court in *Daubert* recognized a new test in the federal courts. This test requires that the scientific evidence or testimony be able to assist the trier of fact to understand the evidence or to determine a fact in issue. In addition, the expert testimony had to consist of scientific or technical knowledge or experience supported by appropriate validation. This "knowledge" can be determined by considering five factors, including whether it can be (and has been) tested; whether the theory or technique has been subjected to peer review and publication; its known or potential rate of error; the existence and maintenance of standards controlling the technique's operation; and the *Frye* standard for degree of general acceptance within the relevant scientific community.

The problem was that many state courts refused to adopt the new standard. In addition, subsequent federal circuit and Supreme Court decisions modified the *Daubert* standard to the extent that most courts had difficulty figuring out how the standard could be applied. This confusion does not appear to be getting better. The following case shows how this standard might, in the future, change many of the long-accepted areas of scientific evidence. In the following case from a Pennsylvania federal district court, the judge deals with a request from defendants to exclude fingerprint identification evidence. The defendants claim that this evidence, which has been accepted as reliable scientific evidence for almost a hundred years, fails to meet the newer *Daubert* standard of testing and scientific knowledge.

CASE

United States v. Plaza

179 F. Supp. 2d 492 (2002)

Pollak, J.

Currently before the court is defendants' Motion to Preclude the United States from Introducing Latent Fingerprint Identification Evidence, in which defendants contend that evidence relating to fingerprints fails to conform to the standard for admitting expert testimony ... Daubert v. Merrell Dow...

continued

....

Absence of Testing of Fingerprint Techniques

[T]he government had little success in identifying scientific testing that tended to establish the reliability of fingerprint identifications. By contrast, defense testimony strongly suggested that fingerprint identification techniques have not been tested in a manner that could be properly characterized as scientific. Particularly pointed was the testimony of forensic scientist David Stoney, the Director of the McCrone Research Institute in Chicago. According to Dr. Stoney:

"The determination that a fingerprint examiner makes . . . when comparing a latent fingerprint with a known fingerprint, specifically the determination that there is sufficient basis for an absolute identification is not a scientific determination. It is a subjective determination standard. It is a subjective determination without objective standards to it."

....

VI. Admission of Fingerprint Testimony

[I]t is the court's view that the ACE-V fingerprint identification regime is hard to square with Daubert. The one Daubert factor that ACE-V satisfies in significant fashion is the fourth factor: ACE-V has attained general acceptance within the American fingerprint examiner community. But the caveat must be added that, in the court's view, the domain of knowledge occupied by fingerprint examiners should be described... by the word "technical," rather than by the word "scientific," the word the government deploys. [T]he court finds that ACE-V does not adequately satisfy the "scientific" criterion of testing (the first Daubert factor) or the "scientific" criterion of peer review (the second Daubert factor). Further, the court finds that the information of record is unpersuasive, one way or another, as to ACE-V's "scientific" rate of error (the first aspect of Daubert's third factor), and that, at the critical evaluation stage, ACE-V does not operate under uniformly accepted "scientific" standards (the second aspect of Daubert's third factor).

Since the court finds that ACE-V does not meet Daubert's testing, peer review, and standards criteria, and that information as to ACE-V's rate of error is in limbo, the expected conclusion would be that the government should be precluded from presenting any fingerprint testimony. But that conclusion—apparently putting at naught a century of judicial acquiescence in fingerprint identification processes—would be unwarrantably heavy-handed. The Daubert difficulty with the ACE-V process is by no means total. The difficulty comes into play at the stage at ... the evaluation stage. By contrast, the antecedent analysis and comparison stages are, according to the testimony, "objective": analysis of the rolled and latent prints and comparison of what the examiner has observed in the two prints. Up to the evaluation stage, the ACE-V fingerprint examiner's testimony is descriptive, not judgmental. Accordingly, this court will permit the government to present testimony by fingerprint examiners who, suitably qualified as "expert" examiners by virtue of training and experience, may (1) describe how the rolled and latent fingerprints at issue in this case were obtained, (2) identify and place before the jury the fingerprints and such magnifications thereof as may be required to show minute details, and (3) point out observed similarities (and differences) between any latent print and any rolled print the government contends are attributable to the same person. What such expert witnesses will not be permitted to do is to present "evaluation" testimony as to their "opinion" that a particular latent print is in fact the print of a particular person. The defendants will be permitted to present their own fingerprint experts to counter the government's fingerprint testimony, but defense experts will also be precluded from presenting "evaluation" testimony. Government counsel and defense counsel will, in closing arguments, be free to argue to the jury that, on the basis of the jury's observation of a particular latent print and a particular rolled print, the jury may find the existence, or the non-existence, of a match between the prints...

Although the judge in the *Plaza* case subsequently changed his mind and allowed this fingerprint evidence, it illustrates the current problems in interpreting *Daubert* and provides a glimpse into probable future issues involving scientific evidence and expert testimony. This is further illustrated by the cases in this country in which fingerprints were incorrectly classified. An example of this was the Madrid terrorist bombing, where Spanish authorities submitted digital copies of latent prints to the FBI's IAFIS fingerprint identification system. The search produced a short list of potential matches, from which FBI examiners identified the print as coming from Brandon Mayfield, a former Army lieutenant and Oregon attorney. The prints were independently analyzed and the results were confirmed by an outside experienced fingerprint expert. However, later testing by Spanish authorities matched the prints to a different man and the FBI issued an apology to Mr. Mayfield.[9]

A related future concern is whether our legal professionals and judges will be adequately grounded in "scientific knowledge" in order to meet the challenges in proving the new standard. If the standard is no longer what is "generally accepted" in the scientific community and instead requires an understanding of different scientific methodologies and procedures, the lawyers and judges of the future will need to prepare for this.

In a recent Wisconsin case, the prosecution in a criminal case obtained an arrest warrant based on a suspect's DNA code without knowing the identity of the suspect. The suspect was later identified and arrested when his DNA was obtained and matched in a different matter. Science and technology are changing the nature of our society and have had a significant impact on our legal process as well.

The children of today are learning computers at a very early age. They are growing up around wireless technology, Internet, computer graphics, and animation as we grew up around the technological revolution of our age—color television and the cordless phone! These children will become the legal professionals of the future, and will affect the gathering and presentation of crime scene evidence.

Trends In Crime Scene Search Laws

As evidenced by the trend of court decisions in recent years, future courts will continue to follow the *Mincey* standard that there is no crime scene exception to the search warrant requirement of the Fourth Amendment. The rule will continue to be that a warrantless search must be "strictly circumscribed by the exigencies which justify its initiation."[10]

However, the two major exceptions to the search warrant requirement, *exigency* and *consent* will continue to drive warrant exceptions to crime scene searches. The general rule will continue to be that warrants are generally required to search a person's home or his person unless there is consent or "the exigencies of the situation" make the needs of law enforcement so compelling that the warrantless search is objectively reasonable under the Fourth Amendment.[11]

In addition, courts will continue to follow the Supreme Court decision that once officers are inside the crime scene under exigency circumstances, they may "remain there for a reasonable time to investigate" and that evidence "discovered in the course of such investigation is admissible at trial."[12]

CSI Effect

In the future, television will not only continue to be popular, but we will be able to view our favorite shows on our cell phones, in our cars, at work, or simply out for a walk with our *TV pods*. New television shows and televised courtroom proceedings will still focus on crime scene investigation and we will still be viewing reruns of CSI. As a result, jurors in criminal trials will not only have a better understanding of crime scene investigation, but will expect that forensic analysis be conducted at all crime scenes, and will be expecting testimony from criminalists to be key to the case. This has been called the **CSI Effect** and this phenomena will continue to disturb legal professionals at trial, resulting in specific training for attorneys in the questioning of prospective jurors in an attempt to prevent or channel this effect.

PRACTICE TIP 13.1

Resource for Future Directions in Crime Scene Investigation

Here is an interesting Internet resource for keeping track of new changes in forensics and crime scene investigation, as well as future recommendations and trends. It is a is a collaboration between the FBI and the Society of Police Futurists International (PFI):

FBI Futures Working Group
http://www.fbi.gov/hq/td/fwg/workhome.htm

SUMMARY

For crime scene investigation, the "future" started with many recent innovations, including the adaptation of the laser, DNA, and computer technology for law enforcement purposes. Technological advances and innovations in crime scene investigation and criminalistics are expected to continue at a rapid pace in the future. New advances in crime scene investigation and criminalistics will be driven by four key factors: improving existing forensic tools and technologies, miniaturization, automation, and standardization. There are many forensic tools and technologies in use at crime scenes and crime labs. The future need will be to further test and improve these existing tools and technologies, making them better, smaller, and easier to use in the field. New innovation in forensic tools and technology is being driven in large part by the need for *miniaturization*; to make things smaller and easier to use in the field. Referred to as *lab-on-a-chip*, this technology uses microchips to develop smaller, more efficient forensic instrumentation, now only found in full size at the crime lab. These miniaturized instruments, including DNA testing, will be used at crime scenes to more quickly discover, identify, and analyze evidence. It will be like bringing an entire crime lab to a crime scene in a shoebox. *Automation* is the electronic connectivity technology that will allow faster and more open sharing, retrieval, and analysis of information, directly from the crime scene. *Teleforensics* is the remote viewing of a crime scene through electronically transmitted images. Teleforensics has tremendous potential for future applications in crime scene investigation. Using *robotics*, teleforensics can further safety issues by checking a scene for victims or suspects, protect the crime scene and evidence from contamination, document the scene before it is disturbed by processing personnel, and identify and analyze important evidence.

In providing crime lab services in the future, it is expected that there will be more consolidation, standardization, and regionalization. Currently, crime labs are not regulated and lack standardized testing and quality control criteria. In the future, these concerns will be addressed through government regulation. States and the federal government will enact laws regulating crime labs and personnel. Standardized testing, quality control, and analyst qualification criteria will be required and regulated by government agencies, or through mandated accreditation and review by the ASCLD.

As with innovations in forensics, law and legal procedure in the future will be impacted by technology. There will be changes in how scientific evidence is viewed by the courts, and the laws pertaining to crime scene search will be relaxed. At trial, the forensic witness or investigator will use *Evidence Presentation Software* programs for exhibiting evidence on monitors throughout the courtroom, and computer animation and graphics to illustrate and explain the crime scene evidence or forensic testing. The **CSI Effect** will continue to disturb legal professionals at trial, resulting in specific training for attorneys in the questioning of prospective jurors in an attempt to prevent or channel this effect.

KEY TERMS

Alternate Light Sources   Laser Profilometry System

Automation   Laser Trajectory Projection

Computer Animation Evidence   Miniaturization

Electrostatic Lifting   Photogrammetry

Evidence Presentation Software   Pictometry

Gas Chromatograph   Robotics

GPS   Teleforensics

Image Processing Software   Thermal Imaging

Lab-On-A-Chip

REVIEW QUESTIONS

After completing your reading, you should be able to demonstrate a better understanding of the learning concepts by answering the following questions:

1. Explain what *Lab-on-a-Chip* means.

2. Define *miniaturization* as it applies to crime scene investigation. Give an example.

3. Discuss how *automation* will be utilized in the future for crime scene investigations.

4. Describe how *teleforensics* is used now and how it might be used in the future.

5. Assess the current problem of standardization in crime labs and personnel, and what might be done in the future to address these problems.

6. Identify the future trends and issues in laws governing crime scene investigations.

7. Explain what the *CSI Effect* is and how it may continue to affect the presentation of crime scene evidence in future trials.

CRITICAL THINKING QUESTIONS 13.1

What do you think is the most important aspect in each of the following drivers for future change in crime scene investigations and criminalistics, and why:

1. Miniaturization
2. Automation
3. Teleforensics
4. Standardization

FORENSIC RESEARCH USING THE INTERNET

1. Search the Internet for recommendations or predictions of future changes to crime scene investigation or criminalistics. List and assess these predictions.

PRACTICE SKILLS

1. Describe the changes that you think will take place in crime scene investigation or criminalistics in future years as a result of technology. What else is needed?

2. What areas of law that pertain to crime scene investigation do you think will change in the future? Give some examples of these changes.

WEB SITES

Futures Working Group

http://www.fbi.gov/hq/td/fwg/workhome.htm

ENDNOTES

[1] For more on this, see the article by Vogel, Julie. Finding and Collecting Evidence, *Law Enforcement Technology*, June 2002

[2] The National Institute of Justice and Advances in Forensic Science and Technology, *Technology Center Bulletin*

[3] For more on this, see Pictometry: Aerial Photography on Steroids, *Law Enforcement Technology*, July 2002

[4] Dr. Chris Lennard, How Miniaturisation of Analytical Equipment Will Change the Nature of Crime Scene Examination, INTERPOL Forensic Science Symposium, Lyon, France, October 2001

[5] The National Institute of Justice and Advances in Forensic Science and Technology, *Technology Center Bulletin*

[6] Report by the California State Auditor, *Forensic Laboratories: Many Face Challenges Beyond Accreditation to Assure the Highest Quality Services*, December 1998

[7] William Schwabe, 1999. *Needs and Prospects for Crime-Fighting Technology*, Santa Monica, CA: Rand Corporation

[8] Report by the California State Auditor, *Forensic Laboratories: Many Face Challenges Beyond Accreditation to Assure the Highest Quality Services*, December 1998

[9] FBI Press Room, Press Release, Statement on Brandon Mayfield Case, May 24, 2004

[10] *Mincey v. Arizona* 437 U.S. 385 (1978)

[11] *McDonald v. United States*, 335 U.S. 451

[12] *Michigan v. Tyler* 436 U.S. 499 (1978)

GLOSSARY

A

abuse of discretion   The standard of review that an appellate court should apply in reviewing a trial court's decision to admit or exclude expert testimony under Daubert.

accelerant   A catalyst in the starting and spreading of a fire.

AFIS   Computerized fingerprint database, *Automated Fingerprint Identification System*.

alligatoring   A charring of wood that is checked and resembles the pattern of an alligator's scales.

alternate light sources   Specialized forensic lighting, such as high-intensity ultraviolet light, used to detect trace evidence at a crime scene.

arch   Fingerprint pattern in which the friction ridges enter on one side and tend to flow out the other side with a rise or wave in the center.

associative or linking evidence   Evidence that helps to identify a suspect and link that suspect to a crime scene.

authentication   Part of laying a foundation, where a witness testifies that evidence is what it purports to be.

automation   Connectivity technology allowing faster and more open sharing, retrieval, and analysis of information, directly from the crime scene.

B

balancing test   A test that weighs probative value of evidence against its prejudicial effect.

ballistics   Science of projectiles in motion; used to examine firearms and the bullets fired from them.

baseline method   A method of sketching commonly used outdoors that establishes an imaginary straight line from one fixed point up a certain measured distance and over at a right angle to evidence.

beyond a reasonable doubt   Burden of proof in criminal action. Requires trier of fact to believe something to be almost certainly true and leaving no reasonable doubt.

brady motion   A motion to dismiss a case because evidence favorable to the accused has been suppressed by the state, either willfully or inadvertently; resulting in prejudice to the defendant.

bulb   Rounded area at end of each finger.

burden of proof   The duty to meet a certain standard or establish the requisite degree of belief in the mind of the trier of fact regarding the evidence submitted.

C

cadaveric spasm   Called a "death grip," an immediate stiffening of a hand or arm upon sudden, violent death.

case law   Judge-made law based on court decisions. Term is used today interchangeably with common law.

chain of custody   The proper preservation and protection of crime scene evidence in order to insure its physical and legal integrity.

circle search pattern   A search pattern used for outside areas, where a stake is placed in the ground, a rope tied to it, and knots tied at intervals of 3 feet. Searchers hold the rope at the knots and conduct a circular search, moving to the next knot when each circle is completed.

circumstantial evidence or proof   Evidence that proves a disputed fact indirectly by first proving another fact. From this other fact an inference may be drawn as to the original disputed fact.

class characteristics   Characteristics of physical evidence that are common to a group of objects or persons.

CODIS   FBI national DNA database.

common law   Case law. A uniform set of laws for a state or country based on court decisions.

computer animation evidence   A newer form of demonstrative evidence that utilizes sophisticated computer-generated graphics and animation to illustrate and reconstruct evidence or crime scenes.

concentric fractures   Circle cracks in glass, radiating out to form circles around the point of the blow.

concept of identity   A concept that although no two objects are identical, there are many factors that combine to establish identity to a certain mathematical probability.

consent   Permission by a person who has authority to grant it authorizing officers to enter and conduct an initial investigation of a crime scene.

constitution   The United States's founding document that establishes framework of government and laws. Supreme law of the land.

core   Center of the pattern area.

corpus delicti   Latin for "body of the crime," or the elements necessary to prove that a crime has been committed.

crime   Act or omission to act that violates a law for which there is a prescribed sanction or punishment.

crime lab   Laboratory where evidence from crime scenes is tested and analyzed.

crime reports   Documentation of the initial reporting and investigation of a crime.

crime scene   Location where crime was committed or continued.

crime scene investigation   A methodical investigation initially carried out at the crime scene to determine what happened, how it happened, why it happened, and who or what was responsible.

crime scene reconstruction   Recreating of a crime scene, or parts of it, in order to prepare a case for trial, verify information from the original scene, or to continue an investigation.

criminalist   One who applies science and scientific method to crime scene investigation.

criminalistics   Application of science and scientific method to crime scene investigation.

criminology   Behavioral study of crime and criminals.

cross-examine   Questioning of a witness by the opposing party on matters within the scope of the direct examination, usually to discredit the testimony of the witness or to develop facts that may help the cross-examiner's case.

cross-projection method (or exploded view)   A method of sketching that shows walls, doors and windows as if the room had been flattened or collapsed.

CSI Effect   Influence of popular *CSI* television shows on jurors' expectations of what criminalistics can and should do in a criminal investigation.

D

dactylography   Study of fingerprint identification and classification.

Daubert Standard   An adaptation of the Reliability Test for determining the admissibility of scientific evidence by weighing probative value of scientific testing and its reliability against the test's potential for prejudice.

deductive reasoning or deduction   To narrow reasoning from the general to the specific.

delta Point on the ridge formation of fingerprint located within the pattern area nearest to the divergence of the type lines.

demonstrative evidence Demonstrates, illustrates, or recreates evidence that has already been presented or a point or matter that needs further explanation.

density gradient tube technique Used to compare soil specimens.

derivative evidence rule From the *Exclusionary Rule:* any evidence obtained as a result of the original search being unlawful is also unlawful.

direct evidence Evidence that proves a disputed fact directly, through an eyewitness, for example.

direct examination Initial questioning of a witness by the party that called the witness to the stand

direct proof Evidence that proves a disputed fact directly.

DNA Deoxyribonucleic acid, found in the cells of every person, contains a unique genetic code that can be profiled for positive identification of that individual.

documentary evidence Evidence in the form of writings or records, including letters, notes, contracts, printings, pictures, or recordings.

due process Constitutional protections extended to suspects and defendant in a criminal investigation.

due process clause Constitutional protection under the Fourteenth Amendment that provides a person with the right to reasonable notice of charges and the right to confront witnesses and evidence against him.

dusting Use of fingerprint powders to detect and visualize latent prints at a crime scene.

E

electrostatic lifting Electrostatic dust-lifting film that collects dust from a surface to the film, allowing an impression to be lifted without damage to the impression.

elements of a crime Every part of a definition for a particular crime must be established and proven in order to convict a defendant of that crime.

exchange theory Whenever two surfaces come into contact with each other, there is a partial transfer or exchange of material from one to the other.

evidence Anything that tends to prove or disprove a fact at issue in a criminal action.

evidence control unit Specially-trained personnel who manage the receipt, handling, packaging, transfer, and storage of evidence.

evidence law Body of rules that help to govern conduct and determine what will be admissible in criminal proceedings and trials.

evidence logs Logs that document evidence collected at the scene.

evidence presentation software A computer program specially designed for the organizing of evidence exhibits and the animated presentation of evidence.

exchange theory Whenever two surfaces come into contact with each other, there is a partial transfer or exchange of material from one to the other.

exclusionary rule A legal rule, established by case law, that prohibits the admission of illegally obtained evidence in a criminal action.

exculpatory evidence Evidence used to clear a party of blame or guilt.

exhibit An item offered in evidence that is properly marked for later identification.

exigency Emergency. The initial response to a crime scene is considered to be an exigent or emergency circumstance.

expert witness A witness qualified by specialized skills or knowledge whose testimony or opinion can assist the trier of fact to better understand evidence in issue.

F

federal rules of evidence   Statutory evidentiary rules enacted by Congress in 1975 and used in all federal courts, and as a model for many states.

felony   Serious crime, generally punishable by more than one year of imprisonment.

forensic evidence and testing   Crime scene evidence and subsequent analysis of it that has a scientific or highly technical basis, requiring an expert witness with specialized knowledge to assist the trier of fact to understand it.

forensic science   Application of science and scientific method to criminal investigation and law.

Fourth Amendment   Constitutional Amendment establishing standard for search warrant and protections against unreasonable search and seizure.

fruits of the poisonous tree doctrine   From the *Exclusionary Rule:* any evidence obtained as a result of the original search being unlawful is also unlawful.

Frye Test   Scientific evidence is admissible only if the principle upon which it is based is "sufficiently established to have general acceptance in the field to which it belongs."

G

gas chromatograph   A crime lab testing instrument that analyzes by separating substances into their components.

gatekeeper   Role of the trial judge in ensuring relevance and reliability of scientific evidence.

general acceptance test   Scientific evidence is admissible only if the principle upon which it is based is "sufficiently established to have general acceptance in the field to which it belongs."

GPS   Global positioning system used in criminal investigation for tracking and determining locational positioning.

grand jury indictment   A process of charging someone with a crime, where a grand jury is convened to determine if probable cause exists.

grid search pattern   A more thorough method of searching that uses two strip or lane searches over the same area but continuing again at right angles.

gunshot residue (GSR) test   Detects the presence of gunshot residue from a fired weapon.

H

hearsay   A statement made out-of-court and offered in court as evidence to prove the truth of the assertion made in the statement.

Henry System   First fingerprint classification system, developed in 1901 at Scotland Yard, by Sir Edward Henry.

I

IAFIS   FBI's national fingerprint database, *Integrated Automated Fingerprint Identification System.*

IBIS   Integrated Ballistic Identification System.

identification   Part of laying a foundation, where a witness testifies that he or she can recognize a piece of evidence and identify it.

igniters   Something used to start a fire, like matches or candles.

image processing software   Specialized software that enhances digital images at crime scenes or on victims that need more detail shown, such as fingerprints or bite marks.

impeachment   Attacking the credibility of a witness in order to convince the jury that the testimony given is not truthful or that the witness is unreliable.

impressed toolmarks   Negative image or impression left by a tool that is brought into contact with a softer surface with no lateral movement between the objects at the moment of contact.

inculpatory evidence Evidence used to incriminate or prove guilt.

individual or individualizing characteristics When the characteristics of physical evidence can be identified as having originated from a particular person or source.

inference A deduction of fact that may logically be drawn from another fact.

information A process of charging someone with a crime, where a prosecutor files a paper with the court.

investigation From the Latin *investigare*, meaning to track, inquire into, search for, or examine systematically.

J

judicial notice When a judge recognizes and accepts a certain fact that is commonly known in the community or capable of accurate and ready determination.

L

laboratory information management system (LIMS) Automated evidence-tracking system.

lab-on-a-chip Use of microchips to develop smaller, more efficient forensic identification and testing instruments.

lane or strip search pattern A method of searching in which investigators start at one side of their search zone and walk back and forth over imaginary lanes or strips no wider than their shoulders.

laser profilometry system Three-dimensional laser scanning equipment able to compare, analyze, transmit and store images of evidence

laser trajectory projection Use of laser to determine trajectory and path of a bullet.

latent Not readily visible.

latent prints Fingerprints that are not readily seen but can be developed by forensic methods.

lay witness A person who testifies at trial, generally from firsthand knowledge about a fact at issue.

laying a foundation Presenting evidence that sets the groundwork for other evidence, authenticating and identifying the evidence.

legal integrity of evidence The principle that evidence must not be tampered with, altered, substituted, or falsified.

legal relevance Even when relevant, evidence is not admissible if it violates any other evidence rule or law.

lifting The process of removing a latent print, discovered at a crime scene.

logical relevance When evidence tends to prove or disprove a fact in issue.

loop Fingerprint pattern in which the ridges flow inward and recurve back toward the point of origin.

luminol A chemical test used to detect hidden blood at a crime scene.

M

masking Attempt to cover up or conceal a crime with another crime.

matchable characteristics Identifying features that might prove the evidence is from the same source as the sample.

means Ability to commit a particular crime.

miniaturization Use of microchips to develop smaller, more efficient forensic identification and testing instruments.

misdemeanor Less serious crime, punishable by less than one year of incarceration.

modus operandi (m.o.) Method of operation. How a criminal commits a crime.

m.o.m. Motive, opportunity, and means to commit a particular crime.

motion to suppress A legal motion filed before trial that seeks to suppress or exclude certain evidence from being admitted.

motive Reason why a crime was committed.

O

object   To challenge evidence or testimony introduced at trial.

onus probandi   Burden of proof.

opportunity   Time and availability to be able to commit a particular crime.

P

past memory recorded   When the witness is unable to refresh memory by reviewing notes or writing, the witness may not testify, but the document may be read from into evidence.

personal knowledge   A lay witness must be able to testify from a firsthand perception of having seen, heard, felt, touched, or smelled something.

physical evidence   Objects or materials that can be seen, touched, or felt, such as the murder weapon, blood stains, or fingerprints.

photogrammetry   Computerized method used to map and precisely measure a crime scene and the objects in it from digital photographs.

pictometry   Aerial photography that can map and depict images in 3D.

plain view doctrine   Officers may seize any evidence observed in plain view while lawfully on premises.

point of departure (POD)   Areas at crime scene where offender exited crime scene.

point of entry (POE)   Areas at crime scene where offender entered to commit a crime.

point of impact (POI)   Areas at crime scene where ransacking occurred or objects were moved or disturbed.

point of origin (POO)   The location at a scene where the fire was started.

postmortem lividity   Settling of blood in the body after death.

precedent   A court decision that serves as a rule of law or standard to be looked at in deciding subsequent cases.

preliminary hearing   A court hearing, before a judge only, where prosecution must present, and defense is allowed to challenge, evidence to show probable cause that a crime has been committed and that the defendant committed the crime.

preponderance of evidence   Burden of proof in a civil action. Plaintiff must produce sufficient evidence to persuade the trier of fact that what plaintiff claims is more likely true than not true.

present memory refreshed   When the witness is permitted to refer to writing or notes in order to jog memory.

prima facie   Translates to "at first sight" and means that at first sight, all of the elements for a particular crime have been established.

probable cause   Standard of proof required for search warrants and arrests in criminal actions. Requires that evidence be considered "more probable than not" in proving what is alleged.

probable cause hearing   A court hearing, before a judge only, where prosecution must present, and defense is allowed to challenge, evidence to show probable cause that a crime has been committed and that the defendant committed the crime.

probability theory   Attempts to define the mathematical or statistical probability of a certain event occurring or an object having certain characteristics, usually in determining identity.

probative   Tends to prove something.

probative value   Whether evidence submitted proves something relevant to the case.

procedural law   Rules that set forth legal process and tell us how to enforce the law.

protective sweep   A brief search of a crime scene, limited in scope to checking for suspects.

Q

questioned documents   Analysis and comparison of documents for identification purposes.

R

radial fractures   Triangular lines in glass that radiate outward from point of impact.

rarity   Evidence found at the crime scene that seems out of place.

reasonable expectation of privacy   Standard set by *Katz v. United States*, 389 U.S. 347 (1967) and still used today to determine validity of searches under the Fourth Amendment.

reasonable person test   This test asks what a "reasonable person" would have done given the circumstances.

reasonable suspicion   Standard of proof required for a law enforcement officer to stop and question a person. Based on the officer's reasonable suspicion that the person has committed a crime, is committing a crime, or is about to commit a crime.

rectangular coordinate method   A method of sketching that uses two adjacent walls at right angles to each other as fixed points from which straight-line distances are measured to the evidence.

redirecting   Altering a crime scene in order to shift focus from offender or protect the family.

relevancy   A basic requirement for the admissibility of evidence is that it tends to prove or disprove a fact in issue.

reliability test   Determines admissibility of forensic evidence and testing by weighing probative value and reliability of scientific testing against the test's potential for prejudice.

ridge characteristics   Identifying characteristics on the friction ridges of fingerprints.

rigor mortis   Stiffening of body after death.

robotics   Technology associated with the design and use of robots.

rules of criminal procedure   Statutory laws and approved court rules governing procedural aspects of criminal investigations, and search and seizure.

S

scientific evidence and testing   Crime scene evidence and subsequent analysis of it that has a scientific or highly technical basis, requiring an expert witness with specialized knowledge to assist the trier of fact to understand it.

serology   Scientific study of blood and its properties.

set theory   All objects can be divided and subdivided into various sets on the basis of their properties.

signature   An action or ritual that some serial criminals perform at a crime scene that leaves a form of a psychological "calling card."

solvability factors   Factors at a crime scene that law enforcement officials have no control over, but that may affect the solving of the crime.

spiral search pattern   A popular and adaptable method of searching where an investigator searches in a clockwise circle, beginning at the outside of the circle and works inward sweeping in a spiral toward the impact area of the crime scene.

staging   Intentional altering of a crime scene to mislead the investigation.

standard of comparison   A sample that is compared to evidence to determine whether both are identical or from the same source.

statutory law   Laws passed by legislature.

striated toolmarks   Parallel striation markings produced when a tool is brought into contact with a softer surface and there is lateral movement between the surfaces at the moment of contact.

substantive law   Defines the law, providing elements and sanctions.

T

teleforensics   Remote viewing of a crime scene through electronically transmitted images.

testimonial evidence   Oral or "spoken" evidence presented by witnesses who come into court to give their testimony under oath.

theory of the case   The initial hypothesis of what crime was committed, how it was committed, and where.

thermal imaging   Imaging technology that detects and converts infrared radiation into heat images based on relative warmth.

3-d or vertical projection method   A method of sketching used to show dimension and depth; shows a building as if you were standing in front.

totality of the circumstances test   This test looks at all of the facts in a particular situation in trying to determine if an action was warranted.

toxicology   Detection and study of poisons.

trace evidence   Minute amounts of evidence, such as fibers, hairs, or specks of dirt.

trace metal detection technique (TMDT)   Field test that determines whether a person has held a metallic object such as a knife, pipe, or firearm.

trailer   Flammable liquid or materials placed along a line to spread a fire from one area to another.

transfer theory   Whenever two surfaces come into contact with each other, there is a partial transfer or exchange of material from one to the other.

trajectory   Path of a bullet.

triangulation method   A method of sketching that uses triangular lines as straight line measurements from two fixed points to the evidence being sketched.

trophy   Item that some serial criminals take from the victim or crime scene as a form of memento or souvenir of the crime.

type lines   Ridges that determine the pattern area of loops and whorls.

V

validation studies   A form of proficiency testing performed to ensure that a crime laboratory and its personnel are meeting certain professional standards.

voiceprints   Voice identification based on analysis and comparisons of voice recording samples.

voir dire   Meaning *to tell the truth*, the process of questioning by defense and prosecution of prospective jurors.

W

whorl   Fingerprint pattern with recurving ridges that flow in a circle or spiral.

Z

zone or sector search pattern   Designed for large or complex crime scenes, this method of searching divides the entire scene into square zones, where investigators then use one of the standard search patterns for each individual zone.

INDEX

D

E

F

J

K

L